Stewart E. Cooper, PhD, ABPP
James Archer, Jr., PhD, ABPP
Leighton C. Whitaker, PhD, ABPP
Editors

Case Book
of Brief Psychotherapy
with College Students

Case Book of Brief Psychotherapy with College Students has been co-published simultaneously as *Journal of College Student Psychotherapy*, Volume 16, Numbers 1/2 2001 and 3/4 2002.

Pre-publication
REVIEWS,
COMMENTARIES,
EVALUATIONS . . .

"IMPRESSIVE. . . . A FASCINATING GROUP OF CASE STUDIES. Effectively demonstrates how time-sensitive therapy can be successfully integrated with a developmental approach. An excellent addition to the library of all clinicians working with college-aged clients and AN IDEAL TEXT."

Bob McGrath, PsyD, ABPP
Director, Counseling and Consultation Services, University of Wisconsin, Madison

The Haworth Press, Inc.

Case Book of Brief Psychotherapy with College Students

Case Book of Brief Psychotherapy with College Students has been co-published simultaneously as *Journal of College Student Psychotherapy*, Volume 16, Numbers 1/2 2001 and 3/4 2002.

The *Journal of College Student Psychotherapy* Monographic "Separates"

Below is a list of "separates," which in serials librarianship means a special issue simultaneously published as a special journal issue or double-issue *and* as a "separate" hardbound monograph. (This is a format which we also call a "DocuSerial.")

"Separates" are published because specialized libraries or professionals may wish to purchase a specific thematic issue by itself in a format which can be separately cataloged and shelved, as opposed to purchasing the journal on an on-going basis. Faculty members may also more easily consider a "separate" for classroom adoption.

"Separates" are carefully classified separately with the major book jobbers so that the journal tie-in can be noted on new book order slips to avoid duplicate purchasing.

You may wish to visit Haworth's website at . . .

http://www.HaworthPress.com

. . . to search our online catalog for complete tables of contents of these separates and related publications.

You may also call 1-800-HAWORTH (outside US/Canada: 607-722-5857), or Fax 1-800-895-0582 (outside US/Canada: 607-771-0012), or e-mail at:

getinfo@haworthpressinc.com

Case Book of Brief Psychotherapy with College Students, edited by Stewart E. Cooper, PhD, ABPP, James Archer, Jr., PhD, ABPP, and Leighton C. Whitaker, PhD, ABPP (Vol. 16, No. 1/2, 2001 and 3/4, 2002). *"IMPRESSIVE. . . . A FASCINATING GROUP OF CASE STUDIES. Effectively demonstrates how time-sensitive therapy can be successfully integrated with a developmental approach. An excellent addition to the library of all clinicians working with college-aged clients and AN IDEAL TEXT." (Bob McGrath, PsyD, ABPP, Director, Counseling and Consultation Services, University of Wisconsin, Madison)*

Helping Students Adapt to Graduate School: Making the Grade, by Committee on the College Student, Group for the Advancement of Psychiatry (Vol. 14, No. 2, 1999). *"Breaks new ground by giving professors and students a guide to the graduate school experience. . . . Thoughtful and clear in both description and prescription; it will benefit both students and their advisors. . . . This is a very readable and helpful resource." (Robert M. Randolph, PhD, Senior Associate Dean, Office of the Dean of Students and Undergraduate Education, Massachusetts Institute of Technology, Cambridge, Massachusetts)*

Campus Violence: Kinds, Causes, and Cures, edited by Leighton C. Whitaker, PhD, and Jeffrey W. Pollard, PhD (Vol. 8, No. 1/2/3, 1994). *"An indispensable reference work for health educators, administrators, and mental health professionals." (Journal of American College Health)*

College Student Development, edited by Leighton C. Whitaker, PhD, and Richard E. Slimak, PhD (Vol. 6, No. 3/4, 1993). *"Provides college counselors and therapists with some of the most important developmental perspectives needed in today's work with students." (Educational Book Review)*

College Student Suicide, edited by Leighton C. Whitaker, PhD, and Richard E. Slimak, PhD (Vol. 4, No. 3/4, 1990). *"Belongs in the hands and minds of everyone who works with suicidal students in post-secondary education. . . . Would also be a good text for graduate courses in counseling, social work, psychology, or student services." (Suicide Information & Education Center (SIEC) Current Awareness Bulletin)*

The Bulimic College Student: Evaluation, Treatment, and Prevention, edited by Leighton C. Whitaker, PhD, and William N. Davis, PhD (Vol. 3, No. 2/3/4, 1989). *"An excellent tool for college mental health professionals . . . Practical information and guidelines are provided to help college personnel develop programs for the prevention and treatment of bulimia." (Journal of Nutritional Education)*

Alcoholism/Chemical Dependency and the College Student, edited by Timothy M. Rivinus, MD (Vol. 2, No. 3/4, 1988). *"This volume is a compilation of articles on several dimensions of the campus substance abuse problems. . . . A must for the clinician's and the administrator's reading list." (Michael Liepman, MD, Providence VA Medical Center, Rhode Island)*

Parental Concerns in College Student Mental Health, edited by Leighton C. Whitaker, PhD (Vol. 2, No. 1/2, 1988). *"A useful reference for parents and professionals concerning the everyday, yet hardly routine, psychological issues of the college student." (American Journal of Psychotherapy)*

Case Book
of Brief Psychotherapy
with College Students

Stewart E. Cooper, PhD, ABPP
James Archer, Jr., PhD, ABPP
Leighton C. Whitaker, PhD, ABPP
Editors

Case Book of Brief Psychotherapy with College Students has been co-published simultaneously as *Journal of College Student Psychotherapy*, Volume 16, Numbers 1/2 2001 and 3/4 2002.

The Haworth Press, Inc.
New York • London • Oxford

Case Book of Brief Psychotherapy with College Students has been co-published simultaneously as *Journal of College Student Psychotherapy*™, Volume 16, Numbers 1/2 2001 and 3/4 2002.

Cover design by Thomas J. Mayshock Jr.

Library of Congress Cataloging-in-Publication Data

Case book of brief psychotherapy with college students / Stewart E. Cooper, James Archer, Jr., Leighton C. Whitaker, editors.
  p. cm.
"Co-published simultaneously as Journal of college student psychotherapy, volume 16, numbers 1/2 2001and 3/4 2002."
  Includes bibliographical references and index.
  ISBN 0-7890-1429-7 (alk. paper) – ISBN 0-7890-1430-0 (alk. paper)
  1. College students–Mental health. 2. Brief psychotherapy. 3. Brief psychotherapy for teenagers. I. Cooper, Stewart Edwin, 1953- II. Archer, James. III. Whitaker, Leighton C. IV. Journal of college student psychotherapy.
  RC451.4.S7 C37 2002
  616.89'14–dc21
                                                                          2002017170

Indexing, Abstracting & Website/Internet Coverage

This section provides you with a list of major indexing & abstracting services. That is to say, each service began covering this periodical during the year noted in the right column. Most Websites which are listed below have indicated that they will either post, disseminate, compile, archive, cite or alter their own Website users with research-based content from this work. (This list is as current as the copyright date of this publication.)

Abstracting, Website/Indexing Coverage . . . . Year When Coverage Began

- **Applied Social Sciences Index & Abstracts (ASSIA) (Online: ASSI via Data-Star) (CDRom: ASSIA Plus) <http://www.bowker-saur.co.uk>** 1987

- **BUBL Information Service, An Internet-based Information Service for the UK higher education community <URL:http://bubl.ac.uk/>** 1995

- **CNPIEC Reference Guide: Chinese National Directory of Foreign Periodicals** 1995

- **Contents Pages in Education** 1987

- **Educational Administration Abstracts (EAA)** 1991

- **e-psyche, LLC <www.e-psyche.net>** 2001

- **Family & Society Studies Worldwide <www.nisc.com>** 1986

- **FINDEX <www.publist.com>** 1999

- **Higher Education Abstracts, providing the latest in research & theory in more than 140 major topics.** 1987

- **International Bulletin of Bibliography on Education** 1992

(continued)

Special Bibliographic Notes related to special journal issues (separates) and indexing/abstracting:

- indexing/abstracting services in this list will also cover material in any "separate" that is co-published simultaneously with Haworth's special thematic journal issue or DocuSerial. Indexing/abstracting usually covers material at the article/chapter level.
- monographic co-editions are intended for either non-subscribers or libraries which intend to purchase a second copy for their circulating collections.
- monographic co-editions are reported to all jobbers/wholesalers/approval plans. The source journal is listed as the "series" to assist the prevention of duplicate purchasing in the same manner utilized for books-in-series.
- to facilitate user/access services all indexing/abstracting services are encouraged to utilize the co-indexing entry note indicated at the bottom of the first page of each article/chapter/contribution.
- this is intended to assist a library user of any reference tool (whether print, electronic, online, or CD-ROM) to locate the monographic version if the library has purchased this version but not a subscription to the source journal.
- individual articles/chapters in any Haworth publication are also available through the Haworth Document Delivery Service (HDDS).

Case Book of Brief Psychotherapy with College Students

CONTENTS

ABOUT THE EDITORS

Stewart E. Cooper, PhD, ABPP, Counseling/Research Methodology, Indiana University, has served as Director of Counseling Services for the past eleven years and is Professor of Psychology and Director of the Graduate Psychology Program at Valparaiso University. He earned his BA in psychology and his MS in counseling at Indiana University. Before joining the staff at Valparaiso University, he was a staff psychologist at the University of Missouri at Rolla. He holds a Diplomate in Counseling Psychology from the American Board of Professional Psychology (ABPP) and is a Fellow of Division 13 (Consulting Psychology) of the American Psychological Association.

His research has focused on the application of multivariate perspectives and methods to diverse counseling-psychology topics. He has published more than 50 articles, book chapters, and monographs on prevention, psychometric analysis, substance abuse, dual-career issues, organizational consultation, and sex therapy, mostly on the college population and their mental health issues. He is coauthor with Archer of *Counseling and Mental Health Services on Campus: A Handbook of Contemporary Practices* (1998). He currently serves as case section editor for *Consulting Psychology Journal,* and he has been a reviewer for *Psychology Reports.*

Dr. Cooper completed a term in 1999 as a member of the governing board of the Association of University and College Counseling Center Directors (AUCCCD) and serves as the organization's liaison to Division 17 (Counseling Psychology) of the American Psychological Association. He has performed lead and support roles on college counseling center accreditation visits and has made numerous regional and national presentations on college mental health topics. He is a member of the Professional Practice Advisory Committee of Division 17 and was 1998 APA Convention program chair for Division 13. He does clinical work, supervision, outreach and consultation, administration, teaching, and research.

James Archer, Jr., PhD, ABPP, Counseling Psychology, Michigan State University) is professor of counselor education and psychology at the University of Florida, where he was director of the counseling center for thirteen years. For the ten previous years he was psychologist and associate director of the University of Delaware counseling center. He holds a BA in history from the University of Rochester, and an MA in counseling from San Francisco State University. He is a Diplomate in Counseling Psychology of the American Board of Professional Psychology (ABPP), and a Fellow of Division 17 (Counseling) of the American Psychological Association.

Archer's main professional interests are college student counseling and prevention. He has written two books, *Anxiety and Stress Management* (2nd edition, 1991, Accelerated Development) and *Counseling College Students* (1991, Continuum), and co-authored two others, *Multicultural Relations on Campus* (1991, Accelerated Development), and *Counseling and Mental Health Services on Campus: A Handbook of Contemporary Practices* (1998, Jossey Bass). He has also written numerous chapters and journal articles on prevention and college student mental health, and a co-authored monograph in *The Counseling Psychologist* on counseling centers in the 1990s. He has served on the editorial boards of the *Journal of College Student Development,* the *Journal for Specialists in Group Work,* and the *Journal of Counseling and Development.*

He served as president of the International Association of Counseling Services, was chairperson of the Association of University and College Counseling Center Directors (AUCCCD), served on accreditation teams for college counseling centers and has been a consultant for college and university counseling and mental health services.

Leighton C. Whitaker, PhD, ABPP, private practice, is Adjunct Clinical Professor at Widener University's Institute for Graduate Clinical Psychology, Editor of the *Journal of College Student Psychotherapy,* and Consulting Editor for Mental Health of the *Journal of American College Health.* He is a Fellow of the Society for Personality Assessment and the American College Health Association and was chair of the Association's Mental Health Section. Previously, he was Associate Professor and Director of Adult Psychology, University of Colorado Health Sciences Center; Professor and Director, University of Massachusetts Mental Health Services; Director of Swarthmore College Psychological Services; and Consultant to the U.S. Department of Labor's Job Corps Program. Dr. Whitaker holds a BA from Swarthmore College and a PhD from Wayne State University. He has a Diplomate in clinical psychology from the American Board of Professional Psychology.

His 80 professional publications address clinical and social subjects, including the *Whitaker Index of Schizophrenic Thinking* (Western Psychological Services, 1980), *Schizophrenic Disorders* (Plenum Press, 1992), *Campus Violence* (edited with J. Pollard, The Haworth Press, Inc., 1994), *Collective Violence* (edited with H. Hall, CRC Press, 1999), and *Understanding and Preventing Violence: The Psychology of Human Destructiveness* (CRC Press, 2000). Currently, he teaches, writes and presents about college student mental health, violence prevention, and schizophrenic disorders.

About the Contributors

Vivian Barnette (PhD Western Michigan University) is Senior Staff Psychologist at the University of Oregon where she is the Group and Eating Disorder Coordinator and Multicultural Seminar Leader. She holds many professional memberships and has contributed to the field of counseling psychology at numerous conferences on local and national levels. She completed her internship at the University of Iowa and her major research interests are: depression, anxiety, diversity and minority issues, crisis intervention, and supervision.

Jeff E. Brooks-Harris (PhD Ohio State University) is a psychologist and practicum coordinator at the Counseling and Student Development Center at the University of Hawaii at Manoa. His professional interests include psychotherapy integration, psychotherapy training, workshop design, and facilitation skills. He is coauthor of *Workshops: Designing and Facilitating Experiential Learning* (1999, Sage Publishing).

Edward A. Delgado-Romero (PhD University of Notre Dame) is Clinical Assistant Professor at the University of Florida Counseling Center and Assistant Director for Clinical Services and affiliate faculty member of the Counseling Psychology Program. His main interest is multicultural psychology in the university environment with emphasis on issues that affect Hispanic/Latino/a students. He has authored articles and made presentations on racism, using racial identity models in therapy, ecological psychology, and research productivity.

David A. Diana (MA University of Dayton) is Director of Alcohol & Other Drug Programs at Hobart & William Smith Colleges. He is a New York Credentialed Alcohol and Substance Counselor and a Michigan Limited Licensed Psychologist. Currently he is responsible for a comprehensive substance abuse prevention and counseling program. He has worked in community mental health and directed the counseling center at

Aquinas College in Grand Rapids, Michigan. His professional interests include brief interventions with college students to reduce alcohol-related harm, clinical strategies that combine social norms and harm reduction approaches, and co-existing mental health and substance abuse disorders. His involvement with a Consortium of New York State providers working with the Office of Mental Health and the Office of Alcoholism and Substance Abuse Services has led to changes in improving the continuity of care for those with both mental health and substance abuse disorders.

Steve K. Dubrow-Eichel (PhD University of Pennsylvania) is a counseling psychologist in private practice. He is a co-founder of RETIRN, a group practice that specializes in working with individuals and families harmed by "high demand groups," including destructive cults. His doctoral research earned him the John G. Clark Award for Distinguished Scholarship in Cultic Studies in 1990. He is also Supervising Psychologist at the St. Francis Homes for Boys (Bensalem, PA) and Adjunct Professor in the Counseling Psychology program at Chestnut Hill College (Philadelphia, PA). Dr. Dubrow-Eichel is a Diplomate in Counseling Psychology of the American Psychological Association and an American Association of Clinical Hypnosis (ASCH)-Approved Consultant in Clinical Hypnosis. He has written and presented on a broad range of topics, including trauma, addiction, hypnosis, brief and integrative psychotherapy, and the psychology of cultic groups.

Lynda D. Field (PhD University of Denver) is Assistant Professor at Suffolk University. Her research and scholarly interests include a variety of topics related to multicultural competency, biracial adolescents, clinical supervision, psychological assessment, and forensic psychology.

Michael G. S. Gottfried (PhD Arizona State University) did his internship in counseling psychology at Ohio State University Counseling and Consultation Service. He is currently Assistant Director of the Student Counseling and Development Center and Adjunct Professor in the Masters of Counseling Psychology program at Valparaiso University. His primary areas of interest are masculine gender role development and applications of attachment theory to counseling.

Christopher Gunn (PhD University of North Carolina) is a supervisor, consultant, trainer, teacher, and therapist. He graduated cum laude from Davidson College and did his internship at Towson University. He is

Assistant Director of the Counseling & Psychological Services and adjunct graduate faculty at Western Carolina University in Cullowhee, NC and in private practice. He and his son sailed around the world with 600 college students in 1998 as part of his job as the ship psychologist for Semester at Sea.

Brady R. Harnishfeger (PhD Western Michigan University) is Staff Psychologist and Coordinator of Group Services for Counseling and Psychological Services at Indiana University Health Center, Bloomington, Indiana. He has worked in community mental health and university counseling center settings. His professional interests include men's issues, relationship issues, and interpersonal communication. In working with college couples, Brady combines cognitive/behavioral, solution-focused and experiential therapeutic interventions.

Dennis Heitzmann (PhD University of Texas) has been the Director of the Center for Counseling and Psychological Services and Affiliate Professor of Counseling and Clinical Psychology at Penn State University since 1984. Prior to his arrival at Penn State, Dennis served as Director of the Center for Student Development at the University of Memphis and Director of Counseling Services at Rhodes College (Tennessee). He also maintains a private practice in psychology and organizational consulting, and has served as President of the Association for University and College Counseling Center Directors and as President of the International Association of Counseling Services, Inc. He has been an author, consultant, lecturer and program presenter on various mental health topics.

J. Eugene Knott (PhD University of Maryland) is Associate Professor in the Dept. of Human Development & Family Studies at the University of Rhode Island where he was Counseling Center Director. He is a Diplomate of ABPP, member of the Academy of Counseling Psychology, part-time private practice psychologist, and a former president of the Association for Death Education & Counseling. He has been an organizational development consultant, frequent management trainer and presenter for over 30 years. His current research and writing interests focus on leadership succession planning, student development, and various survivor sequelae to death loss.

Philip W. Meilman (PhD University of North Carolina at Chapel Hill) is Director of Counseling and Psychological Services, Courtesy Professor of Human Development, and Associate Professor of Psychology in Clinical Psychiatry at Cornell University. He also serves as Co-director of the Core Alcohol and Drug Survey project, which is based at Southern Illinois University at Carbondale. Prior to his work at Cornell, Dr. Meilman served as Director of the Counseling Center and Research Professor of Psychology at the College of William and Mary. He has published studies on collegiate alcohol use and college mental health issues, and is co-author with Paul Grayson, PhD, of *Beating the College Blues* (Facts on File, Inc., 1999).

Tu A. Ngo (MA) is a doctoral candidate in clinical psychology at the University of Rhode Island. She has an MPH in social behavioral sciences and health services and two years experience with inner-city high school youth. She is now a graduate intern at the University's Counseling Center. Her primary interests are Asian-American mental health, family violence in Asian communities, and cultural influences on health behaviors.

Paula Phillips (MS Oneonta State University, New York) is Director of the Counseling and Human Development Center at Franklin Pierce College. She is a nationally certified counselor, a New Hampshire licensed mental health counselor, and was one of the first NH certified alcohol/other drug counselors. Her early work focused on alcohol/other drug issues. She was co-founder of NECAN (New England Colleges Alcohol/Other Drug Network), as well as initiator of the Alcohol/Other Drug Committee for the New Hampshire College consortium. In recent years, post-modern approaches have captured her interest for discussing issues of empowerment, relationships, systems and meaning making. She has been Adjunct Professor and presenter on a variety of topics including: ethical practices, substance abuse, violence in the family, human development, therapeutic techniques and theories.

Harry L. Piersma (PhD, Purdue University) is a Senior Psychologist in the counseling center at Michigan State University. He is a Diplomate in Clinical Psychology (ABPP). He was Director of Research and Psychology Training at a private psychiatric facility in Grand Rapids, Michigan. Currently, he provides brief and longer-term psychotherapy for undergraduate and graduate students, supervises predoctoral interns and graduate level practica students, teaches and does research. He is a Fellow of the Society for Personality Assessment, and has published widely in areas related to psychological assessment and treatment outcome.

Jeffrey W. Pollard (PhD, ABPP University of Virginia), is Director of Health and Counseling Services and Adjunct Assistant Professor of Psychology at Denison University, Granville, Ohio, serves on the editorial board of the *Journal of College Student Psychotherapy* and formerly served the editorial board of the *Journal of Counseling and Development.* He has published in the areas of substance abuse and campus violence and is co-editor with Leighton Whitaker, PhD, of *Campus Violence: Kinds, Causes and Cures.* He is currently President Elect of the Academy of Counseling Psychology which is affiliated with ABPP and works to advocate for Counseling Psychology and ABPP Board Certified Counseling Psychologists. He is certified by the American Psychological Association Board of Governors College of Professional Psychology in the Treatment of Alcohol and Other Psychoactive Substance Use.

Jaquelyn L. Resnick (PhD University of Florida) is Professor and Director of the University of Florida Counseling Center. For the past five years, she has been on the Board of Directors of the International Association of Counseling Services, Inc. (IACS), the accrediting association for university and college counseling centers and public and private agencies and now serves as past-president. She also has been active in the governance of Association of University and College Counseling Center Directors. Her interests include body image and eating disorders; sexual assault/abuse/harassment, and feminist therapy.

Andrew Shea (PhD The Pennsylvania State University) holds an MA in Family Therapy from Southern Connecticut State University and a Bachelors of Arts in Psychology from Fairfield University. He is a staff psychologist and coordinator of practicum training for Counseling and Psychological Services at the Indiana University Health Center, Bloomington, Indiana. He has worked in residential treatment, hospital, community mental health, in-home treatment programs, and various university counseling centers. His interests include couple's therapy, group therapy, and supervision and training. When treating couples he is influenced by Bowen's Psychodynamic and Minuchin's Structural Family Therapy schools of thought combined with Gottman's interventions.

Paul L. Toth (PhD Indiana University) holds a Master of Divinity from San Francisco Theological Seminary and an AB from Hope College. He is a staff psychologist and coordinator of evaluation and research for Counseling and Psychological Services at Indiana University Health Center, Bloomington, Indiana and is part-time Assistant Professor in the Counseling Psychology Department. He has also served as Assistant Professor in the Counseling Department at the University of Iowa. In his work with couples he employs cognitive/behavioral techniques and is guided by social learning theory. He uses solution-focused, interpersonal communication and Gottman's approaches within this general framework. He is author of articles and book chapters on group counseling and college student grief and loss.

Preface

During the last decade the number of books on brief therapy has mushroomed. These books typically focus on a specific theory, an integrated brief therapy approach, a collection of different brief therapy approaches, or specific applications of brief therapy (with eating disorders, depression, etc.). Little has been written, however, examining brief therapy in a developmental context. In this special volume, we will examine brief therapy in a developmental context with young adults whose clinical problems often relate to or are caused by significant developmental impasses.

Our purpose in presenting this book is to provide case studies to illuminate a variety of brief therapy approaches with young adults who are college students between the ages of 17 and 25. We define brief therapy as limited to 20 or fewer sessions, including very brief and even single session therapy. We have selected diverse cases including men and women, different races and ethnicities, and different sexual orientations. We have selected, as authors, college counselors and psychologists who represent a wide variety of theoretical approaches and work regularly with young people. We asked authors to include basic information on their backgrounds and current positions as well as their counseling approach and any other information they felt was relevant to their particular case. We also asked them to include in the case discussion: (1) description of client; (2) presenting problem; (3) social/cultural history/environmental context; (4) assessment/diagnosis (whatever system the author used); (5) counseling goals; (6) treatment plan (how the goals were to be attained); (7) counseling process (description of the process/interaction); and (8) outcome/termination of counseling. We

[Haworth co-indexing entry note]: "Preface." Cooper, Stewart E., and James Archer, Jr. Co-published simultaneously in *Journal of College Student Psychotherapy* (The Haworth Press, Inc.) Vol. 16, No. 1/2, 2001, pp. xix-xxi; and: *Case Book of Brief Psychotherapy with College Students* (ed: Stewart E. Cooper, James Archer Jr., and Leighton C. Whitaker) The Haworth Press, Inc., 2002, pp. xxi-xxiii. Single or multiple copies of this article are available for a fee from The Haworth Document Delivery Service [1-800-342-9678, 9:00 a.m. - 5:00 p.m. (EST). E-mail address: getinfo@haworthpressinc.com].

xxi

requested two or three segments of their treatment transcripts to illustrate the critical aspects of the counseling.

Authors were required to obtain client permission and/or to disguise case details as appropriate according to American Psychological Association (APA) ethical guidelines. In most cases, authors provided actual transcripts; however, in a few instances they used recollected interview segments to illustrate key points. Authors were also asked to provide a discussion section to integrate the developmental aspects of the case, using their transcripts, and illustrations, and to explain how the therapy was made brief. Finally, authors were required to answer several questions we posed to them, based upon our reading of their case studies.

This book follows a more conceptually oriented text we wrote on college mental health services (Archer & Cooper, 1998). The organization of the present text is fairly simple. Chapter one summarizes developmental theory for the 17-25 year age group with a discussion of some of the brief therapy approaches in use today. Following are the sixteen case studies. Our final section, chapter 18, is a summary and commentary on the cases and approaches that have been presented. Reading this chapter first may assist the reader who wishes to select only some of the case studies. We have valued what well-written casebooks can offer to beginning as well as experienced professionals. We hope that this text makes such a contribution.

This text, *Case Book of Brief Psychotherapy with College Students*, is the eighth in the series of *Journal of College Student Psychotherapy* Monographic "Separates." In this instance, two special thematic double issues of the *Journal* comprise the simultaneously published book. The *Journal* versions are Volume 16, Numbers 1 and 2, and Volume 16, Numbers 3 and 4. Together, the "separates" comprise texts on the major concerns of college and university mental health services.

ACKNOWLEDGMENTS

We (Archer and Cooper) conceived the idea of this book as a follow-up to changes in the field of college mental health we had written and lectured about this past decade. We felt that the concrete examples of a case study approach could be very useful to those working in the field. We would like to express our deep appreciation to each of the contributing authors for their courage to present their work and for their willingness to do multiple revisions of their chapters. We would also like to thank Leighton Whitaker, the third editor, for his encouragement and support of this special issue/book publication and for all of his editorial acumen and work. Finally, we would like to thank Lisa Dorsey, Office Manager at the Valparaiso University Counseling Center, for all her efforts in typing the last several revisions of the manuscript.

Stewart E. Cooper
James Archer, Jr.

Chapter 1:
Introduction

The general principles of brief therapy (timely, focused, goal-oriented, an active therapist, rapid therapeutic alliance) appear to fit well with a developmental approach to counseling young adults. A developmental approach is defined here as counseling that deals primarily with blocks to normal development. Brief counseling that is focused and timely can work very well in this context. By learning to negotiate a developmental crisis or challenge, a young person may be able to overcome blocks to normal development. Such blocks could lead to serious pathology later on if they are not successfully negotiated when they are first encountered as part of normal developmental challenges.

For example, a 17-year-old male college student arrives at a residential college as a shy and rather anxious individual. The general developmental tasks creating difficulties for him appear related to interpersonal skills and perhaps the ability to form intimate relationships. He is unable to form satisfying associations in his freshman year and becomes more and more fearful of forming relationships and of asking women out for dates. Although beginning to feel quite badly about himself, if he is able to get counseling to help him learn the skills and develop the sense of efficacy necessary to develop effective relationships, he will be able to continue his development and realize that he can be a competent interpersonal and sexual being. This counseling might well be rather brief, perhaps focused on skill-building and anxiety-management, with augmentation through participation in an interpersonally oriented counseling group.

[Haworth co-indexing entry note]: "Chapter 1: Introduction." Cooper, Stewart E., James Archer, Jr., and Leighton C. Whitaker. Co-published simultaneously in *Journal of College Student Psychotherapy* (The Haworth Press, Inc.) Vol. 16, No. 1/2, 2001, pp. 1-12; and: *Case Book of Brief Psychotherapy with College Students* (ed: Stewart E. Cooper, James Archer, Jr., and Leighton C. Whitaker) The Haworth Press, Inc., 2002, pp. 1-12. Single or multiple copies of this article are available for a fee from The Haworth Document Delivery Service [1-800-342-9678, 9:00 a.m. - 5:00 p.m. (EST). E-mail address: getinfo@haworthpressinc.com].

1

If the young man does not seek help but graduates from college as an isolated and generally unhappy person, he may move into his twenties having bouts of depression and may never establish a positive identity or sense of self. In developmental language, his identity development and capacity for intimacy are foreclosed. Were he to present himself for counseling at age 28, after having experienced several years of depression and living an isolated life style, counseling would be more complex and take considerably longer.

This is not to say that all developmental problems of young adults are simple and easily solved. A similar young man who comes into counseling with a history of severe physical or emotional abuse would probably find his issues to be much less amenable to a brief intervention. He might need to participate in more intense, lengthy therapy to overcome primal feelings of inadequacy. On the other hand, some contemporary theories of brief counseling suggest that an intermittent brief approach could be used even with this more complex kind of case.

While there are no definitive answers as to what kinds of brief therapy work with what kinds of developmental problems, this book attempts to shed light on this question. In this introductory chapter, we will set the stage for the case studies with young adults by discussing the developmental period covering late adolescence and young adulthood, ages 17-25. We will also provide a summary of the evolution of brief therapy as a treatment format and its current applications.

YOUNG ADULTHOOD

This period is far from easy. Young adults are beginning more life roles than at any other point in their lives (Super, Savickas, & Super, 1996) and most adult psychopathologies emerge at this time (Lefton, 1997). Young adulthood represents a key transitional period between adolescence and adulthood in our society. While young adults have most of the freedom and many of the responsibilities of middle and older adults, they typically lack the economic and personal resources to live completely independent lives. Moreover, our culture's pressures to obtain substantial post-secondary school education or training has accentuated and perhaps prolonged young adulthood as a transition stage. Arnett (2000) has hypothesized a distinct stage in industrialized societies after adolescence that he calls "emerging adulthood."

Young adults can evidence substantial energy and enthusiasm, and yet struggle with incomplete and conflicted identity issues. They are still trying to determine who they are, what their role in life will be, and how they want to relate to others, and often confront psychological conflicts related to their key objectives of separating from family, forming partnerships, beginning careers, and establishing life patterns. Some of these internal conflicts relate to abrupt shifts between childlike dependence and adult independent functioning. Others relate to the vast and sometimes overwhelming amount of options and choices available as well as the highly mixed messages they may have received from the many diverse elements of their personal life experiences. Moreover, the research suggests that gender and ethnicity issues add significant complexity to young adult development. For example, Helm's racial identity model posits that young adulthood is an important time of racial identity development (Helms, 1990).

The study of developmental psychology has provided an extensive context for understanding young adults with problems, by explicating how people grow, mature, and change over the life span. Historically, different facets of development have been studied separately: biological (e.g., Kassin, 1998); cognitive (e.g., Piaget); language (e.g., Chomsky); social (e.g., Bowlby); psychosexual (e.g., Freud); or moral (e.g., Kohberg). Most traditional developmental theorists have espoused a stage of life perspective wherein predictable issues and change occur during differing periods of life (Lefton, 1997). Recent theories have espoused a more complex view with greater attention to sociocultural factors such as gender and minority status and on chaotic events such as the impact of specific significant life experiences (Lefton, 1997).

Still, many older theories remain viable and influential. For example, Erikson's model of psychosocial development has been in virtually every general psychology textbook for the last several decades. His transition to young adulthood model holds that Stage 5 (identity versus role confusion) and Stage 6 (intimacy versus isolation) are critical with young college-aged men and women struggling to achieve mastery of these two domains. Specifically, identity has to do with a person having a sense of who they are, their place in the world, and where they fit; intimacy has to do with learning to relate on a warm, social basis, and forming close, intimate relationship (Erikson, 1968). This formulation has been criticized in recent years regarding its application to women. Critics suggest that women do not necessarily develop identity in the same way as men.

Chickering and Reisser (1993) incorporated Erikson's concepts in their model of college student development. They posit seven factors:

(1) Developing competence–intellectual, physical and manual, interpersonal. (2) Managing emotions–awareness and acknowledgement, appropriate channels for release, balance of self-control and release. (3) Moving through autonomy toward interdependence–emotional independence, instrumental independence, healthy forms of interdependence. (4) Developing mature interpersonal relationships–tolerance and appreciation of differences, capacity for intimacy. (5) Establishing identity–comfort with body and appearance; comfort with gender and sexual orientation; sense of self in social, historical, and cultural context; clarification of self-concept through roles and life-style; sense of self in response to feedback from valued others; self-acceptance and self-esteem; personal stability and integration. (6) Developing purpose–vocational plans and aspirations, personal interests, interpersonal and family commitments. (7) Developing integrity–humanizing values, personalizing values, developing congruence (matching personal values with socially responsible behavior). (Chickering & Reisser, 1993, pp. 45-51)

Daniel Levinson's (1980) concept of Life Structures can also be useful in conceptualizing young adult development; it is based on the premise that life has four distinct eras, each with its own unique qualities, typical challenges, common tasks, and likely life events. The Life Structure represents the particular ways an individual comes to perceive and respond to the social and physical world. Transitions between eras (such as from adolescence to adulthood) can be quite difficult for some and may involve high levels of anxiety and depression.

Robert Havinghurst is a leading integrationist of developmental theories and concepts. In his book, *Developmental Tasks and Education,* Havinghurst (1972) outlined eight development tasks of young adulthood: (1) achieving new and more mature relations with age-mates of both sexes; (2) achieving a masculine or feminine social role; (3) accepting one's physique and using the body effectively; (4) achieving emotional independence of parents and other adults; (5) preparing for marriage and family life; (6) preparing for an economic career; (7) acquiring a set of values and an ethical system as a guide to behavior; and (8) desiring and achieving socially responsible behavior. Each of these tasks is very specific with a basis in biology, psychology, and culture.

Current textbooks on adult development and aging (e.g., Lemme, 1999; Schultz & Salthouse, 1999) are products of the dominant paradigm of psychology in general and developmental psychology specifically in their utilization of compartmentalized knowledge and study. These books cover the life span from early adulthood to death and look at physical and physiological functioning, cognitive and intellectual abilities, personality, social, familial, and intimate relationships, work and retirement, adaptation and mental health, and death and dying. Early adulthood is viewed as a time of peak performing in many areas. Middle and late stages of adulthood are discussed with an emphasis on de-bunking many of the negative myths of aging our society holds. Greater attention is now also being given to the impact of both gender and cultural factors (e.g., race, heritage, economic status, religion, geographic location, etc.).

One subfield of adult development and aging is the cross sectional and longitudinal study of psychological adjustment and psychopathology, viewed as a tentative state emerging from the complex, multifarious challenges of adulthood, particularly of the transitional phases such as adolescence to early adulthood. These transitions can create difficulties that lead to severe disorders such as major depression and schizophrenia. The *Diagnostic and Statistical Manual of Mental Disorders* (DSM-IV) differentiates disorders of childhood and adolescence from disorders of adulthood. Many of the latter emerge in the 17-25 year old age range.

Virtually every young adult seeks outside assistance from friends, teachers, mentors, and family members in working through the issues and complicated choices of this life transition. Some by choice, and others because the challenges are too great or because their personal or interpersonal resources are insufficient, seek professional counseling and therapy. Choca (1996), in summarizing the diathesis-stress model, argues that a given individual may have a biologically, psychologically, or behaviorally based vulnerability to stress. He adds that the heightened pressure of a developmental transition will lead to increased anxiety, disorganization of behavior, and increased defensive maneuvers which, in turn, lead to a pathological exaggeration of personality style and formation of symptoms. Thus, the interaction of personal and environmental factors with the stresses of the young adult transition generates large numbers of individuals with significant personal emotional problems.

A large national study (Baron, 1993) provided insight into the most typical counseling concerns of early young adults. The investigation involved 3,016 clients seeking services in college mental health. Numerous problem categories emerged from factor analyses: (a) autonomy, (b) break-up, (c) values, (d) social discomfort, (e) sleeping problems,

(f) suicidality, (g) body image, (h) career/future, (i) homesick, (j) school concerns, (k) stress. Single item issues involved alcohol/drug problems, death or impending death, ethnic/racial discrimination, rape/sexual assault, sexual identity/orientation, and problem pregnancy/sexually transmitted diseases. Many of these problem areas are related to classic young adult developmental issues.

Just as young adults are unique as a group, so are young adults as clients unique. As a group, there is plasticity and flexibility of response, and in many cases the damage caused by negative life experiences and skill deficits is limited. Patterns of negative and self-destructive behavior are often not yet set and personal identities that include a very negative image of self have not yet jelled. The combinations of all the above makes most young adults good candidates for brief therapy.

BRIEF THERAPY

The concept of brief therapy is not new. Freud reported several cases of single session analyses, and many forms of analytic therapy have been developed as brief approaches. Of course, brief is a relative term and from a psychoanalytic viewpoint brief might mean 30 or 40 sessions. Today, we often think of brief therapy as being as few as 6-10 sessions. Several brief analytic therapies were described the 1970s. Malan's (1976, 1978) ideas about brief therapy generated approaches by Sifneos (1979), Davanloo (1978, 1979) and others, using many of the basic Freudian ideas such as a triangle of conflict (defense, anxiety, and impulse) and a triangle of persons (significant others in the past, current relationships, and therapist). Insight and working through transference are important elements, and from this perspective, are achieved more quickly by taking an active orientation that elicits transference and attempts to keep a narrower focus than traditional psychoanalysis. Mann (1973) proposed a theory that involved exactly 12 sessions with a kind of forced confrontation with loss and individuation. Strupp and Binder (1984) formulated an interpersonal analytic approach emphasizing an active approach that works when problems can be defined in interpersonal terms with the client-therapist relationship as the primary curative force.

The two major cognitive theories of psychotherapy, Beck (1976, 1991) and Ellis (1977, 1993), have always been relatively brief though not originally labeled as such. Part of their original appeal, in reaction to analytic approaches, was their directness and focus. This moved the therapist and the client directly into dealing with cognitions seen as the cause of psychological problems. These cognitive theories have now merged with other behavioral approaches into what is now called cognitive-behavior therapy. The behavior therapies of Wolpe (1990) and Kazdin (1994), based primarily on classic and operant models of learning theory, also stressed a more direct and concrete approach to counseling and therapy. Bandura's (1977) social learning theory also became an important influence on the developing cognitive-behavioral approach to therapy. Additionally, Meichenbaum's stress inoculation model (1985) illustrates how cognitive and behavioral approaches have developed into integrated systems using techniques and approaches from all three of the major streams of learning theory (conditioning, operant, and social learning). Meichenbaum has more recently re-labeled his approach a constructivist cognitive behavioral approach (Meichenbaum, 1993), adding a constructivist point of view to cognitive behavioral therapy.

New brief therapy approaches continue to be developed. Eye Movement Desensitization Therapy (EMDR) (Shapiro, 1995) has also been called a cognitive behavioral approach because of its emphasis on reconditioning and changing negative thought patterns. The use of treatment manuals and protocols is perhaps the most recent evolution of the cognitive behavioral approach. The design of these protocols relies upon the most recent empirical research related to the targeted problem. For example, Bourne (1998) has published a protocol for overcoming a specific phobia that includes a ten-session treatment program.

Strategic approaches to counseling have been important in the evolution of brief therapy. Milton Erickson's work (1954,1977) emphasized the direct and indirect interpersonal influences of the therapist directly and indirectly and included hypnosis, paradoxical, and other strategic interventions that could move the clients quickly. Haley (1963, 1987) and members of the Palo Alto Mental Research Institute continued developing these techniques with an emphasis on current problem solving and strongly influenced the evolution of family therapy and systemic interventions.

The newer, postmodern approaches to counseling, such as solution-focused counseling and narrative therapy, can be used for brief counseling and therapy. Solution focused therapy is, in fact, designed to be a brief approach, and has four basic theoretical assumptions: solutions can be constructed by the client and counselor; clients have the strength and ability to find solutions; emphasizing and expanding upon small changes and a focus on the presenting problem can lead to larger and more systemic change; and change is inevitable. Among the leading solution focused theory writers and practitioners have been deShazer (1985, 1994), Berg and Miller (1992), and O'Hanlon and Weiner-Davis (1989).

Narrative therapy is an approach focusing on helping the client "deconstruct" his or her "problem saturated" story and rewrite a new narrative. Examining the "discourses" or influences on the person's development is part of the deconstruction process with the client considered the expert on his or her own narrative. The counselor does not assume an expert role (Monk, Winsdale, Crocket, & Epston, 1997). Although not originally described as a brief therapy per se, narrative therapy can be accomplished in a few sessions depending upon the case.

Very brief counseling has also been discussed and researched. Talmon (1992) described a study of single session therapy in an HMO setting and Bloom (1981) presented a case study using a single session format. These single-session approaches involved longer sessions than the normal 50-minute hour and often included initial and follow-up phone contact. Pinkerton and Rockwell (1994) discussed counseling situations (many of them developmental) wherein college students needed only one, two, or three sessions.

Many theorists and researchers have offered integrated or eclectic models of brief therapy. Lazarus (1997) described his multimodal approach to brief therapy as eclectic. He uses an assessment system with the BASIC ID (Behavior, Affect, Sensation, Imagery, Cognition, Interpersonal, Drugs/Biology) as a system to assesses and treat clients. Steenbarger (1992), in an extensive review of current brief therapy theory and research, hypothesized a three stage model of brief therapy which included engagement, discrepancy, and consolidation. Cummings and Sayama's (1995) work on intermittent counseling over the life span might also be labeled integrative since they illustrated a variety of methods in their case discussions.

Several authors have compiled collections of different brief therapy approaches. Budman (1995) included approaches to individual, group, and marriage and family counseling. Bloom (1997) offered very brief descriptions of a large number of theories. Budman, Hoyt, and Friedman (1992) provided a collection of first session case studies and transcripts from a variety of approaches.

This brief review covers only a few of the highlights of the many recent publications and theories about brief therapy. In order to examine the general usefulness for brief counseling of young adults in the developmental stage (ages 17-25) covered in this book, it is helpful to generalize some common principles of brief therapy. Bloom (1997) listed the following common elements of brief therapy, adapting them from Koss and Shiang (1994):

1. Prompt and early intervention to aid in resolving immediate problems, in part to avoid more serious and chronic problems in the future.
2. Identification of limited but attainable goals designed to ameliorate the most disabling symptoms and improve coping ability.
3. Contract for time-limited intervention designed to attain specific goals.
4. Principal focus on the here and now rather than on early life events.
5. Active and directive therapists who maintain the focus and organization of therapeutic contacts.
6. Experienced therapists who keep goals in sight, and provide rapid initial assessment of the nature of the problem and the client's resources. (p. 5)

There appear to be several advantages for the use of brief therapy with young adults. First, and perhaps foremost, young adults are in the midst of a relatively early stage of life. Consequently, they have the potential to overcome a variety of problems with a timely and effective counseling intervention to help prevent further psychological or emotional damage. Second, the general vitality and optimism of young people tends to make them good candidates for concise, focused counseling interventions. They are often action-oriented, hopeful, and willing to actively pursue specific goals with the belief that they can move forward once a specific problem is handled. Third, young adults' needs for intervention are often acute. They have less experience in coping with various life traumas and therefore often feel the need to receive immediate counseling services. For example, a young adult experiencing deep depression for the first time is likely to be desperate and have limited coping mechanisms versus an older adult who has experienced periods of depression several times. Yet, the young are typically optimistic and in a stage of life when most things seem soluble.

Although brief therapies typically require an action-orientation on the part of both the client and the therapist, the importance of the therapeutic alliance cannot be overstated. This is particularly important with young adults. A significant part of the challenge to therapists doing effective brief therapy is to develop an effective relationship. Young adult clients usually respond well to active counselors who respect their independence and competencies and who treat them as adults. Therapists have to avoid taking on a parental role that generates resistance. For young adults who have not had positive parenting experiences, a brief yet significant counseling experience with an adult can be profoundly helpful.

Although brief therapy has much to offer the young adult, it is important to note its limitations. Even though some brief therapy theorists claim that any client can be helped with these approaches, many practitioners contend that attempting to do brief therapy with students who have serious problems can be harmful. Hersh (1988) argued strongly for an effective match between type of treatment and student needs. Gelso (1992) cautioned against the lack of research evidence supporting what he termed the "myths" of brief therapy. We urge a considered, but optimistic approach to brief therapy with young adults. It is clearly not the treatment of choice in all cases but appears to have great utility with young adults.

In the following chapters of this book, the reader can examine a variety of creative and brief approaches to counseling young adults. The great promise and incredible difficulties experienced by young people from all walks of life will come alive as therapists describe specific counseling cases. Our final chapter attempts to integrate the specific material presented in each of the cases into several themes and core principles and will contain the highlights we feel each case presents.

Stewart E. Cooper
James Archer, Jr.
Leighton C. Whitaker

REFERENCES

Arnett, J. J. (2000). Emerging adulthood. *American Psychologist*, 55 (5), pp. 469-480.

Bandura, A. (1977). *Social Learning Theory*. Englewood Cliffs, NJ: Prentice Hall.

Baron, A. Jr. (1993). *Report of the Research Consortium of Counseling and Psychological Services in Higher Education*. Austin: University of Texas Counseling Center.

Beck, A. T. (1976). *Cognitive therapy and the emotional disorders*. New York: International Universities Press.

Beck, A. T. (1991). Cognitive therapy: A 30-year retrospective. *American Psychologist*, 46, 368-375.

Berg, I. K., & Miller, S. D. (1992). *Working with the problem drinker: A solution-focused approach.* New York: Norton.

Bloom, B. L. (1997). *Planned Short-Term Psychotherapy: A Clinical Handbook.* (2nd. ed.). Boston: Allyn and Bacon.

Bloom, B. L. (1981). Focused single-session therapy: Initial development and evaluation. In S. Budman (Ed.), *Forms of brief therapy* (pp. 167-216). New York: Guilford Press.

Bourne, E. J. (1998). *Therapist manual: Overcoming specific phobia.* Oakland, CA: New Harbinger Publications.

Budman, S. (1995). *Forms of Brief Therapy.* New York: Guilford Press.

Budman, S. H., Noyt, M.F., & Friedman, S. (1992). *The first session in brief therapy.* New York: Guilford Publications.

Choca, J. P., & Van Denburg, E. J. (1996). *Manual for clinical psychology trainees* (3rd ed.). Levittown, PA: Brunner Mazel.

Cummings, N., & Sayama, M. (1995). *Focused psychotherapy: A casebook of brief, intermittent psychotherapy throughout the life cycle.* New York: Brunner/Mazel.

Davanloo, H. (Ed.). (1978). *Basic principles and techniques in short-term dynamic psychotherapy.* New York: Spectrum.

Davanloo, H. (1979). Techniques of short-term dynamic psychotherapy. *Psychiatric Clinics of North America, 2,* 11-22.

de Shazer, S. (1985). *Keys to solution in brief therapy.* New York: Norton.

de Shazer, S. (1994). *Words were originally magic.* New York: Norton.

Ellis, A., & Grieger, R. (Eds.) (1977). *Handbook of rational-emotive therapy.* New York: Springer.

Ellis, A. (1993). Fundamentals of rational-emotive therapy for the 1990s. In W. Dryden and L. K. Hill (Eds.), *Innovations in rational-emotive therapy* (pp. 1-32). Thousand Oaks, CA: Sage.

Erickson, M. H. (1954). Special techniques of brief hypnosis. *Journal of Clinical and Experimental Hypnosis, 2,* 109-129.

Erickson, M. H. (1977). Hypnotic approaches to therapy. *American Journal of Clinical Hypnosis, 20,* 20-35.

Erikson, E. H. (1968). *Identity: Youth and crisis.* New York: Norton.

Gelso, C. J. (1992). Realities and emerging myths about brief therapy. *The Counseling Psychologist, 20,* 464-461.

Haley, J. (1963). *Strategies of psychotherapy.* New York: Grune & Stratton.

Haley, J. (1987). *Problem-solving therapy* (2d ed). San Francisco: Jossey-Bass.

Havinghurst, R. J. (1972). *Developmental tasks and education* (3d ed.). New York: David McKay Company, Inc.

Helms, J. E. (1990). *Black and white racial identity.* Westport, CT: Praeger.

Hersh, J. (1988). A commentary on brief therapy. *Journal of College Student Psychotherapy, 3,* 55-58.

Kassin, S. (1998). *Psychology* (2nd ed.). Upper Saddle River, NJ: Prentice Hall.

Kazdin, A. E. (1994). *Behavior modification in applied settings* (5th ed.). Pacific Grove, CA: Brooks/Cole.

Koss, M. P., & Shiang, J. (1994). Research on brief psychotherapy. In A. E. Bergin & S. L. Garfield (Eds.), *Handbook of psychotherapy and behavior change* (pp. 664-700). New York: Wiley.

Lazarus, A. (1997). *Brief but comprehensive psychotherapy: The multimodal way.* New York: Springer.

Lefton, L. A. (1997). *Psychology* (6th ed.). Weedham Heights, MA: A Viacom Company.

Lemme, B. H. (1999). *Development in adulthood* (2nd ed.). New York: Allyn and Bacon.

Levinson, D. J. (1980). Toward a conception of the adult life course. In N. J. Smelser & E. H. Erickson (Eds.), *Themes of work and love in adulthood.* (pp. 265-290). Cambridge, MA: Harvard University Press.

Malan, D. H. (1976). *The frontier of brief psychotherapy: An example of the convergence of research and clinical practice.* New York: Plenum.

Malan, D. H. (1978). Principles of technique in short term dynamic psychotherapy. In H. Davanloo (Ed.), *Basic principles and techniques in short-term dynamic psychotherapy.* (pp. 332-342). New York: Spectrum.

Mann, J. M. (1973). *Time limited psychotherapy.* Cambridge, MA: Harvard University Press.

Meichenbaum, D. (1985). *Stress inoculation training.* New York: Pergamon.

Meichenbaum, D. (1993). Changing conceptions of cognitive behavior modification: Retrospect and prospect. *Journal of Consulting and Clinical Psychology*, 61, 202-204.

Monk, G., Winsdale, J., Crocket, K., & Epston, D. (1997). *Narrative therapy in practice.* San Francisco, CA: Jossey Bass.

O'Hanlon, W. H., & Weiner-Davis, M. (1989). *In search of solutions: A new direction in psychotherapy.* New York: Norton.

Pinkerton, R. S., & Rockwell, W. J. (1994). Brief psychotherapy with college students. *Journal of American College Health*, 42, 156-162.

Schulz, R., & Salthouse, T. (1999). *Adult development and aging* (3rd ed.). Upper Saddle River, NJ: Prentice Hall.

Shapiro, D. A. (1995). *Eye movement desensitization and reprocessing: Basic principles, protocols, and procedures.* New York: Guilford.

Sifneos, P. E. (1979). *Short-term dynamic psychotherapy: Evaluation and technique.* New York: Plenum

Steenbarger, B. N. (1992). Toward the science-practice integration in brief counseling and therapy. *The Counseling Psychologist*, 20, 403-450.

Strupp, H. H., & Binder, J. L. (1984). *Psychotherapy in a new key: A guide to time-limited dynamic psychotherapy.* New York: Basic Books.

Super, D. E., Savickas, M. L., & Super, C. M. (1996). The life-span, life-space approach to careers. In D. Brown, L. Brooks & Associates (Eds.), *Career choice and development* (3rd ed.) (pp. 1-170). San Francisco: Jossey-Bass.

Talmon, M. (1990). *Single session therapy.* San Francisco: Jossey-Bass Publishers.

Wolpe, J. (1990) *The practice of behavior therapy* (4th ed.). New York: Pergamon.

Chapter 2:
Flight of the Appalachian Bumblebee: Solution-Oriented Brief Therapy with a Young Adult

Christopher Gunn

SUMMARY. A 19-year-old single Appalachian Caucasian man presented with panic attacks related to a recently developed phobia of bees. Brief solution-oriented therapy, along with the tools of Rational Emotive Behavior Therapy (REBT), was employed successfully to treat this specific phobia. Cultural, familial, gender, and sexual identity issues were also addressed. *[Article copies available for a fee from The Haworth Document Delivery Service: 1-800-342-9678. E-mail address: <getinfo@haworthpressinc. com> Website: <http://www.HaworthPress.com> © 2001 by The Haworth Press, Inc. All rights reserved.]*

KEYWORDS. Specific phobia, solution-oriented therapy

For the past 10 years, I have worked as a psychologist in a university counseling center in the southern Appalachian Mountains. Though my

Address correspondence to: Christopher Gunn, Counseling and Psychological Services, Western Carolina University, Cullowhee, NC 28723 (E-mail: gunn@wcu.edu).

[Haworth co-indexing entry note]: "Chapter 2: Flight of the Appalachian Bumblebee: Solution-Oriented Brief Therapy with a Young Adult." Gunn, Christopher. Co-published simultaneously in *Journal of College Student Psychotherapy* (The Haworth Press, Inc.) Vol. 16, No. 1/2, 2001, pp. 13-25; and: *Case Book of Brief Psychotherapy with College Students* (ed: Stewart E. Cooper, James Archer, Jr., and Leighton C. Whitaker) The Haworth Press, Inc., 2002, pp. 13-25. Single or multiple copies of this article are available for a fee from The Haworth Document Delivery Service [1-800-342-9678, 9:00 a.m. - 5:00 p.m. (EST). E-mail address: getinfo@haworthpressinc.com].

practice at the center continues to be rich and full, I opened a limited private practice about four years ago to experience the unlimited joys of managed care and fee collection. In both settings, I work as a solution-oriented brief therapist, helping clients make desired changes in an efficient manner by focusing on exceptions to the problem, strengths, and possibilities. Some folks call it an eclectic approach; I refer to it as the Malcolm X approach to change: By any means necessary. Well, almost any.

I am a southerner by family and birth, but having spent my teen years near New York City, college and graduate school in North Carolina, a year of study in France, my pre-doc internship in Maryland, and four months sailing around the world, I consider my definition of "home" very inclusive. I am a tall Caucasian male of Scottish decent, complete with red hair and beard, and almost 40. As a parent of a son who recently graduated from high school and an organizer of my 20th high school reunion, I relate well to people of all ages. My practice has been with adolescents on up to retirees. The vast majority of my clients have been Caucasian, Christian, and in the process of pursuing post-secondary education, though I have seen a significant number of clients from diverse religious, racial, sexual identity, and cultural minority groups. I am proud of my cross-cultural competence and positive reputation for such. In addition to my education, I believe I owe this multicultural skill and appreciation to open-minded and active parents and numerous travel experiences.

Anxiety disorders have become a specialty of mine, in part, because I find them extremely responsive to cognitive-behavioral and strategic interventions. I am a fan of the cognitive-behavioral principles of Ellis, Beck, and Meichenbaum, and I am well versed in the assorted works of the strategic Milton Erickson spin-offs (e.g., Jay Haley, Stephen Gilligan, Bill O'Hanlon, Jeffrey Zeig; see Zeig and Gilligan, 1990). And finally, I find Reid Wilson's (1996) work, *Don't Panic,* invaluable in the treatment of a variety of disorders along the anxiety continuum.

BIOGRAPHIC SKETCH OF CLIENT

Jonah was a 19-year-old, single Caucasian male of average height, thin build, and crew-cut hair (under his baseball cap), who presented at my private practice at the suggestion of his mother (who found my name through her Employee Assistance Program). Jonah presented as a neatly dressed, polite, friendly, energetic, and animated young man who, with his strong southern mountain accent, enjoyed telling a good story. "Yes, sir, I can tell 'em like the old-timers can!" He was clearly oriented and bright, attending a community college and working part-time with plans to transfer into a 4-year college, major in criminal justice, and become a police officer like his elder brother. He and his brother, Joshua, 23, lived together, only minutes from their parents who were in their late 40s.

PRESENTING PROBLEM

Jonah began to have (what he called) "panic attacks" three months prior to seeking help while working as a lifeguard at a community swimming pool. He presented in crisis due to his having had such an attack during the previous weekend in which he felt "out right hot," nauseous, tightness in his chest and back, and had racing thoughts about bee stings and dying. He noted that his fear of bees was "way out of control," and further, that this fear was originally triggered by his father's getting stung and having a strong allergic reaction when Jonah was a child. There was no history of Jonah having this allergy; he reported having been stung as a child and "it didn't even swell up." Earlier that summer, Jonah had to treat a young boy in anaphylactic shock at the pool. Afterward, he acknowledged that he was primed to react strongly. He reported that he had begun to avoid situations that had a high potential for the presence of bees such as going to the trash dump, or walking barefoot in the yard. He then generalized this fear and avoided still other situations, such as riding with the car windows down or going hunting with his brother.

In addition to frequent, what I called, "anxiety attacks," Jonah reported decreased appetite, increased difficulty falling asleep, and disturbed concentration. He thought his resting pulse was high and had seen his family physician who had been treating him for years for his "regular irregularity" (irritable bowels). Jonah reported she had told him he was "fine" and had prescribed an antidepressant "as needed" to reduce his bee anxiety; he was not interested in taking meds for "this bee thing," though he was taking medication for an acne condition. He felt his friendships were severely affected by his bee anxiety, for he had difficulty explaining why he did not want to go out or join in certain activities with them. And his motivation lessened for some activities and classes.

DSM IV DIAGNOSIS

Axis I	300.29	Specific Phobia, Animal Type (bees).
Axis II	V71.09	No Diagnosis. Did not meet criteria for Obsessive Compulsive Disorder (OCD) or Obsessive Compulsive Personality Disorder (OCPD), but some OCD characteristics were evident.
Axis III		Irritable Bowel Syndrome (IBS), gaseous burping, facial acne.
Axis IV		Problems related to environmental setting (Presence of bees).
Axis V	55	

I concluded that "specific phobia" as described by DSM-IV could account for the range of Jonah's symptoms better than a diagnosis of "panic attack" and that "specific phobia" more accurately described the feared stimulus. I used the more inclusive term "anxiety attack" instead of "panic attacks" to help Jonah see his less severe physiological reactions to bees as significant symptoms. However, my clinical treatment of these "anxiety attacks" included cognitive-behavioral interventions and was quite similar to my treatment of panic attacks.

FAMILY / PERSONAL / CULTURAL HISTORY

During the intake interview, I learned of Jonah's history of OCD characteristics and gastrointestinal complaints. He reported "worryin' about 'nothin' " and having an upset stomach frequently, beginning back in elementary school. He remembered that as a child he thought "more about things" than his peers, often asking more questions and needing to be reassured. "My mamma always called me a 'nervous boy.' I suppose she's right." To "better" himself he had recently chosen to reduce his caffeine intake (e.g., coffee, soda), but continued to use nicotine (chewing tobacco) daily. His father and brother and numerous other family members smoked cigarettes and dipped regularly.

He presented a relatively unremarkable psychosocial history as the younger of two sons born to parents who were still happily married, gainfully employed, did not drink alcohol, and were not abusive. He knew of no family history of anxiety disorders, though he noted his mother's long-standing fear and dislike of cats. Maternal grandfather and great uncle were and continued to be alcoholic. "They drink well past the point of return and there's no stopping them anyhow," he commented. Jonah reported his family relationships as "very close." They were practicing Methodists who had frequent gatherings/reunions with extended family, most of whom lived in the region.

Jonah had been dating Jessica for two years; at intake, she was a senior in his hometown high school. He reported the relationship as sexually active and "just fine, thank you." He described a good network of friends, mostly from his school and places of employment.

CASE CONCEPTUALIZATION AND TREATMENT GOAL

Jonah wanted to be free of this "embarrassing fear" and "to be able to do all the things I've always done." I was aware of his Axis II OCD characteristics to "worry"; I suspected these anxieties worked their ways through and out of Jonah's body in somatic and cognitive ways. I believed successful treatment of his Axis I Specific Phobia was possible through a focused, brief approach. Thus, the goal was to reduce, if not eliminate his bee phobia, and the plan was to use a solution-oriented approach with cognitive-behavioral techniques.

MULTICULTURAL CONSIDERATIONS

- As is true of many Appalachian mountain families, some cultural rules are antithetic to counseling, particularly: "Don't ask for help," and "don't talk about personal problems outside the family."
- The strong traditional roles of men in Jonah's family were also a strike against Jonah talking to another man about his feelings.
- I'm not a hunter or avid sports fan, so I was a bit concerned at the start that this might limit my credibility as someone Jonah could relate to and trust.
- My neutral (some say "northern") accent might cost me points.
- Though Jonah could talk, I could instantly tell Jonah preferred "doing" to "talking."

TREATMENT / INTERVENTIONS / COUNSELING PROCESS

During the intake we began cognitive-behavioral work by discussing the specifics of the stimuli that triggered numerous thoughts and reactive behaviors. Jonah immediately recognized the power of his cognitions (i.e., thoughts of bees) and voiced his preference for an approach that used cognitions over the other approaches I highlighted (e.g., medication evaluation, relaxation training). He eagerly agreed to monitor his anxiety attacks (within the "ABC's" of Ellis' Rational Emotive Behavior Therapy–REBT), and I encouraged him to experience the anxiety fully to collect accurate data ("symptom prescription" via Ericksonian therapists). We agreed to meet the following week and to make plans to alter the most anxiety-producing thoughts so he might begin to experience some relief ("offering hope" via Irving Yalom, among others, and the "meta-communication" of Ericksonians).

Jonah returned the next week experiencing much less anxiety and "not a single panic attack" since we last met. He felt the ABC's had helped him catch his thoughts "before they got out of control" in two instances when he had been "hit" by flying insects (not bees). He reported using deep breathing at times, which also helped him redirect his thoughts and reduce anxiety. He was relieved and pleased with the rapid positive changes and wanted to know more about this cognitive-behavioral approach.

Jonah: So, it's my thoughts that are making this worse?

T: Yes. It's like your thoughts are throwing a switch that sends a message to your body that you are in great danger when you really aren't. The switch gets flipped when it's not supposed to and your body reacts like it's tied to the railroad tracks and the train is coming.

Jonah: That's what it feels like all right. And I didn't use to think so much about bees, much less be so afraid of them.

T: Right. But, for whatever reasons, you do think a lot about them now. It's like a big, steep steel gutter has developed in your brain for thoughts about bees. As soon as the thought appears, it heads down this gutter, picking up speed and power until it hits the bottom where the switch gets flipped and your body reacts with anxiety. The trick is to identify and divert those first thoughts before they get to the steel gutter.

Jonah: Like catching myself with that bug and saying, "it's not a bee and even if it were I doubt its sting would kill me."

Jonah took to the approach quickly and with vigor. As we continued to talk, he noted some "weird things I do," giving me more details about his compulsive behaviors and rituals. He admitted to repositioning his drinking glass on the table several times while eating, and tapping on his shoe in a certain order while sitting and watching TV. He went on to note he had probably been doing these things for about three years. He also noted how, as a child, he saw his grandfather die of cancer over time. I listened, supported, and empathized as he told me things he thought his psychologist should know. Though he was reluctant, he agreed to see a local psychiatrist for a medication evaluation; while I thought meds might help, I mostly wanted a second opinion on his possible Obsessive Compulsive Personality Disorder.

In the second and third sessions, Jonah continued to reduce symptoms and slowly expand his activity level. I would challenge him to try a "next step" activity and, without having developed a formal hierarchy of behaviors, he was successful in selecting activities that were feasible (e.g., riding in his truck with the passenger window down). He seemed to enjoy relating successes at the beginning of each meeting and then would tell me more about family dynamics. He noted how he was different from his father and brother in that he was more sensitive to feelings–his own and other people's. He talked about his great uncle who had died a few years before who also had been different from most family members; he had been more into the arts and more expressive than other men in the family. After I highlighted the strong traditional gender and family roles at play, Jonah conveyed (in a lowered voice) that he had just learned the previous year that his deceased uncle had been gay. This was a "big deal" in his family.

In the fourth and fifth sessions, Jonah became more proficient at disputing his own irrational beliefs and reported continued progress at reducing his anxiety about bees. However, he still had not gone back into the woods, felt his concentration was not back up to par, and had noticed an increase in some of his compulsions. On the other hand, he had seen the movie "As Good As It Gets" about an obsessive compulsive man and felt hopeful that his "nervousness" was not terminal. He talked more about rigid family roles and his being "different," but quickly denied ever having any questions about his own sexuality. At the close of the fifth meeting, Jonah attributed much of his progress to sources outside of his control.

> Jonah: Yep, now with fall ending and winter coming on, there're less and less bees to be botherin' me. I'm sure this is why I'm doing better. Sure, the ABC's still help, but soon there won't be any more bees.
>
> T: And then when spring comes, your anxiety attacks will start all over again?
>
> Jonah: Well, I guess so.
>
> T: Could be, but I think you're the one who's made the difference. In fact, I might encourage you to *dispute* your belief that it's the weather and give yourself more credit for your progress.
>
> Jonah: Like, "where's the evidence that there are less bees now and that's why I'm better?"
>
> T: Exactly.
>
> Jonah: Well, I have gone to places where I've seen bees–like the dump–and I've done much better.
>
> T: Right. And that was just a few days ago. And I bet, even in the dead of winter, if some resurrected bee makes it into your sights, you'll be able to handle it.
>
> Jonah: Yeah, you're right.
>
> T: So, then it's not the weather, it's you and your new thinking.
>
> Jonah: Well, Doc, you got me there!

Before our next meeting, Jonah saw the psychiatrist who had not recommended medication, given the dramatic progress he had made with counseling alone. The psychiatrist, like me, felt his OCD characteristics were just that and did not require pharmacotherapy at this point.

In our sixth session, Jonah reported his pleasure with the psychiatrist's pronouncement as well as his recent success at driving with all windows down and going into the woods with his brother. He felt his "good long talk with my mother and with God" had been very helpful. Symptoms of anxiety were gone. He expressed much relief and satisfaction with getting back to "normal." He told me that he now recognized his "unique style" and approach to people, different than other men in the family, and that now he was more comfortable in "maturing into adulthood." We reviewed treatment, consolidated learnings, previewed potential relapses, and agreed to end counseling. Jonah had difficulty saying goodbye, in part, "because I like to BS with you." As I do with all clients, I gave him an open invite to return, even if nothing was "wrong."

OUTCOME / TERMINATION

I had met with Jonah weekly for the six weeks following the intake session and he continued to make progress until our termination. I felt outcomes were likely to be positive due to the relief he showed and felt during intake and in the changes he reported in the first session. He was ready to be in counseling, wanting to get over the bee phobia and to explore his family's gender roles in light of how he felt "different." I did not hear from him after our termination so, in line with good brief therapy practices, I called him about 10 weeks after. He reported doing "well" and had had no more anxiety about bees. He was taking a psychology class and was considering majoring in psychology instead of criminal justice. He sounded healthy and happy and was appreciative of the call.

DISCUSSION

In reflecting on the case, I asked myself three questions: Did Jonah have an Obsessive Compulsive Personality Disorder? No, I don't think so, as he did not meet the criteria for perfectionism or preoccupation with details, rules, lists, et cetera. Was Specific Phobia more accurate than OCD or a Panic Disorder on Axis I? Yes, the diagnosis of specific phobia was more accurate and more helpful to focus the treatment. Was Jonah gay? Or at least questioning his sexual identity? I know as a caring and competent professional I'm supposed to launch into an insightful and dynamic discussion of the etiological underpinnings of his bee phobia and the likelihood of symptom substitution, but as a solution-oriented psychologist, I stayed with the client's presenting complaint. Jonah did not present his sexual identity as the pressing issue. I think it is best to help clients solve the problems they present in the most effective, least intrusive way possible. Such an approach also lays the positive groundwork for any counseling the client might seek in the future.

QUESTIONS

1. *You list several characteristics of Appalachian Mountain culture that are antithetical to counseling, yet you seemed able to establish a quick and therapeutic relationship with this client. Can you say more about how that occurred? Was it your appearance? You seemed to use metaphors that resonated with him?*

I think Minuchin's emphasis on "joining" with a client (see Berman, 1985) is essential to getting the relationship off to a good start. The therapist must find ways to connect with the client via common interests, humor, language, and/or worldviews. With Jonah, I think I was able to join with him using humor and metaphors similar to his own. He used metaphors that were visual and mechanical. And, sure, my being a white guy with a beard might have helped with my credentials (see Sue & Sue, 1999).

2. *You mentioned in the introduction that you liked Meichenbaum's approach, and his stress inoculation technique includes relaxation training and problem solving components along with cognitive modification. Yet, in this case you chose not to use any formal relaxation training as part of the treatment of bee phobia. Part of your decision was that the client expressed comfort with cognitive approaches. However, can you discuss why you did not more strongly advocate for his learning some form of general relaxation training to directly reduce some of the more somatic general anxiety symptoms like Irritable Bowel Syndrome (IBS)?*

In our first meeting, I laid out some different approaches to treatment including relaxation training. Jonah said he was not very interested in that approach due to his knowing someone who "went through all that" and did not find it particularly helpful. Though I could have returned to this approach later if needed and, perhaps, helped Jonah to have a more positive outlook on relaxation training, I followed the path of least resistance: He expressed interest and a liking for the cognitive approach.

Would relaxation training been helpful to his IBS? I bet so, but he was presenting his IBS as something he had lived with and accepted for quite a while. It was his bee phobia that was unpleasant to him, the presenting complaint; thus I took him at his word that the phobia was most ready for change.

3. *You chose not to explore the issue of sexual orientation, although there seemed to be clear hints that the client might have questions/doubts in this area. You note that as a solution-focused therapist you felt comfortable treating the presenting problem without delving into underlying issues. Was part of your decision based on any assumptions that his cultural background would make it impossible (or at least very difficult) for him to deal with this issue with you? How would you respond to an argument that the sexual identity issue might have been more pressing than it seemed and that his "hints" were designed to get your permission to further explore sexual orientation?*

Your question presupposes that there are or were "underlying issues" to his bee phobia. I chose to meet the client where he was, to focus on and treat his presenting complaint of the bee phobia. As you can see from my write-up, I did explore family gender roles with him and gave him direct and meta-communications that I was willing and able to talk about his gender and sexual identity, if he chose, and that I was accepting of homosexuality as non-pathological. I believe my messages were clear: If he wanted to now or in the future to discuss such issues, I was open and willing.

And, yes, I think discussing anything other than heterosexuality (and even that!) was difficult for him due to certain cultural norms. I have been pleasantly surprised, however, to find a number of "stereotypical" southern and mountain folks–my clients, friends, and family–to have "no problem" with homosexuality after a friend or family member of their's comes out. Part of the Appalachian Mountain culture, I believe, allows great room for differences as long as no threat to others is perceived.

4. Do you usually call brief therapy clients several weeks after the end of counseling to check on their progress? Do they know you are going to do this ahead of time? What do you do when post-therapy progress has not been good?

Yes, I try to call clients a couple of months after therapy has ended to allow me some greater closure and, ideally, a chance for clients to review, consolidate and reinforce positive changes. I typically ask clients in closing if it would be okay if I called or dropped them a postcard, and no client has turned me down yet! If post-therapy progress has not been good or at the level the client had hoped for, I typically invite them back in for a "check-up" or for a "booster" session to see what might be helpful. I have found clients to be appreciative of this call and concern no matter the therapy outcomes or their desire for actual follow-through.

5. How would you have responded had your psychiatric consultant recommended ongoing antidepressants as a means to reduce anxiety and control some of the general anxiety symptoms?

I would have responded positively, for there are usually at least ten ways to skin a cat (Where did that metaphor come from anyway?! I don't know anyone who still does or ever did skin a cat . . .). For a more in-depth discussion I'll refer you to Wilson's (1996) coverage of medications for anxiety disorders. In brief, Wilson concludes from the literature that of the patients with panic disorder who are placed on antidepressants, 75 to 80 percent significantly improve (p. 282). However, it should be noted that these improvements are primarily physiological and less so affective and cognitive, and that all medications have side effects. I have found that for some clients with painful and disruptive "anxiety attacks," medication can provide relief of some of their symptoms which allows them to use psychotherapy in a more effective and efficient manner so they might later benefit from longer-lasting changes as a result of counseling.

REFERENCES

Beck, A.T., Emery, G, & Greenberg, R.L. (1990). *Anxiety disorders and phobias: A cognitive perspective*. New York: Basic Books.
Bergman, J. S. (1985). *Fishing for barracuda: Pragmatics of brief systemic therapy*. New York: W.W. Norton & Company.

Bloom, B. L. (1997). *Planned short-term psychotherapy: A clinical handbook (2nd ed.).* Boston: Allyn and Bacon.

Cade, B., & O'Hanlon, W.H. (1993). *A brief guide to brief therapy.* New York: W.W. Norton & Company.

Ellis, A. (1996). *Better, deeper, and more enduring brief therapy: The rational emotive behavior therapy approach.* New York: Brunner/Mazel, Publishers.

Haley, J. (1963). *Strategies of psychotherapy.* New York: Grune & Stratton.

Haley, J. (1981). *Reflections on therapy and other essays.* Washington, DC: The Family Therapy Institute.

Haley, J. (1984). *Ordeal therapy: Unusual ways to change behavior.* San Francisco: Jossey-Bass Publishers.

Keefe, S. E. (Ed.). (1988). *Appalachian mental health.* Lexington, KY: The University Press of Kentucky.

Meichenbaum, D. (1985). *Stress inoculation training.* NY: Pergamon Press.

O'Hanlon, W. H. (1987). *Taproots: Underlying principles of Milton Erickson's therapy and hypnosis.* New York: W.W. Norton & Company

O'Hanlon, W. H., & Bertolino, B. (1998). *Even from a broken web: Brief, respectful solution-oriented therapy for sexual abuse and trauma.* NY: John Wiley & Sons.

O'Hanlon, W. H., & Weiner-Davis, M. (1989). *In search of solutions: A new direction in psychotherapy.* New York: W.W. Norton & Company.

O'Hanlon, B., & Wilk, J. (1987). *Shifting contexts: The generation of effective psychotherapy.* New York: The Guilford Press.

Sue, D. W., & Sue, D. (1999). *Counseling the culturally different: Theory and practice (3rd ed.).* New York: John Wiley & sons.

Walter, J. L., & Peller, J. E. (1992). *Becoming solution-focused in brief therapy.* New York: Brunner/Mazel Publishers.

Wilson, R. R. (1996). *Don't panic: Taking control of anxiety attacks.* New York: Harper Collins.

Zeig, J. K., & Gilligan, S. G. (1990). *Brief therapy: Myths, methods, and metaphors.* New York: Brunner/Mazel, Publishers.

Chapter 3:
Resolving PTSD Through
Time Limited Dynamic Psychotherapy

Vivian Barnette

SUMMARY. The effect of short-term psychodynamic therapy with a young and highly motivated African-American student athlete presenting with posttraumatic stress syndrome-delayed onset was examined. In 12 sessions, the client successfully addressed several issues including: rape, spirituality, race, and family dynamics. *[Article copies available for a fee from The Haworth Document Delivery Service: 1-800-342-9678. E-mail address: <getinfo@haworthpressinc.com> Website: <http://www.HaworthPress. com> © 2001 by The Haworth Press, Inc. All rights reserved.]*

KEYWORDS. Resistance, culture, trust, brief psychotherapy

I found my love for psychology as I worked as a certified therapeutic recreation specialist. One aspect of therapeutic recreation is leisure counseling. As I began working with minority children in low income housing areas and watching them develop and internalize positive self-esteem, in spite of their circumstances, I realized the importance of

Address correspondence to: Vivian Barnette, University Counseling Center, University of Oregon, 1590 E. 13th Avenue, Eugene, OR 97403 (E-mail: barnette@oregon. uoregon.edu).

[Haworth co-indexing entry note]: "Chapter 3: Resolving PTSD Through Time Limited Dynamic Psychotherapy." Barnette, Vivian. Co-published simultaneously in *Journal of College Student Psychotherapy* (The Haworth Press, Inc.) Vol. 16, No. 1/2, 2001, pp. 27-41; and: *Case Book of Brief Psychotherapy with College Students* (ed: Stewart E. Cooper, James Archer, Jr., and Leighton C. Whitaker) The Haworth Press, Inc., 2002, pp. 27-41. Single or multiple copies of this article are available for a fee from The Haworth Document Delivery Service [1-800-342-9678, 9:00 a.m. - 5:00 p.m. (EST). E-mail address: getinfo@haworthpressinc.com].

counseling and the significant impact I could make on people as a psychologist. Since counseling psychology focuses on the healthy aspects of the individual, I am attracted to this area of study and place great emphasis on prevention and performance enhancement. Therefore, I entered the field of counseling psychology with a specific desire to help people reframe and/or change their negative views of life. I have found that therapy allows me to give hope and encourage possibility thinking to many who may be suffering internally and/or externally from the ills of life. I believe my work with AJ is a great example of how my educational background, race/culture identity, and spirituality nicely integrated so I could help AJ find significance and relevance in her life.

As a developing psychologist, at the University of Iowa, I was trained in short-term psychotherapy. Although exposed to various models of short-term psychotherapy, such as Mann (1991) and Sifneos (1990), my interest and professional training seemed more closely aligned with the underpinnings of Time Limited Dynamic Psychotherapy, (TLDP). I had been an advocate for long-term therapy; however, since my training, I have been positively influenced by the effectiveness and satisfaction of many of my clients as a result of our short-term psychotherapy. I realize that this model may not be appropriate for all clients but it has been beneficial to many.

According to Strupp and Binder (1984), the task in TLDP is to identify and examine certain themes from a client's internal object relations repertoire that are not responsive to current interpersonal realities and, therefore, may maladaptively influence that client's experiences and behavior in many interpersonal settings. Many of these themes take the form of maladaptive interpersonal relationships, including the relationship with the therapist. Therefore, it was important for me in each case to: (a) create a safe environment; (b) allow these patterns to be enacted; (c) help my client see what she is doing; and (d) encourage her to question and/or identify underlying maladaptive patterns.

BIOGRAPHICAL SKETCH OF CLIENT

AJ was a 20-year-old African American heterosexual female junior who presented as articulate, alert and oriented to person, place, and time. She appeared to be a healthy, well-built athlete (on a University sports team), pleasant, and soft-spoken young woman. She made good eye contact during sessions, was usually dressed casually and groomed appropriately. Although she appeared to be straightforward with her self-report, her facial expressions were only 70% congruent with her verbalizations. Her psychomotor activity was slightly impaired and her affect restricted. Her memory (except for difficulty remembering details of a rape) and cognition appeared to be intact; there was no evidence of delusions or hallucinations. She had "nightmares" about her recent rape once or twice weekly, lasting approximately 30 minutes to an hour. She reported having insomnia during those nights, finding it difficult to fall back asleep. She also reported having a vague suicidal and homicidal ideation/plan six months ago, but denied acting out on them. AJ reported that her mood was dysphoric (i.e., depressed, angry, irritable, and frustrated) and noted decreased motivation and concentration.

PRESENTING PROBLEM

AJ's family and fiancé suggested that she seek counseling, but she only made an initial contact with the University Counseling Center and did not return for therapy. AJ was then self-referred with symptoms of Posttraumatic Stress Syndrome Disorder (PTSD) since five African-American men who were members of a sports team raped her approximately one year previously. She reported having nightmares and frequent thoughts about the event, fears she would be raped again, no sexual desire, and the sense that "even the touch of the skin hurts [her]." She felt that her sexual assault was interfering with her current relationship with her fiancé.

DSM IV Diagnosis

Axis I	309.81	PTSD with Delayed Onset.
Axis II	799.9	Diagnosis Deferred on Axis II.
Axis III	Headaches and Menstrual Cramps.	
Axis IV	Problems with support group (conflicted relationship with roommate, absence of close friendships).	
Axis V	GAF = 60	

FAMILY/PERSONAL HISTORY

AJ was raised in a large Midwestern town with parents who were married to each other (first marriage), college-educated, worked in education and were in good health. She reported a "good" relationship with them. She described her father as "highly respected by others, very intelligent" and "He is like Bill Cosby" and "I am my daddy's little girl. I have always been favored by him. We have a 'special' relationship and we talk everyday." AJ said that her mother is very supportive of her and "always put her children first and she understands me." AJ's sister was 23 and a college graduate while her 18-year-old brother was a college student. She reported "little communication with them, yet, [we have a] good relationship." AJ described her family as "healthy, happy, and very positive" and said holidays were "always fun." The only sad memory AJ reported was when she learned that her father "cheated" on her mother.

AJ reported that her grade school/middle school years were "good" ones but in high school she had few "girl" friends whereas "I always had boyfriends"; she said "(I) almost never keep friends . . . never close friends," and she had no close relationships at the University. She told a teammate player, in confidence, about the rape and this information was "passed on to the entire team." She said she prefers to "stay by herself."

Her only notable medical reports were sleepwalking one to two times in her life, current use of Ibuprofen 200-400 mg once weekly for migraine headaches lasting about two hours, and menstrual cramps lasting about two hours per month. AJ said she is performing about "average" academically and had no long-range goals.

AJ noted two significant relationships at the University, one with a Caucasian athlete at a nearby college. She said it was while visiting him that she was raped by five of his African American teammates, having been first teased by the men about dating a "white man" and told she needed to "get with some real men." Prior to the rape she had attended a picnic with several members of the football team, and that evening was the only female drinking with them in their room when she was raped. She did not remember "all the details" of the event, did not press charges, and broke-up with her boyfriend shortly afterward.

Presently, AJ is engaged to a Caucasian male whom she has known for 11 months. Neither had any other friends. She informed her fiancé of her rape, and found him very supportive but not understanding when she is unable to "make love" with him. Initially she had no trouble making love with him, but within the last four to six months "even his touch" bothered her. AJ complained that her fiancé only wants sex with her and that she finds sex to be bad, ugly, disgusting, and wrong.

AJ stated she used to enjoy reading and watching movies, especially comedies, but since the assault had felt sick to her stomach watching violent or strong sexual content movies, and found her love for playing sports has decreased! Although from a "very strong Christian family," AJ was not actively involved in church or its spiritual practices.

CASE CONCEPTUALIZATION

AJ is experiencing Post Traumatic Stress Disorder (PTSD) with Delayed Onset including: (1) re-experience of the Event (rape): (a) physiologic reactivity when exposed to cues (making love with her fiancé), (b) internal cues causing distress (thinking about having sex and what father thinks about it), (c) dreams (nightmares) of the event, and (d) external cues (fiancé touching her); (2) avoidance of stimuli: (a) avoiding stimuli (movies that have strong sexual content) associated with the rape, (b) has no future goals, (c) recall of rape is impaired, (d) affect is restricted, (e) interest in activities has decreased, and (f) detached from others; (3) increased arousal symptoms: (a) concentration is impaired, (b) angry outbursts, (c) sleep disturbance: trouble staying asleep, and (d) insomnia (DSM-IV, 1994). The rape has contributed to her decline in interpersonal functioning with her fiancé. AJ's coping mechanisms include angry outbursts, isolating herself from significant others and internalizing her hurt and pain, and when with her family, displays a facade to mask her guilt and shame. Though sharing her distress and painful experience with her fianceé, she felt misunderstood by him.

Living with fear she may be attacked again, she kept a knife under her bed. Her low self-esteem and confidence often kept her from participating in leisure activities and pursuits. But her family thought she was "doing fine" because she often told them that to keep them from worrying about her. Initially, she told her father she was in therapy for "relationship issues." Because of father's strong belief regarding "sex before marriage is sin," AJ chose to keep her counseling sessions private for fear he would think badly of her. The latter probably increased her ambivalent and negative feelings about sex towards self and fiancé.

MULTICULTURAL CONSIDERATIONS

Upon initial contact, AJ admitted she was "surprised" to have a Black therapist. She felt apprehensive and somewhat ambivalent about beginning therapy and I worked to help her feel comfortable and more at ease. AJ felt shameful and embarrassed about telling me of her presenting issue: "What will she think of me?; What are her beliefs about what I would like to share with her?; I must be brave and keep my emotions under control."

As an African American female therapist working with an African American female client, I know that incorrect assumptions can be made by the client and therapist. However, only a few of these were found to be true in this case and they were discussed with AJ. I believe AJ was expecting to see a White therapist because of her first visit to the counseling center a year ago. When I introduced myself, her eyes seem to lighten up, then suddenly she dropped them as if she were ashamed.

As I began to explore the symptoms that are common with PTSD with delayed onset, I informed/educated her about the symptoms she was experiencing. This seemed to make her feel more comfortable and confident in my competence as a therapist.

Clients from same ethnic group as the therapist often appear interested in knowing about one's training and knowledge, especially with African Americans. This may not be acknowledged or apparent at the onset of therapy but, as therapy continues, it is often discussed, perhaps due to the relatively low utilization of counseling services by African Americans. Many African American clients are unfamiliar with the therapy process. AJ entered therapy with the "quick fix it" and the "read me like a book/Jerry Springer" mentality. She was under the impression that therapy would only last a few sessions.

The nature of family ties is another important consideration when working with clients like AJ. A strong supportive family does not mean an open and understanding one. Although her family seemed to be close and supportive, AJ was uncomfortable talking to them about "the rape." Although she reported talking with her father daily, she did not disclose what was really going on with her though father appeared to be extremely influential in her development and current interpersonal relationships. Similarly, AJ reported she did not communicate with her siblings but had a good relationship with them, which may sound odd but many African American families may indicate close, yet emotionally distant relationships.

AJ stated, following the rape, that her family was initially angry and "ready to kill those guys." Then, her father questioned her about her judgment and decision making skills. AJ felt she let her family down by placing herself in an "awkward position" by drinking and being alone in their room.

According to AJ, her family felt that she was "over [her] trauma," and she wanted to keep them "in the dark" about her decision to come into therapy to discuss her rape; "I don't want them to worry about me anymore." Often, this attitude of protecting the family is reflected in the culture of African Americans. Issues such as rape and incest may be kept within the family and never discussed openly.

Another area of seeming contradiction was spirituality. AJ reported coming from a "strong Christian family" which might account for her ambivalent feelings about sex before marriage. Although not a practicing Christian, she appeared to have a core belief that sex before marriage was a sin.

TREATMENT/INTERVENTIONS

AJ was seen for 12 sessions of 15 offered. The first four sessions were spent establishing rapport and hearing her story. The Life History Survey suggested several areas she wanted to explore in therapy: (1) improve her relationship with her fiancé; (2) increase her self-esteem; and (3) "clear issues in her head." AJ came to the fourth session with her fiancé because she wanted me to meet him and, apparently, to see my reaction. We discussed my hypothesis alone together in the session; AJ admitted that it was important for her to know my "true reaction" to her significant other. Sessions five and six focused on her then current maladaptive behavior, assessing the danger to herself and others and teaching her about possible consequences. As therapy progressed into sessions seven through ten, AJ experienced resistance, transformation, and contrasting. During the termination sessions 11 and 12, she stressed change in herself and integrated/stabilized new cognitions/meanings about herself, as well as understood her family dynamics and spirituality.

It was necessary for me to provide a therapeutic holding environment for as long as it took her to feel comfortable and at ease with disclosing her story. After carefully listening and reviewing AJ's taped narration regarding the rape, I realized that she was not talking about the experience but how she thought her father felt about her having sex. AJ then recognized how her perception and/or belief was affecting her current relationship with her fiancé. She realized, that often, what her fiancé says about sex sounds similar to what her father says, thus, making it difficult to have sexual intercourse with him as indicated in the transcript of session 8:

T: Good morning AJ.

AJ: Good morning (said with a smile).

T: How has it been since the last time we met?

(Long Pause)

AJ: I thought about what we discussed last week about me hearing my father's voice when my fiancé spoke to me.

T: hmmh hum

AJ: I know that he has a strong belief about no sex before marriage and I am . . . well his favorite. I just feel like . . . I don't know . . .

T: What is it that you feel?

AJ: I feel torn. I want to be intimate with my fiancé and at the same time be the daughter my father wants me to be . . .

T: I see, you seem to be feeling ambivalent about your loyalties.

AJ: Exactly, I want to be okay with both. I love both of them and . . . it is just so hard.

T: I wonder if that is possible for you to feel good about both significant men in your life?

(Paused with a look of hope)

AJ: I think that my father really does know that my fiancé and I are together intimately.

T: What gives you that impression?

AJ: I am always at my fiancé's place and my father calls me there, sometimes.

T: So if this is true, what's making it difficult for you to talk candidly with your father about your decision to have sex before marriage? It sounds like the two of you have a close relationship in regards to talking on a daily basis.

AJ: Yes, it's true we talk but not about what is really going on with me.

T: What do you mean about what's "really going on" with you?

AJ: I want to believe that I am not sleeping around and that I am living a "Christian life."

T: What are your views on the Christian belief as it relates to your situation of having sex before marriage?

AJ: I was raised to believe that sex outside of marriage is wrong!

T: Have your beliefs changed?

AJ: I guess, I still believe that it is wrong!

T: Is there anything else you believe about sex?

AJ: Yes, I feel dirty, guilty, and ashamed. My attitude towards sex makes it hard for my fiancé because I can't go all the way with him.

T: How does he respond when you behave this way?

AJ: He is very understanding and patient. I just can't be intimate with him–too many memories of the rape, my father's voice, and my beliefs.

T: You look really sad . . . I wonder if there are other ways you could communicate to your fiancé your love for him?

AJ: I am sure there are–I just don't know how to do them! Can you tell me how because I think he may break-up with me if I don't perform soon?

T: Do you believe your relationship is in jeopardy?

AJ: Not really, but I just can't imagine him staying around much longer . . .

T: Is he pressuring you to be intimate with him?

AJ: No, I just feel bad about not being able to go all the way with him.

T: First, how would you feel if I asked you to change the word "sex" to "intimacy or making love" when you talk about "going all the way" with your fiancé?

(Her face appeared to light up)

> AJ: Yes, that does sound better . . . I like that!

> T: Good, now let's think of some ways you can be intimate without making love to your fiancé. Additionally, how about we establish some boundaries in regards to how intimate you want to be with your fiancé?

> AJ: Okay!

> T: What are some of the thing you like to do?

(AJ begins to name some of the things such as going to the movies and to dinner, and we talked about how important it will be for her to explain to her fiancé what her expectations would be for the night. AJ agreed and stated she was looking forward to having a "lovely" evening with her fiancé. Additionally, we talked about how she might communicate with her father.)

> T: You mentioned earlier that you would like to share more of your "deeper" concerns with your father.

> AJ: I definitely would–I am just afraid of what he might think of me.

> T: From previous sessions, I have gotten the feeling that your father cares for you deeply and wants you to enjoy life. When you told him about the rape, you said he was first angry, sad, and then very supportive of you.

> AJ: Yes, that's true and he does care a lot about me!

> T: It sounds like your father loves you unconditionally.

> AJ: Yes, he does. He has been there for me. He is just great!

> T: He sounds like it . . . and I believe that you are able to convey your concerns to your father in a manner in which he will understand you.

AJ: Yes, I believe I can too. Thanks for your confidence in me.

(The latter part of therapy ended with AJ and I role-playing ways she might consider talking with her father, including how she might address her religious beliefs.)

During the course of therapy, AJ completed many homework assignments, and many of those dealt with anger management and self-esteem/self-concept issues. Brief psychodynamic, reality, and cognitive-behavioral therapy were used integratively to improve and change AJ's level of psychological functioning. In Time Limited Dynamic Psychotherapy, the primary goal was to foster positive changes in interpersonal functioning. Interpersonal problems are conceptualized in a specific format called the Cyclical Maladaptive Pattern (CMP). This model examined *Acts of Self*. In this area the public and private actions can vary in degrees from person to person depending upon how accessible they are to one's awareness. AJ's public acts were displayed as quiet, passive, no real problems, loner while her private actions–did not believe she was worthy or capable of love. Typically, AJ was quiet and only talked when asked questions. She rarely initiated conversations. When she entered therapy, she reported feeling lonely and not connecting with other students and she minimized her presenting issue. She often reported not seeing herself as romantically desirable. I then helped her evaluate *Expectations about other's reactions*. This category focuses on how one imagines a reaction from others. AJ believed she made poor decisions and thus may be seen by others as helpless. She continued to play the role as "daddy's little girl." Next, we looked at *Acts of others towards self*. Usually, a person that has maladaptive patterns of thinking misjudges the interpersonal meanings of other's actions in a way that confirms his/her feared expectations. In this case, AJ experienced multiple abuses–sexual, neglect, and emotional. Family thinks she should be finished with her grieving. This abuse is connected with her identity as an African-American woman, struggling with who she is and with whom she feels safe. Finally, we explored *Acts of self towards self*. This category examines how a person treats him or herself. AJ suppresses her anger by pretending she is doing fine when talking with her family. She refused to engage intimately with her fiancé because of her anger toward men (power struggle). She punished herself through isolation. I assisted AJ with understanding her past and current maladaptive patterns of thinking, as well as her relationship with me as her therapist. Reality therapy kept her in touch with what was happening to her currently and what she could do about it. Cognitive behavioral therapy helped her to practice outside what she had learned in therapy, as well as examine maladaptive situations. AJ also learned some relaxation techniques, was educated about PTSD and encouraged to participate in group therapy when she feels she is ready.

I felt competent when working with AJ. The issues of race, interracial dating, rape, and spirituality were addressed. AJ reported feeling relieved that I was open, honest, and positive about these issues. I believe her perceptions of my compassion and ability to build rapport has been as helpful, if not more, than her increased knowledge of rape trauma syndrome. Trust appeared to have been key in helping AJ resolve her issues.

QUESTIONS

1. *You mentioned that the establishment of trust was crucial in this case. What were the important elements in the development of that trust? Was the fact that you are African-American crucial?*

Establishing trust was crucial in working with AJ. Our trusting relationship was the foundation and the key to her success. Initially, AJ's non-verbal behavior communicated that she was guarded, mistrustful and somewhat frustrated with the idea of being in therapy. She seemed to want me to resolve all of her issues by offering her suggestions and advice. It was during this time that I felt the need to revisit the counseling process and remind her of what she could expect. Additionally, I discussed with AJ what coming to therapy might feel like for her. She readily agreed when I talked about being defensive. AJ stated, "Wow, how did you know that I was feeling uncomfortable considering I was trying to appear just the opposite?" I smiled and stated, "You communicate very well with your body language!" This dialogue was the beginning of a trusting relationship. She felt she could speak candidly to me about her thoughts and feelings in regard to therapy. Almost immediately, her defenses were lowered as evidenced by her openness about her thoughts and feelings regarding herself, family, significant other, and me.

In regard to my racial identity, I sensed that AJ was a little uncomfortable with me. In fact, she stated later as our relationship developed that she was embarrassed to tell me what had happened to her and wondered if I would believe her. She also stated she felt I would judge her decisions regarding dating a white male and "hanging out with the team." I knew that I needed to connect with AJ in order to provide the therapy she needed. It was important for me to be aware of how my racial identity might impact this relationship. When I disclosed my feelings about interracial dating, rape, and being her therapist, AJ, reported feeling like she could talk with me and would often state "our time is up already." I believe my racial identity helped her tremendously.

2. *What were the key elements in getting this work done in only 12 sessions? You accomplished a great deal in 12 sessions, including some analytic work helping AJ understand how her relationship with her father was affecting her.*

One of the most important things I have learned as a therapist is to convey to my clients (particularly minority clients with Axis I diagnoses) the belief that they may be helped and returned to "normal" functioning, and that it may not be necessary to remain in therapy for several months. I introduce to them the brief therapy model and suggest (depending on the issue) the average number of sessions it may take. Usually this attitude toward clients' presenting issues empowers and encourages them in the following manner: (1) they can get better and may not be as disturbed as they may be thinking; (2) they know therapy is not going to interrupt their lives too long and they may terminate therapy with a "sweet taste in their mouths" which I feel will encourage them to re-enter when needed; and (3) they realize and expect to work in order to see change.

When I approached therapy from this perspective with AJ, she reported feeling hopeful about the process. Her attitude was evident throughout therapy as she began to practice what she had learned. I also knew that AJ had entered therapy previously with another therapist and did not return; I believe she was psychologically ready then but something blocked her. It was important for me to present therapy in a way that she would want to return.

3. *You mentioned that AJ experienced resistance, transformation, and contrasting in sessions seven through ten. How did each of these processes manifest during this period?*

Resistance was being shown when AJ skipped a couple of sessions. I was concerned that she might be experiencing some difficulty with participating in therapy. When I called AJ, her interpersonal style and verbal confirmation over the telephone suggested to me that she needed some time to "practice" and experience her new attitude towards self and others. She admitted to being afraid of losing control. She stated, "I can't believe how quickly I am changing. My boyfriend is very excited about my progress in therapy. He gets upset when I miss." I explained to her that the process of change was activated primarily by her motivation and desire and encouraged her to return to therapy.

It was crucial for me to be a good enough adult model to help AJ through her resistance, transference, and other meaning contrasts in order to promote change. I helped AJ alter some of her covert and overt behaviors. I began to talk less in therapy about what was happening and spent more time being gentle, respectful, supportive, yet persistent. My choice of words was serious when I talked with her. Once I said to AJ, "You are a diamond!" In the next session, she stated she had never thought about herself as a rare gem. "This was great for me to hear . . . I can't tell you how much it meant to me in regards to how I am seeing myself, now." I was able to impact AJ's rigid and negative meaning and encourage new meaning constructions. It was then she was able to construct a "good" AJ.

These processes came quickly for AJ because of her desire and the support from her significant other (fiancé) as he was witnessing a change in her. AJ worked at incorporating suggestions and reporting what did and did not work for her the next session.

4. *In the case conceptualization section, you report on AJ's father and family's reactions once she told them about the rape. What led her to tell them what happened and were these family issues ever resolved?*

AJ decided to tell her family about the rape because of the shame and guilt she was feeling. Her family's reaction towards this trauma terrified her. She reported feeling like she was to blame for the rape. Through trust and belief in the therapy process, AJ was able to verbalize "I am not to blame for what happened to me." As her cognitions changed from punishing to more understanding and less blaming, she reported feeling stronger and more confident. Toward the middle of the therapy, AJ informed her family about being in therapy. Initially, according to AJ, her family was surprised because they had assumed she was "over her trauma." However, she reported that they were very supportive and commended her on seeking professional help. According to AJ, "my mother disclosed to me that she had also been raped and she told me that she wished she had sought out professional help, too!" This powerful disclosure encouraged and strengthened AJ to continue moving forward. She reported feeling very proud of herself throughout therapy.

REFERENCES

Diagnostic and statistical manual of mental disorders (1994), (4th ed.), American Psychiatric Association, Washington, DC.

Mann, J. (1991). Time limited psychotherapy. In P. Crits-Christoph & J. P. Barber (Eds.), *Handbook of short-term dynamic psychotherapy* (pp. 17-44). New York: Basic Books.

Sifneos, P. E. (1990). Short-term anxiety-provoking psychotherapy (STAPP) termination-outcome and videotaping. In J. K. Zeig & S. G. Gilligan (Eds), *Brief therapy: Myths, methods, and metaphors* (pp. 318-326). New York: Brunner/Mazel.

Stupp, H. H., & Binder, J. L. (1984). *Psychotherapy in a new key: A guide to time-limited dynamic psychotherapy.* New York: Basic Books.

Chapter 4:
From Hate to Healing:
Sexual Assault Recovery

Jaquelyn L. Resnick

SUMMARY. This case demonstrates the use of brief therapy with a young woman who experienced a vicious sexual assault within a dating relationship. Complex family of origin issues and prior history of problematic relationships, including a stalking episode, complicated her response. The recovery process is elaborated in terms of specific critical incidents within a feminist context. *[Article copies available for a fee from The Haworth Document Delivery Service: 1-800-342-9678. E-mail address: <getinfo@haworthpressinc.com> Website: <http://www.HaworthPress.com> © 2001 by The Haworth Press, Inc. All rights reserved.]*

KEYWORDS. Sexual assault recovery, brief therapy

As a psychologist working at a university counseling center, providing brief therapy is an essential skill. When invited to contribute to this book, I thought about the often complex presenting problems we encounter and the challenge we face to offer quality interventions within a time limited context. Pam's story came to mind as illustrative of what

---

Address correspondence to: Jaquelyn L. Resnick, Counseling Center, University of Florida, PO Box 114100, Gainesville, FL 32611-4100 (E-mail: resnick@counsel. ufl.edu).

[Haworth co-indexing entry note]: "Chapter 4: From Hate to Healing: Sexual Assault Recovery." Resnick, Jaquelyn L. Co-published simultaneously in *Journal of College Student Psychotherapy* (The Haworth Press, Inc.) Vol. 16, No. 1/2, 2001, pp. 43-63; and: *Case Book of Brief Psychotherapy with College Students* (ed: Stewart E. Cooper, James Archer, Jr., and Leighton C. Whitaker) The Haworth Press, Inc., 2002, pp. 43-63. Single or multiple copies of this article are available for a fee from The Haworth Document Delivery Service [1-800-342-9678, 9:00 a.m. - 5:00 p.m. (EST). E-mail address: getinfo@haworthpressinc.com].

can occur within brief therapy for a client who might typically be considered as requiring longer-term intervention. In our setting, brief therapy is defined as up to 15 sessions, with extension of individual sessions possible under specific circumstances following case review; referral to group can also occur. The typical number of client sessions has a bimodal distribution, with about one third being seen for one session and the remainder seen for more than one session. The average number of sessions per client is seven. Nearly one-half of the clients have experienced previous counseling and three-quarters describe their problem as "very disruptive."

My approach to counseling is best described as eclectic (incorporating elements of humanistic, psychodynamic and cognitive therapy) with an underlying feminist therapy base. Influences in my work include formative training in humanistic-existential-phenomenological psychology (Jourard, 1964; May, 1958; Rogers, 1961). The interpersonal perspective of Kell and Mueller (1966) on impact and change in counseling relationships further affected my understanding of the therapeutic relationship. I have been profoundly impacted by feminism. Specifically, the principles of feminist therapy (Brodsky & Hare-Mustin, 1980; Brown, 1994) have been integrated into my work with all clients. Lastly, I want to acknowledge Herman (1992), who has written the definitive book to date on trauma and recovery.

I find it a privilege to be a partner in the therapeutic relationship and bring to the therapy my belief in people's resilience and capacity to change. I am a woman, Caucasian, in my mid-50s, with over 30 years experience as a therapist. Though a generalist, over the years I have developed specialization in counseling issues affecting women, particularly sexual assault/abuse/harassment and eating disorders. The client I have chosen to write about is a young woman who experienced a sexual assault in a dating relationship. She was seen for a total of 12 sessions including the initial intake interview.

CLIENT DESCRIPTION

Pam, a 19-year-old Caucasian female, is medium height, average weight, casually dressed, and typically did not wear make-up. She was a first year student at the university at the time of her intake. Her parents suggested that she come to counseling, as did some of her friends; all of them regarded her as "needing help." She was very reluctant to seek assistance herself although not denying that she might need it. She had a friend getting counseling at our Center, which provided encouragement for her. When I went to meet her in our reception area, her head was buried deep into her books and she actively avoided eye contact with me. She appeared anxious and frightened.

PRESENTING PROBLEM

Pam was dealing with the sequelae of a date rape that occurred three months previously, when she was home for the weekend. She told no one about the incident and drove herself back to school the same day but her pain was so great that she finally told a residence life assistant who reported the incident as required by the campus sexual assault protocol. The Housing counselor-in-residence was called and Pam spoke with him. She stated to me that she was in denial and did not want to talk with anyone at that time, especially not a male. Due to her injuries, she was transported to the emergency room at the university hospital where she received medical treatment. She had significant vaginal tears, both internally and externally, and a bleeding uterus. Pam was treated and released. She refused to talk with police or allow them to take evidence. The perpetrator, Wes, was several years older than Pam, and lived in a community near Pam's hometown. Although Pam's friend introduced them at a party, their relationship was based mainly on Internet contacts. They did have some limited face-to-face interactions and some prior consensual sex. Pam now sees Wes as highly manipulative but at the time they were in a relationship she thought he was a "sensitive male." Pam subsequently found out that Wes was facing sexual molestation charges in his home jurisdiction. Wes claimed that his father molested him as a child, and Pam said she felt sorry for him and wanted to protect him, even after learning of the charges.

When Pam finally told her mother about the incident a few weeks later, she reported that her mother was appalled and insisted Pam go to the State's Attorney Office to report the assault. Wes had threatened Pam after he found out that she talked to this office, and he sent her e-mails denying the assault occurred. Pam "wanted everything to go back to the way it was," so she initially kept in contact with and supported Wes. At his request, she washed her panties to get rid of the remaining evidence. Pam said she had been stupid and deceived. She reported her mother treated her as if she had done something wrong and as if she had AIDS or another disease. Her best friend laughed at her when she disclosed the incident to her. Pam subsequently became fearful of and angry towards men. On her intake sheet, she wrote, "raped on –/–/– [i] hate all males [,] males are scum [,] do not give me a male." She reported recently screaming and cursing at a male friend when he showed interest in her and wondered if these feelings would ever change. Pam said her mother accused her of being a lesbian in view of her male bashing comments.

Pam's initial presentation, with only intermittent eye contact, jerky movements and strange, wary comments diminished as the intake interview continued but hostile expressions and extreme self-blame replaced her wariness. She spoke sharply, loudly at times, and used rough language with intensity and anger.

SOCIAL AND CULTURAL
HISTORY/ENVIRONMENTAL CONTEXT

Pam was the only child of parents in an intact marriage. The family was middle class Caucasian, and fundamentalist Christian, living in the South. Pam reported her parents had "bigoted" views about people different from them. Her father worked in the service sector and mother was a health professional. Father's heavy drinking sometimes affected his work while mother had an unstable work history with repeated, significant interpersonal problems with co-workers. Pam characterized her mother as critical, controlling and intrusive and her father as more laid back and not very present while she was growing up. Paternal grandfather was described as a mean and controlling man of wealth, who "beat his wife and treated her like a slave." Grandfather owned the house the family lived in, and he paid for her college tuition. She felt that he had power over some of her decisions but had not seen him in over three years and refused to do so because he is so demeaning of others.

Pam was a bright young woman successful in an academically accelerated program and active in extracurricular activities. She rarely brought friends home, however, due to her problematic parents. She had experience with courts of law after involvement in a stalking case during high school. Pam said she never wanted to involve the court system but her mother insisted that she pursue the case even after Pam wanted to drop it. The case was not satisfactorily resolved despite obtaining restraining orders, and Pam said she "doesn't trust the system." Pam also had a history of being in dysfunctional relationships with unsuitable men. Despite her complicated history, Pam had no prior counseling.

Her family believed that religious faith is all that is needed to resolve problems and viewed psychological interventions with mistrust.

ASSESSMENT/DIAGNOSIS/CONCEPTUALIZATION

In the aftermath of the acquaintance rape, Pam had symptoms consistent with rape trauma syndrome/posttraumatic stress disorder (PTSD). Pam was deeply affected by the rape. She had intrusive distressing recollections of the event even as she tried to minimize the impact and didn't want to talk about it. She experienced disruption in studying and social activities. She felt violated and betrayed, yet blamed herself for being "stupid." She associated men in general with the rape excepting her father whom she characterized as having been understanding throughout the ordeal, but also powerless and ineffectual. Pam was angry about her mother's control and invasion of her privacy as well as grandfather's fiscal control. Pam's family of origin issues, past history of being stalked, and prior dysfunctional relationships with men complicated her response to the rape. People who suffer complex after-effects of chronic trauma can be misdiagnosed as personality disorders. Given Pam's presentation, this perspective was considered in the initial assessment.

TREATMENT GOALS AND PLANNING

Goals

- Facilitate recovery process from sexual assault
  Decrease symptoms of PTSD
  Separate angry feelings towards perpetrator from feelings toward all men
  Restore her sense of being herself rather than a tainted self
- Address family of origin relationships, particularly conflict with her mother
  Engage in individuation from mother
  Develop boundaries in relationship with mother
- Improve her self-esteem
  Evaluate self in a less critical, more humane manner
  Establish more realistic, less perfectionistic expectations

Plan

- Normalize her feelings in context of rape trauma syndrome, incorporating sociocultural messages and feminist conceptualizations
- Establish trust and safety in therapy relationship
- Empower Pam in the therapeutic relationship
- Use cognitive interventions to reframe negative "self talk"
- Support her coping strategies, identifying where she has been resilient
- Identify destructive behaviors and provide alternative options
- Explore ways in which her family of origin issues have complicated dealing with the assault
- Identify specific situations where she can strategize and implement boundaries, separating self from others
- Work on safety in relationships with others
- Identify situations where she can begin to try new behaviors leading to feeling empowered in relationships with others
- Practice communication skills that are assertive (not aggressive)

COUNSELING PROCESS

Herman (1992) wrote that the core experiences of psychological trauma are disempowerment and disconnection from others. The recovery process occurs in a healing relationship based on the empowerment of the survivor and the creation of new connections. These were the guiding principles in this counseling process. I find that these themes tend to cycle, while deepening, over the course of counseling and I have characterized the sessions below in terms of predominant emergent themes. In doing so, the evolution is not linear, because the process is more complex and circuitous than that.

Session #1 [Safety, boundary setting, empowerment, dealing with self-blame]

Establishing a trusting relationship and a safe environment where control could be restored marked the initial sessions. Pam defined the content and concerns to be discussed. As counselor, I provided validation of her feelings while at the same time confronting and challenging her negative, self-defeating behavior and integrating the overriding themes which were brought into most sessions: (1) trauma recovery;

and (2) the developmental issues around individuation from family, identity formation, and establishment of intimate relationships, complicated by dysfunctional family of origin issues.

In early sessions we worked on conflict with mother, addressing small ways in which Pam could begin to feel some power and control, such as developing boundaries around mother's intrusive phone calls and helping Pam define her own level of self-disclosure. I framed Pam's desire for some privacy and independence as appropriate developmental goals and encouraged her to observe her interactions with family and identify opportunities to make choices for herself. Pam was angry with her mother because she (Pam) could never be "good enough"; mother wanted her to be perfect and rejected imperfections of any kind. Pam identified with her father whom she said had no privacy and was controlled by mother. She was tearful, fearful and bitter about mother's judgment if she had contacted AIDS. I was supportive and helped Pam clarify and deepen her thoughts about her family.

Session # 2 [Introducing empowering behaviors]

Pam: My dad doesn't have a private life, either. She's (mother) in control . . . Everything has to be "just so" with her. She controls others. Her hand is always on you. Ever since I was little, I was expected to tell her everything or be punished . . . I feel conditioned, like Pavlov's dog. I don't know what to do.

T: Would you like some help in gaining more control?

Pam: I would. I don't like being dependent. That's what it is. It is a weakness.

[Pam discussed mother's conditional love, her protectiveness and bragging and questioned whether her mother really loved her at all.]

T: How do you feel about your mother?

Pam: I don't want her dead or anything, but I'm tired of her conditional love and her wanting me to be perfect . . . My dad wasn't there for me in the first half of my life–I mean he was there but he didn't take me to dance lessons, etc. He will be there for me now. He already has been. He didn't react like she did [to the assault].

T: He didn't blame you or treat you like you were damaged goods.

Pam: My mother is jealous of my relationship with my dad. She is jealous of our time together and wants to know why I wouldn't be with her instead of him. She is jealous if I tell him things and not her. But I trust him, not her.

[Pam describes phone calls from home and how she winds up telling mother everything.]

T: How often do you speak to your family?

Pam: Once a week. They will call me if I don't call them.

T: Is that amount OK or too much? Does the amount bother you or is it more the content of the calls?

Pam: [Silence] . . . I guess you could say it is the content–it is the control. I always feel like she is in control.

T: Would you like that to change?

Pam: Yes.

T: Would you like help in making that happen?

Pam: Yes, if possible.

T: Because we could work on that. We could see what happens when you are on the phone and see if there are any places where you might have some choice about what you want to say or how you can answer a question.

Pam was able to describe extracurricular activities she had gotten involved in, beginning the process of re-engagement. She also exercised several times a week for stress relief. She regarded any men that she encountered as "neutered," and disclosed that a male friend in her club confronted her about "male bashing." She got so angry with him that she revealed that she had been assaulted. When he told her that he was glad she revealed that, that he could better understand her, Pam was disgusted. Pam did not trust that sentiment and was very upset that she told him and did not want to face him at the club event that night because she was so ashamed of herself. I confronted Pam on her reaction to deeply address the repetitive and severe self-blame she chronically engaged in. She showed a wide range of emotions during this session, revealing the hurt and pain underneath the anger while still holding on to the angry feelings.

Session # 3 [Dealing with self-blame]

Pam: I cannot look him [a male friend] in the eye. I don't feel like a whole person ever since that happened. I feel like I have the plague. Especially around guys.

T: We need to pause a minute here, and attend to what you are saying.

Pam: To what?

T: To how hard you are being on yourself. To how much you sound like your mother calling yourself diseased and less than whole.

Pam: Well I am, I'm not her perfect daughter anymore. I have had sex. I may have AIDS. She will disown me if she finds out that I have AIDS.

T: Look how mean you are being to yourself–just really mean . . .

How would you treat a friend who had been raped? Would you blame her?

Pam: No, I would not.

T: Well, you are no different. There is no double standard. You have not done anything to be ashamed of.

Pam: I feel it. Those are my feelings. I am diseased. My own mother has said so. And my best friend laughed at me when I told her. Maybe because I am a perfectionist–always have been, just to please her. I feel ashamed not to be the perfect daughter. She told me, later, "please don't tell anyone what happened." She is ashamed of me. How can I not feel shame when my own mother does?

T: What would you tell your daughter if she had been raped?

Pam: I don't know. I couldn't tell her anything.

T: What would you *want* to say to her?

Pam: Nothing. [Pause] . . . I would want to hug her tight and tell her I loved her and that she would be safe.

T: Yes, you would want to embrace her, tell her you loved her, and that she would be safe. She would deserve to hear that message. Your mother wasn't able to tell you that, was she? Sometimes people are ignorant about these things, or are fearful about the "just" world, so they try to make it right by assigning blame. That happened to you, didn't it? You got the blaming messages instead of the loving ones you deserved to hear.

Pam: Yes, but I am still to blame.

T: What do you think that could you have done differently?

[She described how "stupid "she was, how different Wes was from the person he portrayed himself to be on the Internet, he was much more self-centered, and how she did not believe him.]

T: What are you ashamed of?

Pam: Minor things . . . .

T: Like what?

[She describes a variety of other things she regards as imperfections.]

T: What are you ashamed about regarding the assault? Why can't you look Rob in the eye today? You have to give yourself a different message than your mother gave you.

Pam: What do you mean?

T: Do you hear me giving you a different message?

Pam: What do you mean? You're supposed to be helping me, to be steering me back towards being normal.

T: I just want to know if you are hearing a different message from me, or if you cannot hear it because there is no room for a different message?

Pam: I hear it but you are not as important as my mother or my friend.

T: I know I am not as important as they are to you. Of course not. But I just want to know if you have some room to consider a different message, because when you see Rob today, you will have a choice–whether you want him to view you as someone who is damaged, who should be ashamed, or if you are someone, the person you have always been, a good person who has had something bad and painful happen to her, but who deserves to be loved, not to be blamed.

Sessions #4-5 [Relationships with men, power, control and vulnerability]

Pam continued to report on her relationship with mother, noting the positive changes as Pam changed, yet being suspicious of those changes and wondering when her mother would ambush her next. She also discussed a relationship with a male friend, how she "slept" with him for several nights at his place, "as a friend." She was then upset when she awoke one night to find that he was "groping" her. Pam had been attracted to him because he "allowed me to abuse him." She indicated she knew this was "not normal" but took pride in this an example of being in control.

The next session involved feelings about receiving too much attention from another male (roommate of her male friend) and her discomfort around his unwelcome, harassing behaviors. Her ways of responding to him were indirect and left her frustrated and powerless. We were able to identify other ways she could handle the situation that could put her in greater control and allow her to set some limits with her friend.

Session #4 [Relationships with men]

[Note: She had described the groping incident that occurred.]

> Pam: I'm not ready for a relationship. I curled up in a fetal position and cried. I told him [about the rape], so now he knows. He kept trying to be so nice to me–that crap about he was glad I told him, that he has a friend this has happened to, and that he thought it was good that I was getting counseling. That made me feel sick. I was revolted.
>
> T: How was it that you got involved with him?
>
> Pam: I like it that he let me abuse him.
>
> T: What do you mean?
>
> Pam: Punch, pinch, slap (she smiles)
>
> T: How did this happen?
>
> Pam: It started with me smacking him when he said something I did not like. He saw it as playful. (But I wasn't playing–I just liked it. I was in control.) Then we got into wrestling and scratching. Until that night . . . I'm just not ready for a sexual relationship.
>
> T: What made you think that nothing would come of it if you slept with him? Did you not feel you were putting yourself in a vulnerable place?
>
> Pam: I slept with him before and nothing happened . . . He has three roommates they would hear me if I screamed. His roommates let me beat up on him.
>
> T: What do you mean?
>
> Pam: I left marks on him, scratched him (smiles). I liked watching him be in pain, seeing the pain in his face, his eyes.
>
> T: What did you like?

Pam: I had a feeling of power and control. I had a feeling of control . . . I know it sounds sick. Mostly I don't feel I have control because of my mother.

T: Is there any place you feel like you do have control?

Pam: The only thing I have control over is my diet–isn't that pathetic?

T: What do you mean?

Pam: I am a strict vegetarian–no meat, eggs, dairy. It is important to me; it defines me. That's the only thing I have control over. I don't have control over my sex life. I have the ability to say no but that doesn't mean I am in control . . . I felt safe with him. He was a doormat. He let me abuse him, then I would be sweet and nice to him, after I abused him. I just loved it. It is an abnormal obsession. I am not ashamed of it.

T: You're even proud of it.

Pam: Riiiight–I know it is sick.

T: You really want to be in control.

Pam: Yeah–(starts sobbing).

T: I wonder what other ways you can be in control besides abusing someone?

Pam: I can't stand cruelty to animals and would never abuse animals, but humans . . . I don't know. The past two relationships I had hinged on this abuse . . . I did make marks on his back. I was drunk. It was like scars under his shirt the next day. I was proud of it. I made my mark. I owned him. That was my property . . . I liked him and he didn't like that, so I changed, and then he lost interest in me. I did not have control. He was abusive to me–in words. He called me names and he was nasty. I didn't have control. I lost myself, and then, it was the end.

Session #6 [Acting out]

Pam reported that she was highly stressed by school and her PTSD related concerns. She went out to dinner and a movie with a friend in an effort to decompress. While pleasant, it did not provide the expected relief. She then went to a party, where she drank eight drinks, with the hopes of getting drunk. She succeeded. She was "set off" by a comment from a male and "lost it." She started screaming, crying, locked herself in a bathroom and had a "temper tantrum." Several friends took her home. In the car, she continued the tantrum and told them of the rape. She feels very ashamed and has "shut down," withdrawing from friends and not even going on-line, an extreme sign in her view. Pam exploded with pent-up rage and knew it felt good, yet had little idea of her impact on others. We contextualized what occurred and planned to explore other ways to deal with her rage. She had constructive activities planned for the Spring Break, which was coming up soon.

Sessions #7-9 [Reconciling with self; self-care and self-regulation; experimentation]

Following the break, Pam carried out plans that indicated increased self-acceptance and caring. She initiated topics that she wanted to talk about: academic concerns and plans, relationship with mother (who was just fired from her job) and the resultant financial pressures she felt would be on her for the summer. I confronted her about the ways in which she "needled" her mother and sometimes instigated conflict when mother did not. Pam was able to engage in productive exploration. She had good eye contact, displayed a wide range of emotion, and asked, "what next" at the end of the session, as she wanted some things to think about and work on during the week. She continued to experience difficulties in various relationships with male friends, but did not resort to destructive behaviors to cope. She even decided to give up alcohol for Lent. Pam noted that she no longer felt ashamed about the rape and was pleasantly surprised by this development. She had some thoughts about the assault this weekend (the 6-month anniversary) but they were not overwhelming.

By next session, she had started a new, long distance relationship with a male whom she met at a social event over the Break. Their major mode of interaction was extensive daily Internet communication. She wanted to visit him the following weekend. I confronted her about the relationship and questioned some of the choices she was making. She was not pleased to be confronted about the discrepancies between expressed goals and actual behaviors. She did not wish to explore or examine any aspect of the consequences of taking such a trip. Unfortunately, her car broke down during the return drive, and she called her parents to pick her up. The broken car and unauthorized trip reinforced her image as the imperfect child. She called in to reschedule her counseling appointment for the week, as she was stuck out of town on our appointment day. She was then able to process the events, including why a long distance relationship with a male would be so attractive to her. We also explored the triangulation in her family and her role in contributing to the problem.

Session #10 [Telling her story]

Pam had resisted telling her story of the sexual assault up to this time. I would bring it up or refer to it from time to time, saying to her that I believed it would be important for her to tell the story, as part of the recovery process, but that she could do so when she felt ready. It seemed to me that the acting out that occurred previously was indicative of some "spillover" which was getting harder to contain, and that it was likely time for her to share her account with me which I invited her to do, with an explanation of why I thought it was important now. My explanation resonated with her. With some initial reluctance, hesitancy and self-doubt, she used the session to recount the events the night of the assault. She clearly had felt negated and overpowered, yet wondered whether that mattered because there had been prior consensual sex and the pre-intercourse sexual acts that night were consensual. We were able to process the difference between those behaviors and the aggressive, nonconsensual violence that transpired later that night.

Sessions #11-12 [Resolution and termination]

Pam resumed her studies and was able to prepare for final exams. She went for her HIV test during which she cried the whole time. However, she did not dwell on this in session. I inquired about the impact on her "telling her story." She said she faced some difficulties but found she wanted to tell some friends about what happened. She chose to take it easy the coming summer (a clear vote for self-care) and asserted her plan to her mother. She inquired about the requirements for a retroactive medical withdrawal for the previous term and said she wanted to consider it as an option, because she had really hurt her grade point average

(GPA) and now was concerned about how it would affect her plans for graduate study. Pam showed a wide range of emotions, some teariness but also much energy and humor, maintaining an acerbic wit but without the hostility and rancor present earlier.

In our final session, Pam relayed a story about a fight about her mother's intrusiveness. This time, Pam reported on how she handled it by writing a mock e-mail spoofing her mother and her extreme religious beliefs. She felt better for having written a "wicked" letter and decided she did not have to send it. Pam indicated that her HIV test came back negative and brought up on her own that this was our last session and asked what we should talk about. I suggested we review her progress and discuss any current concerns. Pam was able to articulate the changes she experienced, including important ways in which she now perceived the sexual assault differently than before. She noted that it had become a much less intrusive issue for her. She said she had moved on in her life and "feels stitched." Her current concerns centered on her studies and going home for the summer. She still had some pain about parental relationships but was able to keep her boundaries and not lose herself. She found herself less affected by the "jabs."

OUTCOME/TERMINATION OF COUNSELING

The termination date was influenced by the end of the semester, a timetable we were aware of from the outset. Initially Pam had not wanted to commit to any ongoing counseling, but once she agreed that it would be helpful to continue, we knew that April would bring a decision point, as Pam was going home for the summer. The termination of counseling was predictable and mutually agreed on. Many counseling goals were accomplished and her PTSD symptoms were alleviated. Pam will need to work on boundaries, both in family and in intimate relationships, firming up our beginning work. She will need to put into practice and further integrate her self-care and self-acceptance. I asked if she would like a referral to a counselor in her hometown to continue this work, or whether she would like to continue the process on her own. Not surprisingly, she opted for the latter. I was able to support her choice and validate her confidence in her ability to apply what she had learned in counseling. We discussed the possibility that she could get stuck and need some help. We identified possible warning signs and framed help seeking as a proactive, self-caring step, should it be warranted. I told her she could return to the Center the next academic year should she need to consult or want to enter counseling group. She appreciated the offer, seeing it as a safety net if needed. Pam articulated deep thanks to me, conveying a sense not only of acknowledgement but of connection. Pam did not request additional counseling when she returned to school the following year.

DISCUSSION

Recovery from a sexual assault within a dating relationship is almost always more difficult because of the relationship with the perpetrator. The survivor rarely identifies the act as a sexual assault or rape. Further, the survivor is likely to experience considerable guilt and self-blame which can be exacerbated if the client was drinking or using other drugs, and/or went along with the perpetrator to some extent (e.g., went to a bedroom or permitted initial kissing and touching). For Pam, all these elements were present. She doubted she had been raped (and felt she got what she deserved for being so stupid). The tenacity of these beliefs, supported by our sociocultural expectations, is remarkable, especially in the face of Pam's significant injuries that required emergency medical attention.

The recovery process is multi-determined. Many factors impact the outcome, including the particulars of the assault, past history, intrapersonal issues, current support system, culture and environment. Pam had a past history that complicated the recovery process. She had a lengthy experience of being stalked (a kind of chronic traumatization) that was not well resolved. Her family of origin issues included an abusive grandfather who maintained power in the family, an alcoholic father, and an emotionally abusive, unstable mother. At the time of the assault, she had a history of being in dysfunctional relationships with men and of struggling to individuate from an enmeshed family. She had incorporated her mother's perfectionistic expectations for herself, with resultant low self-esteem. She feared being like her mother and identified with her father (though humiliated by his powerlessness). She lacked role models for functioning adults and was confused about what it meant to be a healthy man or woman in our culture. Factors in favor of the recovery process included Pam's past resilience, her ability to be successfully involved in academics and extracurricular activities outside of the family, and her ironic sense of humor.

Pam's issues were similar to developmental issues faced by young adolescents: identity formation, separation from family, and establishing intimate relationships. Due to her complicated family of origin is-sues, her developmental process was complicated in all these areas. Pam's poor boundaries and low self-esteem made her vulnerable to exploitive relationships and she experienced some traumatic conse-quences. Her development was interrupted by the traumatic event of the sexual assault, which challenged her already shaky feelings of power and control and reinforced her negative self-image. In the brief therapy model, the troubled family dynamics could be explored but not as fully as would have been without limits on duration, and we were limited as to how deeply we could process Pam's dependence on relationships with men to define herself. Nevertheless, we were able to sufficiently identify and begin work with these issues so that she could move for-ward. She worked on establishing interpersonal boundaries, both with mother and in relationships with male and female friends. Pam became able to feel empowerment in the present and hope for the future in con-trast to the outset of counseling. The therapy allowed her to restore feel-ings of worthiness, to contain and contextualize the rape rather than let it overwhelm her, and to gain relief from the PTSD symptoms. Pam was able to move to a more functional place with tools in place to continue the work on her own.

QUESTIONS

1. *Can you highlight the elements of this case that allowed you to make considerable progress in a brief period of time?*

I think that I remained focused on the treatment goals and themes identified. Many intriguing aspects of this case would have been tempt-ing to explore further. However, I felt that would require more time and would possibly work against the containment and empowerment that Pam needed to successfully remain in school this term. I trusted that Pam would return to any of those particular issues if processing were es-sential at this juncture and that we could examine them at that point. I felt strongly about choices made in Session 2 (excerpted), where pres-ent themes were incorporated into her discussion of family of origin is-sues. Rather than focus on the pathology, I acknowledged and validated it but moved toward what was happening now, inviting her to collabo-rate and begin to experience some control, which enabled me to gently "test" Pam's openness to explore issues and her ability to engage in the change process. Problems were not minimized but were framed as understandable and not unusual for someone in her circumstances. The confrontation in Session 3 (excerpted) was important as I risked connecting with her at a deeper level, challenging her worldview and introducing alternatives which would promote self-acceptance and nurturance.

Throughout the sessions, I tried to acknowledge places where her resilience, coping and/or choice making were evident, even if not always stemming from constructive actions. We used role-playing and other techniques to re-do scenarios where she had been destructive, as in "What could you do differently if you found yourself in that situation again" (e.g., excerpt in Session 4). I referred many times to the importance of her "telling her story" but allowed her to choose the time to disclose it. She was supported in her control of the timing of the disclosure but not in her efforts to minimize or avoid doing so. I was purposely patient with her without "forgetting." In Session 10, when I indicated that perhaps it was time today to do so, she appeared "ready" and was able, with support, to talk at last about the sexual assault. It was a painful, powerful session that was important for the resolution.

2. *How did transference affect the therapy? Might the fact that you are a woman in the same age range as P's mother have any effect?*

I was quite aware of the fact that I was in the same age range as Pam's mother. I wondered how she would get angry with me or react when she felt she could not please me. This also gave me the opportunity to provide a corrective parenting experience and to be the voice of "the good mother." This differentiation occurred without triangulation, which I was careful to avoid. Her mother was characterized as troubled and unpredictable but as someone who cared about Pam and was showing her caring in her own way (high expectations, extreme protectiveness, and intrusiveness). At one point I was not successful in maintaining this differentiation. Pam decided impulsively to leave town for the weekend to see a new male friend, even though that was risky academically, financially, and interpersonally. Pam was angry when I confronted her prior to the trip, as I tried to align to a care-taking voice within her that had not been adequately developed. Pam wound up seeing me as parental (maternal) in this regard, and was passive aggressive in her response (as she often was with her mother and not usually with me). I saw her as "asking for trouble" and unable to self-regulate. I realized by her initial reaction that she did not want to hear this from me, yet I decided to try it anyhow, hoping that I could connect, or even ignite, a part of her that would offer more safety than she was ready to provide herself at that point. The session after that counseling episode was the only one she missed.

3. *Pam's conflicts about men seemed not to be resolved during therapy. If this perception is accurate, how troubling was this to you?*

I concur that Pam's conflicts about men were not resolved; however, I believe that the resolution process had started. The progress that Pam made in dealing with the sexual assault was notable. As a result, she diminished her male bashing and was beginning to explore more positive relationships with men, albeit only the most initial phases. I would have liked to have further explored this with Pam in this area but was unable to do so because we had reached the end of the term and she was leaving town. Otherwise, we could have had four or five more sessions to pursue this topic. Even with a few more sessions, however, I doubt we would have seen resolution. There is a limit to how much can be accomplished within the framework of the short-term intervention. True integration of change needs time and opportunity to experiment, especially in cases with complicated family history. I was very pleased with the considerable progress that Pam was able to make. I hope that she gained some tools that she can use and that she will be able to continue the process on her own. If, at some point, she was unable to progress alone, if she felt stuck or regressed, I would hope that our counseling experience would make it easier for her to seek help and that she could use a brief intervention to work further on these issues.

4. *You mentioned that clients at your center are sometimes referred to group after their individual sessions. Would this have been appropriate for Pam? If so, what type of group and why?*

Pam was aware that a small group opportunity was available upon her return to the university in the following academic year. She was counter-dependent and therefore unlikely to engage in more counseling than she thought absolutely necessary. Groups offered at the Center that might be helpful would include: "Women's Empowerment," "Me and My Family," and "General Counseling." All of these are process groups that would provide the opportunity to further support Pam in exploring relationship and family of origin issues, and in developing self-esteem. They would also create an environment for her to experience positive and healthy peer relationships.

REFERENCES

Brodsky, A.M., & Hare-Mustin, R.T. (1980). *Psychotherapy with women: An assessment of research and practice*. New York: Guilford.

Brown, L. S. (1994). *Subversive dialogues: Theory in feminist therapy*. New York: Basic Books.

Herman, J. L. (1992). *Trauma and recovery: The aftermath of violence–from domestic abuse to political terror*. New York: Basic Books.

Jourard, S. M. (1964). *The transparent self*. Princeton, NJ: Van Nostrand.

Kell, B.L., & Mueller, W. J. (1966). *Impact and change: A study of counseling relationships*. New York: Appleton-Century-Crofts.

May, R. (1958). The origins and significance of the existential movement in psychology. In R. May, E. Angel, & H.F. Ellenberger (Eds.), *Existence: A new dimension in psychology and psychiatry*. New York: Basic Books.

Rogers, C. (1961). *On becoming a person*. Boston: Houghton-Mifflin.

Chapter 5:
Don't Go There:
Impulse Control in Stage-Specific
Short Term Counseling

Jeffrey W. Pollard

SUMMARY. Impulse control manifested in following or low-level stalking behavior is treated using stage-specific interventions described by Prochaska. This approach suggests that therapy address the particular stage at which the client is working as well as the conditions of the diagnosis. Dialogue is employed to illuminate both stage and therapeutic intervention. *[Article copies available for a fee from The Haworth Document Delivery Service: 1-800-342-9678. E-mail address: <getinfo@haworthpressinc. com> Website: <http://www.HaworthPress.com> © 2001 by The Haworth Press, Inc. All rights reserved.]*

KEYWORDS. Counseling, impulse control, psychotherapy, and transtheoretical analysis

I originally trained with equal parts of Carl Rogers, who consulted to all of us during internship, a Michenbaum-trained operant psychologist, and an Ellis disciple. It was a heady mix, yet by comparison, things

Address correspondence to: Jeffrey W. Pollard, Health and Counseling Services, Denison University, Granville, OH 43023-1368.

[Haworth co-indexing entry note]: "Chapter 5: Don't Go There: Impulse Control in Stage-Specific Short Term Counseling." Pollard, Jeffrey W. Co-published simultaneously in *Journal of College Student Psychotherapy* (The Haworth Press, Inc.) Vol. 16, No. 1/2, 2001, pp. 65-84; and: *Case Book of Brief Psychotherapy with College Students* (ed: Stewart E. Cooper, James Archer, Jr., and Leighton C. Whitaker) The Haworth Press, Inc., 2002, pp. 65-84. Single or multiple copies of this article are available for a fee from The Haworth Document Delivery Service [1-800-342-9678, 9:00 a.m. - 5:00 p.m. (EST). E-mail address: getinfo@ haworthpressinc.com].

seemed so simple in those days–let the client choose the course of therapy, look for the irrational "B," and/or find the reinforcing event. As director of a combined college health and counseling service it has become a challenge to maintain what is a priority for me–carrying a full caseload. Maintaining a caseload has also encouraged me to read and continue my professional training. If I had to label my professional approach today I would say I'm mostly a cognitive/behavioral psychologist (sorry Carl) but there are so many other influences. I am currently particularly drawn to Prochaska's notions of development within the process of therapy and application of technique based on the client's stage of change. My work is also heavily influenced by the first position I held right out of undergraduate school–I was a probation officer. I learned very early on what are for me two unshakable truths about dealing with mandated clients. First, that untreated, these folks would commit another crime and find another victim and second, there is an extraordinarily powerful feeling connected to reaching the unreachable. It is difficult and often emotionally bruising work, but the rewards are palpably satisfying. As a result, I have served on our battered women's shelter advisory board, our county's commission on child sexual abuse, the Ohio Domestic Violence Network, and Ohio's Family Violence Prevention & Services Grant Review and Domestic Violence Advisory Committees.

BACKGROUND

Frank, a 20-year-old college junior economics major, was referred to the University Counseling Service during the second semester of his sophomore year. The referral was made by the university judicial system and his participation in counseling was involuntary. He had been found responsible by the judicial system for failing to stay away from a specified area of the university. Prior to the judicial hearing that resulted in the referral, he had been disciplined by an Area Coordinator. He was to have no contact with another specific student and he was required to remain away from a specified residential area.

He presented with no history of prior psychological treatment and no history in his family of psychiatric diagnosis. He reported no remarkable childhood trauma or violence in the home. Employing the criteria of the *Diagnostic and Statistical Manual of Mental Disorders, IV* (DSM IV) (1994), the issues discussed did not reach criteria for a specific impulse-control disorder. However, this individual had repeatedly failed to resist a self/other-destructive urge. An obsession with another individual was evident and Frank understood that the obsession was unreasonable. The obsession was time consuming and interfered with his functioning, and though it co-existed with impulse-control difficulties, it was not part of a specified diagnosis. His disregard for others was focused on one individual alone and therefore not pervasive. Further, there was no evidence of a history of a conduct disorder or that there was a preoccupation with details, lists, rules, etc. He was not perfectionistic, nor was he overconscientious, overscrupulous or inflexible about morality, or ethics. He was able to discard worn-out or worthless objects and reported that he was not miserly. He related multiple examples of driving while impaired, missing classes, and turning in academic work that was substandard due to his alcohol use. While there was no evidence of alcohol tolerance or withdrawal, there were instances of compulsive behavior while intoxicated. The impulse-control disorder coexisted with an alcohol abuse history; the impulsive behaviors in question were committed exclusively during periods of sobriety. For the purposes of this chapter, specific evaluation and treatment of his alcohol abuse will not be covered.

"The essential feature of Impulse-Control Disorders is the failure to resist an impulse, drive or temptation to perform an act that is harmful to the person or to others. For most of the disorders . . . the individual feels an increasing sense of relief at the time of committing the act. Following the act there may or may not be regret, self-reproach, or guilt" (DSM-IV, p. 609).

The etiology of impulse-control disorders is not known though there are multiple theoretical explanations. Within psychodynamic theory, the common theme is pain reduction. What to the external observer may appear to be greed or irrational behavior is believed to be a disordered attempt to relieve guilt, depression or other psychic pain. Fatigue, overwhelming stimulation and psychological trauma can contribute. Biologically, the limbic system has been implicated along with other regions of the brain. Temporal lobe epilepsy and mixed cerebral dominance are other possible factors in violent impulse displays. Serotonin, 5-hydroxyindoleacetic as well as dopaminergic and noradrenergic systems have all been implicated in various impulse-control disorders. Psychosocial factors such as childhood events, in the form of poor parental modeling, violence in the home, substance abuse, and antisocial tendencies are considered contributory (Kaplan & Sadock, pp. 760-761).

DIAGNOSIS

Axis I   Obsessive-Compulsive Disorder (300.3)
              Alcohol Abuse (305.00)
              Impulse-Control Disorder not otherwise specified
              (312.30)

Axis II   Rule out Obsessive-Compulsive Personality Disorder
              (301.4)
              Rule out Anti-Social Personality Disorder (301.7)
              Diagnosis deferred (799.9)

Axis III   Diagnosis deferred (799.9)

Axis IV   Problems related to interaction with the (university) legal
              system

Axis V   GAF-75 (DSM-IV, 1994)

This collection of dialogues is taken from consecutive sessions with Frank, though not every session is represented. They have been excerpted for the sake of brevity and continuity and are not intended to represent the entirety of the therapy, but rather critical events demonstrating the transition from one stage of change to another. This client was seen nineteen times over a four-month period.

The case is presented employing Transtheoretical Analysis to identify the stages of change in psychotherapy (Prochaska, 1994). Prochaska's model focuses on treatment of both Frank's issues as well as Frank's stage of change. Prochaska argues that attempts to assist clients to change before they have successfully negotiated the appropriate stage for change to occur will result in failure. He describes five basic stages. The first, *Precontemplation* is characterized by individuals' lack of an intention to change any time in the next six months. Many who are referred involuntarily present in this stage. Prochaska suggests that individuals in Precontemplation "may be uninformed or under-informed about the consequences of their behavior." Denial, hostility, and defensiveness also characterize this stage. Prochaska reports defining two naturally occurring motivational forces that create the opportunity for change. The first are developmental events. These are times when individuals employ introspection to consider whether the behavior in which they are participating is appropriate for their stage in life. The second force comprises environmental events with consequences for individual behavior as opportunity to initiate change (Hubble et al., pp. 228-229,

Prochaska, p. 461). It has been suggested that consciousness raising by increasing information about self and the problem, observations, confrontations, interpretations, and bibliotherapy be employed during this stage (Brinthaupt & Lipka, p. 209).

T: So how about telling me what got you here.

Frank: Well . . . I was on Warning Probation and then I got in more trouble so they sent me down here.

T: What kind of trouble?

Frank: I was caught on the East Quad.

T: Why was being on the East Quad such a problem?

Frank: Part of being on Warning Probation was I wasn't supposed to be on the East Quad.

T: You better go all the way back to the beginning and bring me up to date.

Frank: Okay, I'm dating a girl–Jessica–who lives on the East Quad. One day she tells me that she feels like smothered just because I like spending time with her and she asks me to give her some room. But I have other friends on the East Quad and some of her roommates are my friends too, so I went over to see my friends. She got really upset and told to the AC [Area Coordinator]. I had to meet with her in the AC's office. The AC told me to stay away from her and that I wasn't allowed on the East Quad. She wrote a letter saying I couldn't go over there. So I didn't go over to see her anymore, I just went over to see my friends. I got written up for being on East Quad by the RA [Resident Assistant] . . . . and I had to go to Judish and the AC told 'em all that I was in violation of her letter to stay off East Quad because Jessica didn't feel safe around me. What a bunch of bullsh . . . !

T: You're really angry about it, aren't you?

Frank: Wouldn't you be? All I did was go over to see my friends and now I'm on probation. That sucks! Don't I have any rights? I pay a lot of money to go here, why can't I go where everybody else can go? It's all crap! I ought to get a lawyer and sue the hell outta this place.

T: Frank, may I ask you some questions about all this?

Frank: Yeah . . .

T: How long were you and Jessica dating before the trouble started?

Frank: . . . about two weeks.

T: . . . and how many dates had you been on?

Frank: We met at the Hang Out and ever since we just go over to her room.

T: Did you go anywhere else with her?

Frank: What do you mean?

T: Did you guys eat together, or hang in the student union or have class together?

Frank: No

T: Did you meet after classes or go into the village or did she ever come over to your dorm?

Frank: No

T: Did you and Jessica ever talk about your relationship–like were you going to date others, keep it casual or . . .

Frank: No! She won't talk to me. She always says that she doesn't have time or she's busy with her roommates or she's studying or something else lame. Then she just one day decides that she doesn't want to see me anymore.

T: That made you pretty angry too, didn't it?

Frank: Uh huh . . . 'cause I really love her and I haven't had the chance to tell her–I know it will be better when I just get the chance, but her roommates were always butting in.

T: Do you think it's possible that she never felt the way you did?

Frank: No, no–we have a wonderful time and she is perfect for me, I . . . I love her and I want her to know. I'm sure when I just get the chance to talk with her we will be cool.

T: Okay. But after she said she didn't want to see you and the AC had made it clear you were not to go over to the East Quad, why did you return? I know you said that you wanted to see your friends, but . . . weren't you afraid you would get in trouble?

Frank: No, I told you, I didn't go over to see her, I went over to see her roommates and my other friends who live in her building.

In this interaction there are clear signs of hostility, immaturity, and denial. Frank's lack of insight and transparent excuses reveal a pattern. He does not yet understand the effect of his behaviors on the female student, and there are sufficient signs for me to follow in seeking to rule out an obsession manifested in an impulse-control disorder.

Consciousness Raising and Environmental Reevaluation were employed to help Frank progress from Precontemplation to the next stage–Contemplation (Prochaska, pp. 461-467). While this client certainly produced sufficient information to reach criteria for the diagnosis of Substance abuse–Alcohol, there are signs at this point that a problem exists in addition to the substance abuse; principally, his continued references to a relationship with a female student in the present tense even though he had run afoul of the judicial system because she had made it clear she was not interested in him. Alcohol abuse did become an important coexisting issue in this client's therapy, but it is not visited here as alcohol and other drug abuse are dealt with elsewhere in this volume.

At the beginning of the interview, I expressed empathy and understanding for the client's feelings of being coerced into counseling. When dealing with mandated clients, it is important to be willing to return to those feelings whenever the opportunity arises. Eventually the client will recognize that he likely can not avoid doing the work of therapy and still finish the sanction successfully. Candid conversation about the heightened power differential is therefore important if the client is to genuinely seek help (Rooney, pp. 20-21).

After two more sessions in which the interaction continued on the lines discussed previously, another incident involving the university authorities helped motivate the change from Precontemplation to Contemplation.

Contemplation is evidenced by the person's awareness that a problem exists, thinking about overcoming it, and there is no commitment to change (Prochaska, p. 461) indicating only that they are intending to change at some point in the next six months. An acute awareness develops that involves both the pros and cons of changing and that the costs of change will be potentially painful (Hubble, Duncan, Miller, pp. 229-230). People in this stage are not committed to change and are at risk of spending considerable time in contemplation (Brinthaupt & Lipka, p. 205).

T: So tell me, have you seen Jessica recently?

Frank: Yeah and I'm in trouble again too.

T: I'm sorry to hear that, what happened?

Frank: Well, I had to go to the East quad to get some notes for my Ed Psych class 'cause the person who had them lives in the same building as Jessica. She saw me in the hall and called the AC.

T: I take it you have to go back to Judish?

Frank: Yeah, . . . yes I do . . .

T: Tell me what you make of finding yourself in trouble for the same thing all over again?

Frank: I don't know. I really don't see how it's such a big deal–I only went over to get some notes, what's the problem?

T: Did you think that you might run into her?

Frank: I don't know . . .

T: Frank, slow down and ask yourself if you had any hope at all you might see her.

Frank: Sure it would be cool to see her, but I didn't want her to see me, 'cause then I'd get in trouble.

T: Didn't you think that you might possibly be seen by other students who knew you weren't supposed to be over there?

Frank: I guess I didn't think about that.

T: Frank, I know all this has made you very angry. I wonder if you ever feel like hurting Jessica, let's say in order to punish her?

Frank: I am really angry at her.

T: Have you made any plans or had any thoughts to hurt her?

Frank: No . . .

T: Yes, but do you think about hurting her? Do you have a gun or other weapon?

Frank: I'm not sure what you mean by "hurt" her. I sometimes think it would be okay if she hurt inside the way I do, but I don't own a gun or anything. I am not going to hit her or even touch her, . . . that simply isn't cool and I hate it when I see guys treating women like that. But I do wish she knew how it feels, and if that means she would hurt to find out, fine, but I'm not going to do anything to her.

T: Frank, I wonder if you feel that you have a choice about going over and trying to see her?

Frank: What do you mean?

T: Well, let's say you were holding your breath, after a while you wouldn't have a choice except to breathe–its kinda like that. Not going to the East Quad is like holding your breath and going over there is like breathing.

Frank: I never really thought about it that way. Is that possible?

T: Yes it is. One way you may know is that you may be thinking about Jessica a lot.

Frank: I do think about her all the time–I write poems and letters to her. I've made up a design of a tattoo for my ankle with her name worked into this barbed wire look.

T: . . . and do you feel that you really had to go over to the East Quad to be near her?

Frank: Yeah . . .

T: . . . and do you still want to? I mean even as we speak?

Frank: Yeah, I do . . .

T: . . . and I bet you are very aware that the East Quad is just up the hill from the Counseling Center aren't you? And that there oughta be a way to go through the East Quad when you come over here or when you leave?

*Frank: Yea, I was thinking about that on the way over. I need to go to the Theta house from here and the shortest way is straight through East Quad. I wouldn't get in trouble for that would I?

T: Well, I want you to think about what you just suggested. How does that fit with what the folks on Judish said?

**Frank: They say that in no circumstances am I to be on East Quad, but I wouldn't go over there to be on East Quad, just to walk through–I think that should be okay.

T: Sounds like you need to breathe . . .

Frank: Yeah . . .

T: This is exactly what I'm suggesting. You think about Jessica all the time. You write about her, think of having her name permanently tattooed on your body, and you're trying to negotiate with me to give you permission to go on the East Quad. All this when both Jessica and the university have clearly told you that under no circumstances were you are to be around her or on the East Quad. You need to breathe–you don't feel you have a choice, do you?

Frank: . . . no, I don't . . . I love her . . . what am I supposed to do?

T: Would you like to work on this together?

Frank: Do I have to give up loving her?

T: That depends on what you mean by loving her. You do need to be in control of your behavior, and unlike the breathing thing, you can learn to make choices about this.

*, ** Note that during this sequence, Frank tried on two separate occasions to invite me to participate in his obsession. Though it may be tempting to be empathic in these instances, it was important not to join Frank's obsession. I would do well to give a consistent message that Frank's thinking and behavior are voluntary, albeit at this point they don't completely feel that way to him.

I encouraged Frank to reevaluate himself and his current circumstances in order to soften the absence of commitment inherent in the Contemplation Stage (Prochaska, p. 467). At the end of this interaction, Frank began to show signs that he understood that he had a problem and that he is interested in change. During this exchange, it became clear that Frank was unaware that he is making a choice not to comply with the Judicial System's decision. He speaks easily about Jessica, with barely any inquiry from me, and he believes he is compelled and justified to go where he has been forbidden to go. However, Frank is also beginning to develop some insight. The issue of why he feels this way and how this style of interacting developed are not part of this therapy. If he can develop skills to identify his compulsive behavior and deal with it successfully, he will be able to avoid the negative consequences they create in his life.

A preliminary lethality evaluation, including an assessment of the client's access to lethal items as well as his state of mind, is indicated in these circumstances. In this example, conversation about Frank's state of mind reveals that he is personally opposed to violence against women although he clearly harbors a wish for her to "feel his pain." He does not appear to have the critical element of a "feeling of ownership" of the object of his obsession that is often present in so many potentially dangerous individuals. The query as to his access to weapons also produces a negative answer. Here, neither course of questioning reveals cause for serious concern at the time, however, it was imperative to repeat this line of questioning during the course of treating his obsession in order to identify any shift in his potential for violence (Pollard, p. 59).

Preparation, the third Prochaska stage, is characterized by the intention to take immediate action. Clients in this stage often have taken some small steps to change but do not as yet fulfil the criteria for the next stage which is Action (Prochaska, p. 462). Their time horizon for change is usually measured as being within the next month and they often have made plans for the action they will take (Hubble et al., p. 230). This stage has been characterized as transitional rather than stable and reflects movement rather than a state in which clients generally remain for extended periods of time (Brinthaupt & Lipka, p. 205). In this third section of dialogue, Frank began learning to control his compulsive thoughts and behavior.

> T: What do you say to yourself when you think about seeing Jessica or going over to the East Quad?
>
> Frank: I don't know. I just start thinking of a way to go over there, and frankly I don't see why I shouldn't.
>
> T: So, in response to a wish or impulse to see her, you think of a way to do it and you give yourself permission to do so.
>
> Frank: Yeah . . . .?
>
> T: Okay, this is important . . . to gain control over your actions, you must understand that you are making a decision. The decision you are making is this: you are choosing to make a plan to see her and you are encouraging yourself to do it. Those are choices. When you don't listen to the things you say to yourself, you will get that "need to breathe" feeling and you will act out of habit.
>
> Frank: But I'm right about seeing her, if I want to, why shouldn't I?
>
> T: I don't necessarily disagree with you, it's just that you don't think or behave like you have a choice, do you? If you have control over your behavior and you choose to see her, so be it. You'll simply pay the consequence if you get caught, which as I understand it will likely be dismissal from the university, right?
>
> Frank: Yeah . . . so how do I get this control?

T: Okay, first understand that you are already making a choice, and that choice is: after you get an idea, you choose to make a plan and then give yourself permission to follow through with it. You do all this almost automatically without considering other choices you have. You need to use your ability to consider alternatives to your original idea.

Frank: What will that do?

T: Ultimately? . . . it will give you control over your behavior.

Frank: I don't know . . .

T: You sound skeptical–that's good, it means you are thinking about what I have said. Can you do the same about what you say to yourself? Do you ever have doubts about going over to the East Quad?

Frank: *Actually I do . . . sometimes I even drink to make the thoughts go away, but not always.

T: How do those doubts make you feel?

Frank: Actually they scare the hell out of me.

T: Why . . . ?

**Frank: If I get caught and kicked outta here, my parents will kill me. I'll have to go home, go to a community college and I'll never get out of the house.

---

*This clear reference to alcohol consumption as a form of psychological anesthesia was intentionally overlooked at that point as we had other discussions about alcohol, but it is an important piece of information and contributes to the evidence that he is abusing alcohol.
**Note that no attempt is made to suggest or inquire as to the possibility of his wanting to do just exactly that which he states he is afraid to do. The goal of this therapy is to help the client develop choice-making behavior.

T: Do you like the way that feels?

Frank: No . . . absolutely not, but sometimes I don't really care because I love her so much.

Here I helped clarify change by labeling the behavior in which Frank is engaging. By so doing, both Frank and I know exactly what is being discussed to consider changing. This is a critical opportunity to help Frank move away from feeling frightened, trapped and unable to control his behavior. He is having difficulty with his emotions and his newly discovered realization that he feels unable to manage his decision-making and behavior. His confusion provides an opening to demonstrate that his ability to look at his internal dialogue will create opportunities to both feel and act differently.

All that has transpired in the therapy to this point is preparation for change or what Prochaska calls Action. Although forced to participate in counseling the client has given me his trust, and is beginning to see that there are alternatives to the way he is feeling and acting.

Action occurs "when individuals modify their behavior, experiences, and/or environment in order to overcome their problems" (Prochaska, p. 462). This stage is the most active as individuals implement differing strategies of change. It is also unstable and is highly subject to relapse (Brinthaupt & Lipka, pp. 205-206).

T: Can you identify the "need to breathe" feeling?

Frank: Yeah, I think so.

T: How can you tell?

Frank: I get an urge to see her . . . and I feel a pressure right in the middle of my chest. It feels irresistible.

T: I bet some of the urges are stronger than others, and some last longer than others?

Frank: . . . Yes.

T: And some you are able to resist by just gutting them out and others you can't resist and you find yourself on your way over to the East Quad with your heart thumping away.

Frank: . . . Yeah.

T: Can you imagine the strength of these feelings on a scale? Let's say the strongest are a "9" and weakest are a "1"–Okay?

Frank: That's about right too . . .

T: So how often do you have a 7, or an 8?

Frank: Not all that often, maybe once or twice a week . . . I have the little ones all the time.

T: Daily?

Frank: Maybe hourly . . .

T: Okay, and these feelings aren't comfortable at all are they?

Frank: No . . . no not at all.

T: I mentioned that because we all have a tendency to avoid negative feelings. One of the ways you make that "need to breathe" feeling go away is to what . . . ?

Frank: Make a plan and give myself permission?

T: Yes! Absolutely. And it makes you feel better doesn't it?

Frank: Uh huh . . .

T: But it gets you in trouble, so instead of making a plan and then giving yourself permission, we need another way to make the feeling go away right?

Frank: Yeah . . . I guess . . .

T: Okay, when you feel the urge, get the pressure in your chest and have that irresistible feeling, that is a signal for you to begin listening to yourself. First I want you to say to yourself: STOP! Then I want you to take a few long slow breaths, then I want you to begin to think, after all that you can act–Okay?

*Frank: What do I think about?

*Note: Frank is trying to inadvertently move away from the protocol. I try to keep the intervention structure simple and consistent.

T: What do you do first?

Frank: Say STOP . . . .?

T: Then what?

Frank: Breathe . . .

T: Several long slow breaths in and out, just slow down. Then what?

Frank: Think, but I don't know what to think.

T: Fair enough, we will get to it, I promise. Then what?

Frank: Do whatever I have decided to do?

T: Yes, act . . . Okay, you have the steps down: stop, breath, think, act. So when do you do this?

Frank: When I get the urge, the tightness . . .

T: Yes, very good. So, you get the urge, you decide to stop, breathe, think and you need to know how to think this through, right? Well, how do you usually think through a decision?

Frank: I think about what the up side is and what the down side is for each part of the decision.

T: Excellent! See you really don't need as much work on your thinking as you may have thought. You already know how to make a decision, don't you? Use that process here. Consider both the up side and the down side to each alternative you can think of. You just use the skills you already have–plug 'em in right there! . . . would you be willing to keep track of your urges for a couple of weeks? I'd like for you to keep a journal and write in it each and every time you get an urge.

Frank: I guess . . . what should I do?

T: This is very important. I want you to write down each urge you have, how strong it is on the scale of one to ten, and what you wind up doing about it. Okay? Here I'll write that out for you and you can keep it in your journal. Look at it whenever you have an urge. Okay?

Frank: (nods yes)

T: You can't do this wrong, there is no grade. It will help you see what you are dealing with. Next week bring it in and we will look it over together.

During this interaction, Frank learns that he is already modifying his behavior and that he needs to continue to apply his knowledge to his difficulty in order to achieve success. The therapy will continue with further Action steps in order to assist in the change process. Asking for a written journal, identifying feelings, etc., will assure a more stable state of change post-therapy.

Clues in his writing about what is going on in his life, where he is, and who is around when he feels the urge to see Jessica are critical and are explored in-depth. These clues are used to help Frank predict when his obsession is likely to occur and, consequently, when he needs to begin the active decision making process. As he learns about his urges and begins to realize that he already possesses some of the skills necessary to successfully deal with them, he will gain confidence and competence. He will learn the transient nature of urges and that he will be able to identify two different kinds of change: the first in which the urges become less powerful and the second as the urges occur less frequently. Next, his ability to work through the more powerful urges will improve and he will subsequently, finally gain mastery. When clients do not respond fully, other interventions are warranted. Subsequent interventions are chosen based on the level at which progress is slowed (Prochaska, pp. 468-470).

Maintenance, the last stage, is necessary because the old patterns may resurface. Prochaska views maintenance as maintenance of Action, not a static condition in which no change occurs (Prochaska, p. 463). It is important to put in place a system of follow-up sessions spaced out over perhaps four to six weeks between sessions to assess the client's continued progress, the possibility of his developing another obsession, and any change in the lethality potential. Should the client regress, the therapist will then assess to which stage the client has reverted and intervene appropriately. It is most likely that in relapse, the client would return to the contemplation or preparation stage (Prochaska, p. 463).

In this case, I followed the client monthly for the remainder of the school year, after which he and I terminated treatment. No further incidents were brought to my attention and Frank was not seen again in the Counseling Service during his college career.

DISCUSSION

Counseling and clinical psychology in general and college counseling centers in particular are experiencing an increase in demand for treatment of those who display self and other-destructive behaviors. In the cases of those with other-destructive behavior, prevention begs for solutions that create safety from further victimization on campus. As the majority of campuses are gaining experience treating involuntary clients for alcohol-related behavior, a standard of practice to accept involuntary referrals is being reinforced by university administrations (Gallagher, 1991, pp. 1, 5). From within the profession, authors are suggesting increased involvement by professionals in the prevention of victimization (Hage). The Prochaska model blends well with techniques that aid change and create prevention.

QUESTIONS

1. *How would you characterize your counseling approach in this case?*

The approach in this case is cognitive and behavioral. The process of the approach is informed by the stages of Trans-Theoretical Analysis. It was my hope to help Frank identify those internal states/thoughts that maintained his behavior. Through increased awareness, Frank was then able to make choices of which he was previously unaware.

2. *Frank moved through the Prochaska stages of readiness rather rapidly. If Frank had not been ready to move to the next stage, how would you have proceeded?*

The excerpts may have been misleading in that those chosen were for the purpose of demonstration. We also had sessions that addressed the obsession from which no excerpt was taken nor were any excerpts included that dealt with his alcohol abuse. That having been said, yes this client was highly motivated, and as a result, he responded in a way that was counterintuitive to the presentation imagined by many therapists who contemplate providing mandatory counseling. Had he at some point bogged down unduly, a different intervention approach would have been implemented. Prochaska makes a short, yet surprisingly in-depth description of this process in: *Systems of Psychotherapy: A Transtheoretical Analysis* (pp. 466-470). In his analysis Prochaska postulates that for each stage there are appropriate interventions and he arranges them in an ever-deepening order so that, where one fails, the theory calls for the next "deeper" approach.

3. *Alcohol abuse is listed as one of the Axis 1 diagnoses, but it doesn't appear to be a focus of the treatment that was conveyed in these transcripts. How did problems with alcohol abuse affect the counseling and why wasn't it a part of this write-up?*

Treatment of alcohol abuse was not included in the excerpts because it is dealt with in-depth in other chapters of this volume. In my opinion, alcohol or any other drug abuse must be dwelt with first in therapy before other issues can be successfully addressed. This is because substance abuse often takes the place of dealing with internal states of both cognitive dissonance and emotional distress, both of which are necessary for growth and change. The presence of Frank's alcohol abuse made it necessary for me to finish a good deal of that work before beginning with the obsession. While working with the obsession I was continually on the lookout for indicators of Frank's slipping back into abusive patterns or developing an addiction. Abusing clients are at risk of increasing their intake as the work of therapy becomes more difficult.

4. *The basic treatment seems to be a variation of Stress Inoculation, yet little time was spent on teaching the relaxation response or developing a set of coping self-statements. What was your rationale for using a briefer version of this approach?*

The introduction of the notion of decision making can sometimes accomplish both relaxation and coping self-statements. To do so, it was necessary for Frank to slow down and believe he could make the appropriate decision. This approach has worked in my practice with motivated clients. Had it not had the desired effect, teaching relaxation and creating new self-talk would indeed have been the next step.

5. *During the maintenance phase of the treatment, was there any work with Frank to help him use the general approach to other areas of impulsivity?*

No, and in fact that may have been an oversight. I continued to monitor Frank's potential for lethal activity, as any change in that status would create the circumstance for alarm and possible action.

REFERENCES

Brinthaupt, T. M., & Lipka, R. P. (1994). *Changing the self.* Albany, NY: SUNY Press.

Diagnostic and statistical manual of mental disorders (1994) (4th ed.). Washington, DC: American Psychiatric Association.

Gallagher, R. (1991). The annual national survey for counseling center directors. The University of Pittsburgh.

Hage, S. M. (2000). The role of counseling psychology in preventing male violence against female intimates. *The Counseling Psychologist, 28*(6).

Hubble, M. A., Duncan, B. L., & Miller, S. D. (1999). The heart and soul of change: What works in therapy. Washington, DC: American Psychological Association.

Kaplan, H. I., & Sadock, B. J. (1998). *Synopsis of psychiatry.* Philadelphia: Lippincott, Williams & Wilkins.

Pollard, J. W. (1994). Treatment for perpetrators of rape and other violence. In A. Berkowitz (Ed.), *New directions in student affairs, men and rape: Theory, research, and prevention programs in higher education,* No. 65, New York: Jossey Bass.

Prochaska, J. O., & Norcross, J. C. (1994). *Systems of psychotherapy: A transtheoretical analysis,* 3rd Ed. Pacific Grove, CA: Brooks/Cole Publishing.

Rooney, R. H. (1991). *Strategies for work with involuntary clients.* New York: Columbia University Press.

Chapter 6:
Current Conflicts as Mirrors
of Unfinished Business with Mom and Dad

Harry L. Piersma

SUMMARY. This chapter describes brief therapy with Lynn, a college junior enrolled in an athletic training degree program, who presented with anxiety related to her supervisor's criticism of her work. Therapy focused on how she could deal more appropriately with her supervisor in the present, while also looking at how her reactions to supervisory criticism touched off a variety of feelings related to unfinished business with her family of origin, particularly her relationships with her mother and father. *[Article copies available for a fee from The Haworth Document Delivery Service: 1-800-342-9678. E-mail address: <getinfo@haworthpressinc.com> Website: <http://www.HaworthPress.com> © 2001 by The Haworth Press, Inc. All rights reserved.]*

KEYWORDS. Supervisory conflict, brief therapy, family of origin

I work as a Senior Psychologist at the Counseling Center at Michigan State University (MSU). I have worked in this Center for approximately

Address correspondence to: Harry L. Piersma, Michigan State University Counseling Center, 207 Student Services Building, Michigan State University, East Lansing, MI 48824 (E-mail: HarryP@secure.couns.msu.edu).

[Haworth co-indexing entry note]: "Chapter 6: Current Conflicts as Mirrors of Unfinished Business with Mom and Dad." Piersma, Harry L. Co-published simultaneously in *Journal of College Student Psychotherapy* (The Haworth Press, Inc.) Vol. 16, No. 1/2, 2001, pp. 85-100; and: *Case Book of Brief Psychotherapy with College Students* (ed: Stewart E. Cooper, James Archer, Jr., and Leighton C. Whitaker) The Haworth Press, Inc., 2002, pp. 85-100. Single or multiple copies of this article are available for a fee from The Haworth Document Delivery Service [1-800-342-9678, 9:00 a.m. - 5:00 p.m. (EST). E-mail address: getinfo@ haworthpressinc.com].

two years, seeing a variety of clients for individual psychotherapy. In addition, I supervise predoctoral interns and practicum students from the clinical and counseling psychology programs at MSU. Previously, most of my professional career was spent at a private psychiatric facility in the Midwest where I served in a variety of clinical and administrative positions in inpatient, day treatment, and outpatient settings. I also directed an APA-approved internship for many years, and served as director of clinical research. In total, I have had over 25 years of experience working as a clinician, researcher, administrator, and teacher.

I have tried to continually develop my skills as a psychotherapist, and have been exposed to several therapy approaches since my graduate years at Purdue University in the early 1970s. I have been trained in psychodynamic, behavioral, family systems, cognitive and interpersonal modalities, and have been most influenced by models that comprehensively provide: (1) a theoretical framework for understanding human development, (2) a system for assessing what is problematic for an individual's development at the particular time counseling is sought, and (3) methods for intervening to help the individual cope with the problems for which they seek help.

In particular, I have been most influenced in my clinical development by therapy modalities with an interpersonal focus. Two specific interpersonal approaches have been extremely helpful in guiding my approach to short-term therapy at the MSU Counseling Center. The first is Schema-Focused Cognitive Therapy, developed by Jeffrey Young (Young, 1990, 1994). Even though this schema-focused model has its roots in the cognitive therapy framework developed by Aaron Beck, it is a multi-faceted therapy which provides a method for conceptualizing, assessing, and counseling clients. The schema-focused model emphasizes the critical importance of interpersonal elements to understand how an individual's problems developed and how the relationship between client and therapist can help change maladaptive functioning. A second powerful influence on my approach to working with students is based on the work of Lorna Smith Benjamin, whose therapeutic method is brilliantly described in *Interpersonal Diagnosis and Treatment of Personality Disorders* (Benjamin, 1993). Benjamin has developed a model illustrating how interpersonal problems arise in the context of family dynamics, and the necessity to help the client understand these dynamics to improve interpersonal functioning. Finally, I have drawn heavily on the work of Theodore Millon (1996), his influence having been most profound on how an individual's personality dynamics can be understood. Two instruments, the Millon Clinical Multiaxial Inventory-III MCMI-III (Millon, 1994) and the Millon Index of Personality Styles (MIPS; Millon, 1994) have been excellent tools for enabling me to assess clients' Axis I and Axis II dynamics.

CASE DESCRIPTION AND CONCEPTUALIZATION

In this section I will present the case of Lynn, a 21-year-old Caucasian female junior majoring in athletic training. Her presenting complaint centered on anxiety she was experiencing related to conflicts with a supervisor. I will illustrate my use of Young's and Benjamin's models in my brief, focused therapeutic work with this client, and briefly comment on how the Millon inventories assisted me in identifying core interpersonal issues in therapy, as well as conceptualizing the client according to DSM-IV diagnostic nosology.

Lynn presented at the Counseling Center shortly after the beginning of the fall semester. She reported increasing anxiety and distress in coping with her supervisor in the athletic training department. She experienced this supervisor as overly critical, giving as an example recently being "dressed down" by the supervisor because she had filled out a referral for physician consultation but failed to put "Dr." in front of the physician's name. Lynn reported experiencing this criticism as unwarranted, although she also felt that her emotional reaction to this criticism was exaggerated, and thus she was seeking help to better understand why this event was "causing" her so much ongoing distress. She expressed some awareness that her distress was somehow related to her relationships with her parents, but was not sure exactly how.

At this point, I offered to see her for short-term therapy. I discussed our clinic policy of limiting sessions to no more than 12 in any one academic year, and suggested that we meet for a minimum of six sessions, focusing on how Lynn could more effectively understand her conflicts with her supervisor. She would then be in a better position to decide how she wanted to deal with that situation. I explained that I would be working out of a schema-focused model, and gave her a "Client's Guide to Schema-Focused Therapy" (Bricker & Young, 1991), providing an overview of schema-focused therapy, including what schemas are, how they evidence themselves in an individual's life, and how the therapy process can be used to understand and modify dysfunctional schema patterns. In addition, I requested that she complete several assessment instruments developed by Young to evaluate a client's dominant schemas, and how they relate to early life experiences, particularly with parents. Finally, I requested that Lynn complete two psychological tests, the Millon Clinical Multiaxial Inventory (MCMI-III; Millon, 1994) and the Millon Index of Personality Styles (MIPS; Millon, 1994), explaining that these assessment tools would help us better understand the source of her current distress, and that she would be given feedback on the results as part of our work together.

In the next two sessions we did a comprehensive psychosocial history, and discussed my impressions from the psychosocial history, and the psychological testing. Lynn's parents separated when she was two but had never divorced. Father, 62, held a variety of jobs in the federal government. He was described by Lynn as "temperamental, but generally I've gotten along with him." She noted that he e-mailed her almost daily, and that "he's always told me to try my best and that when I have a problem, he usually tells me that everything will be alright, which bugs me." Mother, 51, had worked in various secretarial and receptionist positions. Lynn described a very conflictual relationship with her mother, noting that she has never been good at managing money or her household. She also reported that her mother was emotionally abusive towards her, and had displaced much anger towards Lynn's father onto her. Lynn added that she always had felt responsible for taking care of her mother, despite her mother's abusive behaviors toward her. Mother's emotional abuse of her was illustrated by Lynn's being told as a teenager by her mother: "You should go live with your father, because you've ruined the last 10 years of my life." Lynn said that she coped with her emotionally deprived upbringing by becoming involved in athletics as a child, which led to her eventual interest in pursuing a career as an athletic trainer.

Lynn has one half brother, age 27, who is single, living some distance away. He is a product of mother's first marriage, which ended with the death of her husband in the Vietnam War. Lynn said she was close to her brother, but felt that he was irresponsible with money, much like her mother. Lynn's father also had a previous marriage which ended, according to Lynn, because "my dad said she was an alcoholic and would never be able to take care of herself." Lynn was quite clear in saying that she felt her mother was emotionally abusive to her throughout her childhood, but denied any history of physical or sexual abuse.

Lynn said that in high school she was heavily invested in athletics, including softball, volleyball and field hockey. She said she was a good student with a B plus grade point average (GPA), fairly popular, and dated throughout high school and college, but had never been fully sexually active. She explained: "I usually break up with any boyfriend who wants to get serious because I'm worried that they just want sex and are going to take advantage of me." Throughout college she had volunteered her services to an athletic program for children, because she enjoyed this work, although "it frustrates me to see kids who are abused and I can't do anything about it."

Lynn experienced migraine headaches throughout adolescence and early adulthood. In her sophomore year of college, she underwent a CAT scan and was initially told by a neurologist that she had brain tumors, but a week later she was told that this was not true, that a mistake had been made in reading the scan. She reported continuing anger over how she had been dealt with by the medical profession in this situation. She had never previously sought assistance for mental health concerns and denied any substance use. She said she had questioned her religious faith much during high school but the recent crisis, being told she had brain tumors, had led her to reinvolve herself in a local Lutheran church.

The results from the Millon instruments gave further information helpful to conceptualizing, diagnosing, and developing a short-term treatment plan. The MIPS profile suggested Lynn generally experienced herself as well-adjusted and enjoying life; she presented herself on the MIPS as outgoing, assertive, nurturing of others, yet able to individuate and separate herself when appropriate. Although generally seeing herself as congenial and cooperative with others, the results did suggest that Lynn prefers to make her own decisions and be her own boss. When faced with situations where authorities disagree with her, she is likely to "draw lines in the sand" quickly. She has strongly held values about how to do things best and when dealing with those who monitor her closely and do not allow her much freedom to make her own decisions, she is likely to rebel. The results suggested, however, that in most instances Lynn is able to structure her environment so that she does not have to face conflicts with authorities. The MCMI-III yielded further helpful diagnostic data. Underlying Lynn's relatively well-adjusted external persona is an individual who, at the time of testing, was experiencing a great deal of diffuse anxiety. The highest elevations on the personality scales were on self-defeating, depressive and paranoid which, in the context of the foregoing information, suggested that she experienced much disillusionment and mistrust in interpersonal relationships. She wondered whether true closeness and intimacy with others can be achieved, fearing that, ultimately, others will not be able to meet her emotional needs, and may actually intend to use and take advantage of her. Thus, the Millon results suggest an Axis I diagnosis with anxiety as the most prominent symptom, associated with an external stressor, conflict with a supervisor. Thus, the most accurate diagnosis was Adjustment Disorder with Anxiety. Lynn did not meet criteria for a personality disorder on Axis II, but self-defeating, depressive and paranoid traits were prominent. The test results suggested that in most instances Lynn takes a counter-dependent stance in her relationships with others, due to her underlying fear that emotional closeness will lead ultimately to rejection and/or being abused or taken advantage of by others.

In addition to a DSM-IV formulation, I use Young's and Benjamin's models to develop a richer interpersonal diagnostic formulation, as well as to assist in developing an interpersonally-focused treatment plan. In terms of Young's schema-focused model Lynn reported most identifying with schemas having to do with issues of abandonment, defectiveness/shame, and self-sacrifice. The schema-focused assessment instruments were also consistent with her self-report but also suggested that the unrelenting standards schema was very prominent. In collaborating together, we talked about how these dominant schemas related to her family of origin: mother was extremely critical of her, and provided almost no emotional support or nurturance; father was more supportive, but was not around consistently, and gave Lynn the message that "Everything will be okay if you work hard enough." Given these dynamics, it was understandable that Lynn's surface persona was to appear well-adjusted and in control of every aspect of her life. Underneath, however, she was emotionally deprived and had developed defenses to cope with this deprivation. Her sensitivity to any criticism was understandable given what she had encountered in her relationship with her mother. In adolescence, she had been able to defend against mother's critical nature by withdrawing, and investing herself in athletics. Her conflict with her supervisor could then be understood as touching off major unresolved issues from her past with her parents. She experienced the criticism from her supervisor as unfair and, in reality, it was criticism over a relatively trivial matter, but unlike the situation with mother, she could not withdraw, since she needed to pass the course to achieve her goal of becoming an athletic trainer. The supervisor's criticism also touched off unresolved issues with Lynn's father, particularly her introjected belief that if she works hard enough, everything will be okay. In the case of conflict with the supervisor, she was trying her best but still encountering criticism.

Benjamin's approach to case conceptualization also helped to understand Lynn's situation in terms of how she could best be approached in short-term therapy. Benjamin emphasized the importance of understanding how the client related to major adult figures in early life, particularly the parents. She suggests to clients that what we do as adults often copies patterns we learned with parents, and notes three primary ways patterns are copied: first, to be like the parent in how one relates to others; second, to act toward others as one did towards the parents; third, to treat oneself as the parent treated himself or herself. In Lynn's case, each of these patterns was evident to one degree or another. Like her mother, Lynn could be very critical of others whom she perceived as incompetent. In her relationship with her mother, she eventually gave up trying to get from her the emotional support and acceptance she needed, and withdrew into the world of athletics. In like manner, in most relationships in her current life, Lynn withdrew when she felt the least hint of rejection or criticism. Finally, she introjected her experience of her father by becoming extremely driven and having unrelenting self standards for achievement. In this way, she treated herself as she saw her father treat himself.

All of the foregoing guided my approach to the actual therapeutic work with Lynn. In a short-term model, one has to carefully pick the areas of focus. I carefully delineated all the foregoing conceptual and diagnostic information in my work with Lynn, because without a good understanding of the client's basic character structure, it is difficult for the therapist to effectively target realistic and meaningful goals for short-term therapy. In Lynn's case, my formulation suggested a fairly stable character structure with generally well-functioning defenses. Having completed a thorough assessment, I had a good understanding of why she was coming in for help at that time. Basically, she had been able to structure her life so that she could avoid having to deal with the more painful and unresolved issues of her past, by becoming involved in athletics, getting into an athletic training program, and becoming very skilled, and thus able to develop interpersonal relationships with others in this capacity, without the "risks" involved in more intimate relationships. What was causing her so much conflict with the supervisor was that she was reexperiencing her relationship with her mother; she was being criticized unfairly. She had managed to cope with this earlier in life by disengaging from her mother, withdrawing (sublimating?) into the world of athletics. All of the sudden she finds that her world continues to have a "critical mother," in the form of her supervisor. Her anxiety was so unrelenting because her usual defense from criticism, withdrawal, was not readily available to her. If she were to become a trainer, she could not withdraw, because that would mean loss of her most meaningful objective, athletic training.

TREATMENT

The assessment process was completed after two sessions. In our third session, I summarized the foregoing conceptual information to Lynn, as a way of beginning short-term therapy. I explained to her that in a short-term framework, it is necessary to pick only one or two areas of central focus. Lynn was able to recognize the link between her presenting concern (conflict with the supervisor) and her conflictual relationship with her mother. Together we agreed to focus on the relationship with her mother as the best way to help her understand and deal with her conflicts with her supervisor. We also agreed on another area of focus, which was how she could achieve closer and more intimate relationships with others, both males and females. We contracted for a minimum of four additional sessions to work on these goals. Another issue central to our immediate work together was Lynn's ambivalence about engaging in therapy. In our feedback session, she expressed concern about discussing her relationship with mother. This was illustrated in the following exchange:

> T. We've talked about some of the reasons you are coming in for counseling. Often clients have another part of them that resists, or has second thoughts about coming in. Was that at all true for you?
>
> Lynn: Well, I guess one reason I haven't wanted to come in is I worry about talking about my mom.
>
> T. Your mom?
>
> Lynn: Yes, I don't know . . . well, we've had a lot of problems in the past and I think I've put them behind me.
>
> T. So what might happen if you talk about your mom in counseling?
>
> Lynn: It might make things worse, I mean, it might stir up things I've put to rest.
>
> T. And you're not sure you want to do that?
>
> Lynn: Yes, I don't know if it would be a good thing or not.

I acknowledged that therapy often arouses strong emotions, some of which will be distressing. However, I communicated my belief to Lynn that ultimately she would be better off by engaging in short-term therapy to understand her conflict with her supervisor in the context of her relationship with her mother. I also talked with Lynn about likely transference reactions in view of her personality structure. Given her history and defensively perfectionistic traits, Lynn was particularly sensitive to criticism, and I talked with her about how, if she felt criticized by me at any point, it would be important for her to talk about it with me, so that she didn't simply withdraw from therapy, acting out her feelings rather than talking about them. I also knew that Lynn was sensitive to anyone minimizing her problems, as her father had tended to do whenever she expressed concerns to him. This perception of her father was highlighted in the following dialogue:

> T. You've mentioned about your mother criticizing you when you brought up important concerns to her. How about your dad? How was it when you brought up concerns to him?
>
> Lynn: He's always been much more supportive of me.
>
> T. How so?
>
> Lynn: Well, he wouldn't criticize me–he would listen.
>
> T. And after he listened to your concerns?
>
> Lynn: Usually he would tell me that things would be okay.
>
> T. Okay?
>
> Lynn: Yes, he would say that things will always work out and that you really don't have to worry about anything.

I encouraged Lynn to let me know if at anytime she felt I was underestimating or not understanding what she was telling me about herself. In my work with students, I constantly strive to establish collaboration, emphasizing the dual nature of therapist-client responsibility in the therapeutic process. I felt this would be critically important in my work with Lynn, given her need to feel "in control" over her relationships with others.

In focusing on the conflict with the supervisor, Lynn was able to quickly see how there were parallels between this relationship and her conflicted relationship with her mother. She was able to express some of the underlying despair she had experienced in her early life because mother had been so emotionally unavailable to her. This also led to her talking about another side of her relationship to her mom, feeling that she must take care of mother's emotional needs. Lynn was relieved to sense that I understood that even though she had suffered much because of her mother's emotional unavailability, she still had positive and caring feelings about her. Given Lynn's ability to recognize the relationship between her presenting concerns and her early life experiences, we were quickly able then to talk about how she might deal most productively with her relationship with her supervisor. We role-played how Lynn might approach her supervisor in a direct, assertive, but non-hostile manner to talk about her concerns. We talked considerably about how feelings she experienced earlier in life toward her mother would be present when she talked with her supervisor, but how she could recognize them, manage them, and not simply "act out" on them. She was able to approach her supervisor with, and to her surprise, she was heard and validated for her directness and honesty. Thus, after the first two post-assessment therapy sessions, Lynn had made considerable progress in dealing with her presenting concerns.

Our remaining sessions focused much on Lynn's perfectionism, or "unrelenting standards" in schema-focused terminology. Interestingly, we discovered that Lynn was often her own worst critic (in the present) and was constantly striving to do everything perfectly. Lynn wanted to avoid criticism from her mother; thus, by doing everything "perfectly," she was unconsciously trying to avoid any possibility of being criticized. But another link to the past was even more helpful in Lynn's cognitive and emotional learning about her perfectionism. Even though in one way she felt her father had been the much more supportive of her parents, we discovered that Lynn had the belief that she could only receive approval from her father if she tried her absolute best and, if she tried her absolute best, then she should achieve success. As Lynn talked more about this dynamic in therapy, she was able to understand how her unrelenting standards and perfectionism were hurting her in many areas of her life. I asked her to list some of the ways she saw it as interfering with living life to the fullest. In our next session she related what she discovered:

T. We talked last week about your perfectionism and how that may be related in some ways to your parents. Did you get a chance to write down how some of these perfectionistic traits may actually work against you?

Lynn: I did. I was surprised by what I came up with.

T. Like what?

Lynn: There are so many ways that my being so hard on myself have hurt me. I think it's the major cause of why I have had migraine headaches for so many years. I psychotically take on the whole world, and think I have to be responsible for everything. It also has affected my relationships with friends, who don't like it that I don't have more time for them.

T. So in some ways you're your own worst critic?

Lynn: (becoming tearful) I think I've beat myself up mentally for making the smallest mistakes. And I hold others to these same standards, I expect them to be perfect, and when they are not, I feel overwhelmed and let down.

After this very emotional session, Lynn did not show for her next scheduled session. When I called her, she told me that she had forgot. We rescheduled, and when I saw her the next time, I asked if there might have been any factors involved in her forgetting her last appointment. At this point, Lynn acknowledged that breaking down and crying in our session had "scared" her, and when we explored this further, she said that she felt something bad was going to happen to her. One link we made was how her feelings after our last session were similar to those she had had when she talked with her father about deeper concerns. She had experienced him as uncomfortable when she was "weak," and thus felt rebuffed when she acknowledged distress. At the end of this session we talked about further sessions. We were able to talk about her continued ambivalence about coming in. She acknowledged feeling that she had been helped, but also said she felt scared about going any further. I suggested that we schedule one more session to either finalize our work together, or to contract for more sessions. Lynn agreed.

In our seventh and final session, Lynn said she wanted to discontinue therapy. In these instances, I am usually torn between my desire for the client to go even further and my desire to acknowledge client autonomy. I talked about my ambivalence with Lynn, but validated her decision to discontinue therapy. I also left the door open for her to call me in the future, either for further therapy, or for consultation. We reviewed our work together, and ended therapy in a positive manner.

DISCUSSION

Many aspects of my work with Lynn warrant further discussion. From a developmental perspective, Lynn's presenting problem, persistent and escalating anxiety related to conflict with her supervisor, can be viewed as an inevitable consequence of her entering adulthood. In spite of her best efforts to be as competent and "perfect" as possible, it was inevitable that, as she progressed in her training as an athletic trainer, she would come in contact with supervisors and other authority figures who would be critical of her, "fair" or not, so Lynn would be faced with emotional reactions which would cause her distress because she had not come to terms with how the critical style of her mother influenced her development. Our short-term therapy was effective in helping her gain perspective on why she was so severely troubled by her supervisor's negative comments. By gaining an understanding of her current conflict in relation to her unfinished business with mother, Lynn was eventually able to appropriately assert herself with her supervisor in a non-hostile and non-attacking manner, which allowed some resolution of their difficulties. In addition, therapy helped her begin to understand how her perfectionistic qualities were an unconscious attempt to please not only mother, but father as well. This awareness allowed her to begin to consider how her perfectionism was keeping her from developing more intimate relationships with others.

As I was writing up this case, I became more aware of how much I had hoped that Lynn would continue past our original contract of six sessions, a common occurrence for me in brief therapy with clients such as Lynn, since I saw her as capable of going even further in helping herself if she had continued for another six sessions. In retrospect, I think that our relationship, in which she had become vulnerable and shared some of her deepest concerns, touched off fears that, once again, trying to express her inner self would ultimately lead to disappointment. In retrospect, I would have made greater efforts to have placed this transference issue "on the table."

In reviewing my work with Lynn, I want to emphasize how important I believe a thorough assessment to be in doing short-term work with young adults. Interns whom I have trained often think that because short-term therapy places a premium on rapid intervention, they don't have the time to do a thorough assessment. I argue that good assessment is even more important for short-term therapy than long-term therapy. Assessment leads to a solid diagnostic formulation, which is the best method to determine the appropriateness of a client for brief therapy, as well as which problems should be the focus. To explain further, I have found that short-term therapy is most efficacious for individuals who: (1) present with fairly circumscribed concerns which can be related back to conflicts with key adult figures from childhood, most often the parents, (2) have moderate degrees of anxiety which are driving them into treatment, but do not have anxiety so severe that it interferes with rapidly establishing rapport and quickly intervening, and (3) do not have a debilitating Axis I disorder, such as major depression or bipolar disorder which would complicate an interpersonally-based approach. These areas can only be evaluated if one does good assessment up front. Personally, I find it difficult to do this kind of assessment in less than two sessions.

I also think it is important that the short-term therapist evaluate the severity of Axis II pathology in working with clients. I do believe that even fairly severe character pathology can be dealt with in a short-term model, but recognizing how severe the pathology is and what type it is has a huge impact on realistically setting goals. One of the most difficult tasks in doing short-term therapy is collaborating with the client in defining goals that are achievable. My tendency, having been trained in longer-term therapy methods, is to feel discouraged when clients do not make significant changes in dysfunctional characterological patterns. In the case of Lynn, the thorough evaluation helped me to focus on goals, such as understanding how the conflict with the supervisor could be addressed by helping her recognize the roots of the conflict in her relationship with her mother, which were achievable. Inevitably, if the client and I collaborate well in working on these goals, I find myself (and often the client) wanting to go further and deeper in dealing with dysfunctional interpersonal and emotional patterns. Since this is often not possible given the time-limited constraints in our center, I will do my best to talk with the client about options they have for continuing therapy in the future. I always want to keep in mind that my clients having a positive experience with me in brief therapy will be the most significant factor in their willingness to seek out therapy, whether short-term or long-term, in the future.

One final comment on my work with Lynn illustrates an important element in doing brief therapy with young adults. I have found it helpful to set an initial contract with clients for six sessions, rather than immediately setting a contract for 12 sessions. For young adults the prospect of it taking 12 sessions to get help often seems overwhelming. I like to set six sessions in the initial contract as it gives me time to do a thorough assessment, collaborate with the client in setting a treatment plan, and then working on two or three goals. Then, if the client and I agree, up to six more sessions can be contracted.

QUESTIONS

1. *Can you explain in more detail how your extensive assessment helped you determine the treatment plan?*

First, the assessment process helped me to understand that Lynn's presenting concerns were related to characterological issues. They were not primarily a product of an Axis I disorder, such as dysthymia or major depression. This assessment allowed me to focus immediately on how the conflicts with her supervisor related to issues with the parents ("copy processes" in Benjamin's terms). Also, the assessment helped me to recognize that Lynn's character defenses were generally quite stable. They had served her fairly well during much of her life, at least in terms of managing anxiety. I knew I could focus on her immediate concerns without major interference from transference issues (such as might be encountered with an unstable, highly variable defensive structure present in borderline character patterns).

2. *Do you believe that insight into your formulation that the client's perfectionism was an unconscious attempt to please her mother was an important element in the treatment?*

In retrospect, I believe that Lynn's insight into her perfectionism was largely intellectual. She was able to assent to this insight cognitively, but I don't believe it was really worked through at a core emotional level. In this sense, I don't believe this was a major factor in the treatment.

3. *The client seemed to play out her fear of intimate relationships by opting out of further counseling when she started to feel emotional and vulnerable. How did her feelings towards you, the therapist, affect the earlier part of therapy?*

Lynn approached counseling with a concern she might be criticized (as with her mother) and be "dismissed," or told everything would be okay as with her dad. I was aware of both these facets of her character structure, in part due to the thorough assessment. I tried to prepare her and myself for how they might influence the therapist-client relationship. I believe I did a good job of putting these issues on the table early in therapy. What I didn't fully appreciate was how likely it was that Lynn's character defenses would reestablish once her presenting concerns were addressed. I think what she found most difficult was that I was an adult who did not criticize her or dismiss her. This was perhaps more anxiety-provoking than anything else in the therapy relationship.

4. *How do you think this client would have responded to a lengthier, analytic approach with considerably more time spent on discussing her childhood relationship with her mother?*

I truly wonder whether a longer-term, analytically-oriented approach would have been possible with Lynn, at this time in her life. I think that the "success" she had in dealing with her presenting concern, conflict with her supervisor, led to diminished anxiety. This success led to an understandable, unconscious desire to return to "tried and true" ways of defending against childhood pain. My speculation is that Lynn might be more likely to engage in longer-term work when external stressors become even greater, which might happen when she encounters issues of vulnerability in a close relationship with a boyfriend or spouse.

REFERENCES

Bricker, D.C., & Young, J.E. (1993). *A client's guide to schema-focused therapy.* (Available from the Cognitive Therapy Center of New York, 120 East 56th Street, Suite 530, New York, NY 10022).

Lynns, B. (1996). *Interpersonal diagnosis and treatment of personality disorders* (2nd ed.). New York: Guilford Press.

Millon, T. (1994). *Millon Index of Personality Styles Manual.* San Antonio, TX: Psychological Corporation.

Millon, T. (1997). *Millon Clinical Multiaxial Inventory-III manual* (2nd ed.). Minneapolis, MN: National Computer Systems.

Millon, T., & Davis, R.D. (1996). *Disorders of personality* (2nd ed.). New York: Guilford.

Young, J.E. (1999). *Cognitive therapy for personality disorders: A schema-focused approach.* (3rd ed.). Sarasota, FL: Professional Resource Press.

Young, J.E., & Klosko, J.S. (1994). *Reinventing your life.* New York, NY: Plume.

Chapter 7:
Fostering Development:
A Case of Short Doses of Psychotherapy
Over the Course of a College Career

Philip W. Meilman

SUMMARY. This chapter reports a case of college student psychotherapy involving short "doses" of counseling over the course of a student's four-year college career. During treatment, the student addressed and increasingly came to terms with issues involving relationships with his family, friends, and love interests. By his own report, he gained considerably from this experience. *[Article copies available for a fee from The Haworth Document Delivery Service: 1-800-342-9678. E-mail address: <getinfo@haworthpressinc.com> Website: <http://www.HaworthPress.com> © 2001 by The Haworth Press, Inc. All rights reserved.]*

KEYWORDS. Psychotherapy, college students, counseling, developmental tasks, short-term psychotherapy

---

Address correspondence to: Philip W. Meilman, Counseling and Psychological Services, Cornell University, Gannett Health Center, Ho Plaza, Cornell University, Ithaca, NY 14853 (E-mail: pwm7@cornell.edu).

[Haworth co-indexing entry note]: "Chapter 7: Fostering Development: A Case of Short Doses of Psychotherapy Over the Course of a College Career." Meilman, Philip W. Co-published simultaneously in *Journal of College Student Psychotherapy* (The Haworth Press, Inc.) Vol. 16, No. 1/2, 2001, pp. 101-117; and: *Case Book of Brief Psychotherapy with College Students* (ed: Stewart E. Cooper, James Archer, Jr., and Leighton C. Whitaker) The Haworth Press, Inc., 2002, pp. 101-117. Single or multiple copies of this article are available for a fee from The Haworth Document Delivery Service [1-800-342-9678, 9:00 a.m. - 5:00 p.m. (EST). E-mail address: getinfo@haworthpressinc.com].

I work in the office of Counseling and Psychological Services (CAPS), a division of the health service at Cornell University. In this setting, we treat students at the University with a brief therapy model (12 sessions or fewer during an academic year). Our office is the sole mental health service for the campus. Departmentally, about two-thirds of our time is spent on typical counseling sessions, while about one-third of our efforts go toward managing crises and emergencies.

After 23 years of practice in the field of college mental health, my approach tends to be eclectic, drawing on a variety of approaches customized to fit the particular student and that student's problem. My approach can and does vary within the session, across sessions, and across clients. It can range from cognitive behavioral to short-term dynamic psychotherapy to Freudian dream analysis to practical problem solving to crisis intervention techniques and even to giving advice. Perhaps the unifying principle is the question of "what works most expeditiously for this client with that problem." I believe in achieving significant therapy gains in the briefest possible time.

My main practice areas include substance abuse, intervening in campus community crises, addressing campus climate issues, and working on situations involving both psychological and academic difficulties. College mental health largely pulls for us to be generalists, and over the years I have found facility in handling a variety of complaints involving anxiety and depression and life transition issues; notable exceptions to the list include at least eating disorders and borderline personality disorders.

CASE BACKGROUND

The following case is presented as an illustration of the use of therapy in short, distinct "doses" over the course of a client's college career. The client, Adam, came five distinct and separate times to consult over the course of his four years at school. He came 11 times during the spring of his freshman year, seven times during the spring of his sophomore year, twice during the spring of his junior year, once during the summer between his junior and senior years, and two more times the spring of his senior year. With each episode of counseling he made good headway, and succeeding "doses" of treatment necessitated fewer visits as they built on the work that had already transpired as well as the foundation of our working relationship.

Adam, age 18, a single white Jewish male from the Midwest, first consulted me early in the spring semester of his freshman year. His nuclear family was intact, both parents were professionals, and he had a brother two years his senior.

PRESENTING PROBLEM

On the initial intake form he wrote, "I broke up with my girlfriend, and I feel like I'm in the middle of a crisis. I can't do my work and I'm afraid about my future." On the same form, he circled items to indicate that he was "extremely concerned" about academic issues, anger/hostility, grief, loneliness, meeting people, and relationship issues. He circled that he was "quite a bit concerned" (the next highest category) with respect to anxiety/panic/worry, appearance/weight, depression, employment, grades, self-esteem, and stress.

During the initial visit, Adam made it clear that he was reeling from the breakup of a relationship with his high school girlfriend, Abby, who had chosen to attend college elsewhere. They had not been entirely compatible in high school, and he had expressed anger in the relationship in ways that did not enhance their relationship. In the latter months of high school and the beginning of college, she had pulled back from him, which only compounded his already-significant distress.

At the time of his initial visit, he was not sure he would survive academically. He had signed up for a larger-than-normal courseload, and so we discussed the options of dropping courses, muddling through, or taking a medical leave of absence for mental health reasons if necessary; at the same time I indicated that it was too early to make a decision on this. He was relieved to discover that he had some academic options.

Social/Cultural History/Environmental Context

Cornell has an intense and competitive academic environment. The mythology is that it is the easiest Ivy League college to gain admission to but the hardest from which to graduate. It is large, which can be an advantage in enabling students to find their own niche among a wide variety of options in lifestyle and interests, but can be a disadvantage in that students may sometimes feel anonymous and lost. Most students report that they "love Ithaca," a college town with two universities in it, "centrally isolated" in rural upstate New York.

The institutional culture is best described by the well-known Cornell phrase "freedom with responsibility." Although this concept is meant to speak to the very best in personal and academic freedoms and choices, in real life terms it has historically resulted in a hands-off policy on the part of the institution with respect to student life. In this respect it looks more like a state university or a large urban institution.

Adam entered Cornell as a freshman and completed his degree in four years. He came from a mid-sized city in the Midwest. His family was intact. To the limited extent that he talked about his family, he spoke mostly about his brother who he felt had been quite critical of him over the years. Adam indicated that his father had also adopted a critical attitude toward him at times, and the combination of negative feedback from the father-brother combination was painful to him. He only spoke rarely of his mother, though he indicated at one point that she had also criticized him. No truly distinct picture of the personalities in his family ever became apparent through the counseling. His focus for treatment was on presently experienced difficulties with the people with whom he interacted.

ASSESSMENT/DIAGNOSIS

In our setting, we generally do not use DSM-IV diagnoses unless one of our psychiatrists places a student on psychotropic medications. Our policy is based on a philosophical premise that diagnoses tend to pathologize what may be more appropriately considered as developmental tasks and transitions. Sometimes what would appear to be a long-term or entrenched problem in an older adult is easily addressed and resolved in a traditional college-aged student, which was the case here. Accordingly, in our setting we typically use descriptive labels, which simply describe the problem that the student presents. In the present case, the problem list initially included "depression" and "couples problems." Later on, the list was expanded to include "peer interpersonal problems."

COUNSELING GOALS

The goals of counseling changed over time. My initial task was to help Adam grieve the loss of his relationship with Abby and to help him consider some options with regard to academics. Further along during this first round of counseling, the goals included how to successfully manage relationships whether romantic or non-romantic, including learning to understand and manage his anger.

The second round of counseling, sophomore year, addressed issues of motivation and depression, and attempted to help Adam develop relationships with women. The third round of counseling, junior year, comprised merely two sessions and focused on allaying his fears about depression and his continuing overly cautious approach to women. The fourth round was a single session during the summer between junior and senior years when we again focused on his hesitant approach to women. The fifth and final round, senior year, was two visits again focused on trying to help him become more positive in pursuing relationships.

TREATMENT PLAN

The treatment throughout focused on the issues Adam presented, which were almost always immediate and pressing. Only occasionally did the counseling deal with past life history, and when it did, it was with an eye toward better understanding what was happening in the present and helping him navigate through the challenges and developmental transitions he was facing. The treatment approach was active, perspectives on his situation were offered, options were discussed, and suggestions for action were made where appropriate. We did not focus on transference or countertransference issues, although as a therapist I experienced myself offering a benign, supportive, safe space for him to explore his thinking and behavior in a way that his family had not. He appeared to find this overall approach helpful; had he not found it so, we would have altered it in some fashion to better meet his needs.

COUNSELING PROCESS

Round 1. During the first visit, there was little time for much more than obtaining a description of the then-current deterioration of his relationship with his high school girlfriend Abby, how she had pulled back from him, was superficial in the relationship, together with his resultant anger, his expression of anger toward her, and how her superficiality and his anger conspired to work against their relationship. Adam's affect during this session was noteworthy; he cried in a manner suggesting sheer desperation and, as he talked through his tears, his voice cracked and changed pitch frequently as the tears rolled down his cheeks. He presented himself as the very embodiment of a pained, tortured soul, with a dramatic quality as if it were a bit forced or overdone. Even so, there was no question that he was in significant pain.

Adam talked about his difficulties in performing academically due to his distress over the relationship, and he was genuinely concerned about his academic survival. As is often the case in college mental health when emotional issues adversely affect academic performance, we talked about a range of options including reducing his 20 credit hours to a more manageable load, or muddling through his courses, or even taking a medical leave of absence. Had it been later in the term, we might also have considered the option of extensions or incompletes, but this session occurred at the very beginning of the spring term. He showed no evidence of suicidality and no vegetative signs of depression. We agreed to meet weekly.

He came to the next session reporting he was doing better, though still grieving the loss of the relationship with Abby. He began to look at how he could have done things differently in that relationship and was feeling a good deal of guilt about what he perceived as mistakes on his part. He was especially irritated at himself when, in response to Abby's attempt to be kind to him, he told her off, and the next visit continued on that theme; he was beating up on himself for having sent her an unfortunate note that was angry in tone. I interjected some reality into the discussion by pointing out that the relationship had been in trouble long before he sent that recent note, and that the note did not in itself end the relationship, and that he might do well to stop beating himself over this one unfortunate move.

Adam came back much calmer the following week, having gained perspective. The discussion focused instead on his recognition that he had in the past needed to express and act on feelings whenever he had them, which unfortunately had gotten him into some trouble in relationships. This session was a respite from the pain he had previously expressed, but the very next session he came back experiencing grief in full force, once again beating up on himself for the demise of the relationship with Abby. He said that he wanted her back, but he would not want to ask her because "I know the answer." Since the issue was still unresolved by the end of the session, I gave assigned homework: to consider making a decision as to whether he should leave well enough alone or should re-approach Abby about renewing their relationship.

When he returned, the discussion focused specifically on how he had, in his typical style, beaten himself up, which we associated with criticism from his father, his brother, and to a lesser extent, his mother. We talked about how he had attempted to attach himself to Abby as a way to feel better about himself, and I reframed the breakup as an opportunity to look at how he really felt about himself. I asked him to reflect on the supportive stance that I (and others) had taken when he berated himself, and to consider our stance as an alternative model for how he could treat himself. I also interpreted to him that his anger was a red flag indicating that he needed to work on feeling better about himself.

He came to the next visit feeling much better, seeming to have accepted the idea that he did not have to beat himself up. We talked about how he could realistically work on his shortcomings, particularly anger management, and how he could look at difficult situations as learning opportunities rather than failures. We also discussed how to maintain a good relationship with a close college friend named Joe, even though they had disagreements. This topic continued through the next session when he reported an upsetting verbal argument with Joe. Adam had clearly personalized some frustrations Joe had expressed, reacted defensively, and gotten angry toward Joe in response. I pointed out that the issues at hand were Joe's and Joe's alone:

T: Did you do anything here to create the situation?

Adam: No, this was about something else.

T: Well, I want to emphasize what you just said, I didn't create the situation. So you don't need to personalize it–it's not about you, it's about him. Let me repeat that: It's *not about you, it's about him*. Let's put the issues back where they belong.

Adam: Yeah, it was really about him.

T (later on): You might want to remember the term 'lighten up' to give yourself some perspective and not to turn your interactions into such heavy, serious problems.

The idea behind this message was to give him a strategy to internally break the tension (for himself) in such a situation. Also in this session, he reported having had correspondence with Abby that had some finality. He wept a great deal about the ultimate demise of the relationship. I simply sat with him through his sadness.

He came to the next visit having done very well. He had gotten some positive feedback from an instructor and a female student in one of his classes. He was discovering, he said, that some people actually liked him and that this felt wonderful! He said he could never discover their liking as long as he was so focused on Abby. The remaining two sessions of this first round of treatment focused on friendships with two male students and how he might establish them on a more solid footing. Our discussion enabled him to look objectively at some of his friends' immaturity and possessiveness. I said to him, "I want to point out again that these things are not about you. It's about them. When you think about this, I suggest that you remind yourself, 'It's not about me.' " My remark seemed to have additional impact.

Round 2. Approximately one year later, Adam returned during the midpoint of his spring term complaining of decreasing motivation and depression. On his new intake form he gave as the reason for the visit: "Why I feel so depressed, unmotivated and afraid." He reported that his grades had suffered somewhat and he had had difficulty concentrating. Upon exploration, it turned out that his grandmother had died about a week earlier, which had a great deal to do with his distress. He said that he did not like Cornell's competitive atmosphere, probably because of his past history of rivalry with and criticism from his brother. During the next visit we talked about his lack of career and academic direction, and about how he and Cornell might be somewhat mismatched although he still liked being here. On the third visit he discussed a life-threatening illness of a close family friend and how it had thrown him into some emotional disarray. He worried also about how his mother and brother were doing and he questioned his choice of major, which I took as opportunity to discuss how to manage things when they get out of control. I also pointed out that issues can get very upsetting and he can then be so cerebral that sometimes it may useful to reestablish a balance with recreation. He acknowledged that running and weight lifting, which he had done in the past, might be helpful to him now as a way for him to regain that balance.

The next visit he dealt with two issues: whether he should take a leave of absence and whether he should share his feelings of attraction with Marie, a young woman in his classes. He decided to defer on the latter, but wanted to talk with his parents regarding the former. The visit after that, he was again in distress about making a decision to take time off. We reviewed pros and cons, and I pointed out that there were no apparent dire consequences to either choice. I reminded him that there was no pressing need to decide right then; he could even make the decision in the summer, after the term was over. He also indicated that what he thought at the time was a lack of worry about academics the previous fall might actually have been something more akin to saying "screw it" to being in school at that time.

The remaining two visits of Round 2 were less intense. He was excited and nervous about a summer job at Cornell in a high tech project. We addressed some logistics for the summer, he talked about his hesitancy to approach Marie for fear of being rejected, and he indicated that his family friend's health status had improved. He seemed grateful for the opportunity to have counseling again.

Round 3. A year later (his junior year), Adam came in yet again, complaining that he felt no pleasure, had been irritable, wasn't sleeping consistently well, and thought he was depressed. He wrote on his intake form: "I believe that I am depressed; I feel no pleasure and feel very listless and tired." He garnered the label depression from his mother and his friend Bob. Then he panicked about having depression and feared he would never come out from under it and would never feel pleasure again; that led to suicidal thoughts, with his thinking that, if he were this way another year, he would kill himself, perhaps with a gun or pills, but he had no current intent or plan to kill himself and he contracted for safety.

When we analyzed it, the issue was that he panicked that something might be wrong with him. He also panicked because when Bob said that Bob's girlfriend and Adam were what Bob lived for, Adam did not have the dramatic reaction internally that he thought he should have toward someone making such a profound statement. I speculated that there might be any number of reasons for this, including his past history with male figures (father and brother), fears of intimacy, and realistic concerns about Bob's statement being "too much." I suggested that we needed to look into this further. I also interpreted that he was panicked about the label depression and the implication of some sort of abnormality. I suggested he simply look at what he was experiencing without attaching a value judgment. I discussed with him the fact that life was not problem-free and that the expectation of it being that way was unrealistic. I might have added that his symptoms had followed his self-labeling of panic disorder and depression. I did convey that based on the relatively recent onset of his malaise the past three months and his history of positive psychotherapeutic experiences, I felt confident that he could successfully address the present concerns.

He breathed a huge sigh of relief at the end of the session. Though he had self-medicated with St. John's Wort in the previous two weeks, he told me he hadn't taken it in the last two days and now did not even feel a need for it. I told him that since I was not a psychiatrist, I was unable to provide comment or useful advice about St. John's Wort, but that I was glad that he was feeling better.

By the next visit he was much better, so much so that he did not feel the need for an additional visit. We focused on the reasonableness of his reactions to Bob's comments; he reported that his mother said that comments like Bob's are usually reserved for family or one's future spouse and asked if Adam really wanted that kind of relationship with Bob, which of course Adam did not. We went on to talk about Adam's interest in Marie, and we discussed the idea of taking risks to see if the chemistry between them would work. He was afraid he would be unacceptable to her. I took the opportunity to point out that he is a composite of many characteristics and that relationships between two people were based on how the "total package" was perceived. He felt very good at this session, so good that he decided that he did not need further treatment.

Round 4. Adam returned for a single visit during August between his junior and senior years. At this point he listed the following reason for his visit on the intake form: "I'm attracted to a friend I can't date. Looking for perspective and someone to listen to my thoughts and get feedback." He wanted to talk about how he had not pursued Marie even when she was available, and how he now needs to grieve the fact that she is in a relationship with another man. This led to a productive discussion of how he undermines his self-confidence by comparing himself with others and finding himself lacking. We returned to the idea that he is a mosaic of attributes and how it is possible to find oneself lacking on a particular dimension, but that it is the whole persona and the way all the components come together that makes him unique and special:

> T: If you want to find someone who is better looking than you, you can find that. If you want to find someone who is smarter than you, there are plenty of people at Cornell to go around. If you want to find someone who is more creative, or more dynamic, or funnier, you can find that too. But that's not the point. The point is that only you can put the characteristics together in a way that is uniquely yours. When someone is in a relationship with you, it is the total package that they look at. And there is no other total package just like you.
>
> Adam: I hadn't thought of it that way.

T: Along these lines, I want to caution you not to assume that what you think is attractive to women is actually what they find attractive. It might surprise you but it is very possible that they are looking for something in a partner that you haven't even thought of!

Adam (surprised): Hmmmm . . .

In short, I wanted him to question his own assumption that he was not attractive as a person and thereby undermine himself. I said, "If you do this, you will create a self-fulfilling prophecy where you believe yourself to be unattractive, then you'll act sheepishly or become fearful of approaching women, and then they will not engage with you." This seemed to offer him some perspective.

OUTCOME/TERMINATION OF COUNSELING

Round 5. During the spring of his senior year, Adam came for two more visits. This time, his intake form read as follows: "I am hoping to discuss and receive feedback on my behavior towards a friend and hopefully clarify my feelings. I also want to discuss some unusual mood swings that I've had." During the first visit, he reported some self-destructive daydreams and that he had also dripped candle wax on himself. This occurred in relation to his reactions to Marie, who rejected him in favor of another man. He said he nevertheless felt the need to spend some time around her but did not want to, and then felt guilty because he had not done so. We discussed the fact that he was under no obligation to spend time around her when in fact she was seeing another man. He also reported some images of being on fire and of "a rusty nail up my pisshole." We discussed how the first image might be related to anger (I referenced the concept of "burning with anger") and how the second image might be related to the way in which he felt hurt, rejected, and "stabbed" with respect to his sexual and romantic interests in Marie. These interpretations enabled him to put things in perspective and they helped de-mystify and de-pathologize his daydreams. He seemed greatly relieved.

In our final session, he discussed how angry he was at himself as well as with Marie for not taking risks and for being rejected, and he connected this with the imagery from the previous session. He discussed how he has stayed in a "safe zone" (his term) in terms of relationships:

T: When you use that term it sounds like you're waiting for rigor mortis to set in.

Adam (shocked and surprised): What do you mean?

T: Well, that's what it sounds like. You want things to be perfectly safe and you don't want to be rejected, so you don't make any moves at all. If you continue along this path, you'll die before anything will happen. As I say, it sounds like you're just waiting for rigor mortis to set in.

There was a moment of silence after which he seemed to get in touch with a need to adopt a new strategy. All of a sudden, he appeared to access an internal sense of determination and power; his energy level grew palpably during the session. He left feeling a distinct sense of increased personal power and a willingness to take more risks in relationships.

Given that I had worked with Adam over the course of four years, at the end of the term I sent him a note congratulating him on his graduation and inviting him to stop by to let me know his plans. He did in fact stop in the day after commencement. He had no immediate plans for work and was going to take some time off to sort out his next steps. We reflected on how far he had come, the confidence he had developed over his four years in college, and we wondered aloud how things might look like for him years from now. He departed, expressing considerable appreciation for the work we had done since his freshman year.

DISCUSSION

It is important to consider some of the developmental aspects of this case. For background on developmental issues in the college counseling arena, Grayson (1989) and Margolis (1989) present excellent discussions, and the reader is also referred to Eugenia Hanfmann's (1978) seminal work on college mental health. The developmental aspects of college counseling have been noted almost from the beginnings of the work in our field, as evidenced by Fry's (1942) description of patients at Yale.

In the case at hand, it was clear that the relationship between Adam and the rest of his nuclear family was strained by the history of parental criticism and sibling rivalry. Perhaps because he was gentle in nature and the youngest in the family, Adam had felt hurt by these criticisms and did not directly look to his family for the kind of guidance he really needed, specifically with regard to relationships. Instead he was left with the idea that his reactions were somehow idiosyncratic and defective, and that he did not have much worth or value. It took someone from outside of the family, in the form of a therapist, to provide the supportive, benign adult guidance that was needed to help him find his way. Perhaps this could be considered a kind of re-parenting or mentoring. Though it might have been tempting to read various (and probably unrealistic) meanings into some of the material he discussed, it was especially important to avoid doing so and to present him with commonsense interpretations of the realities of relationships and feelings, not dissimilar to those presented in Grayson and Meilman's (1999) book. That is what Adam seemed to need and what seemed to help him grow. To do other than this would have injured him and done him a disservice.

The quotations in the section marked "Counseling process" were chosen to illustrate three critical points in Adam's therapy. The first, "It's not about you, it's about him," had a significant impact. This message was repeated several times during the course of his treatment. Adam indicated that the resulting perspective helped him regain his footing in dealing with a particular friend and he understood that it applied more generally to other relationships. It helped prepare him for taking his place in the world of relationships, owning what was his and letting others own what was theirs. The second quotation, about "the total package" and regarding what women "were looking for," was designed to challenge Adam's view of himself and his assumptions about what people value. If what he believed were true, then his notion that he was a lost cause would have some validity. But I did not and do not believe it was true, and I feel confident that as he grows older this will become increasingly apparent to him. So I was intentionally establishing a platform for future growth. The third quotation, about "rigor mortis setting in" was chosen for its dramatic effect. Adam had been dancing around taking a risk with Marie for a good 18 months but could never seem to act on it. I intentionally made the point that his life was passing by and, that at the rate he was going, he would die (hence the reference to rigor mortis) before asking her out, if he continued on this path. The bottom line: "Adam, you need to get off your duff!"

With respect to brief treatment, it should be noted that my first impression was that Adam would not be a short-term case; he was so distressed that at the initial visit I would have predicted we would need well over a year just to get through the first round of therapy, so I was surprised that it moved along so quickly. I believe that the common-sense approach, the de-pathologizing nature of interpretations and sug-gestions, the guidance and mentoring function of the therapy, and the help with perspective and relationships enabled his counseling to move along quickly. We did not focus on transference or countertransference interpretations. To do so would have prolonged the treatment without necessarily producing any better result. Once the first course of therapy was completed, the shared knowledge base and ongoing working rela-tionship shortened the next four rounds of therapy; this was most dra-matically demonstrated in Round 3, when he came in fearing that he had major problems and even had some suicidal ideation, yet felt an enor-mous amount of relief in the first visit and completed this round of ther-apy in the second visit. Rounds 3, 4, and 5 could be characterized as "booster shots," not in the traditional sense but in the sense that a good foundation had already been laid and could readily be built upon to help Adam grow.

Adam's Comments

In response to this narrative, Adam wrote the following response for inclusion: "10/8/00 My experiences with Dr. Meilman have been ex-tremely helpful. The first time I met with him I was looking for some-one objective, someone whom I did not feel would be overly critical or judgmental of me, someone off of whom I could bounce my ideas and thoughts. This "safe space" to which he refers was exactly that.

However, in a way my therapy sessions became much more than just a safe space in which to be and to talk. Something that I feel is true about myself is that I think about my problems, issues, and dilemmas enough, but too often I become afraid and timid of making decisions. I lay out my assessment of my problems but instead of forming a plan of action I tend to obsess over and worry about them. Sometimes this takes the form of over-analyzing. It is partly here where my work with Dr. Meilman became much more than just a "safe space" to be in. Rather than wading through a giant marsh of ambivalent feelings, he encour-aged, in a way challenged, me to take the plunge in personal affairs. Witness my homework assignment about calling Abby. I could have prolonged the grief endlessly with the vacant hope of getting back to-gether with her. Instead he seemed to suggest that either I try to recon-nect with her or that I work on accepting that the relationship was over and on how to come to terms with that fact, in order to begin moving on.

More recently, though, his suggestion that I was "waiting for rigor mortis to set in" was a strong wake up call to me that the safe zone, for which I look in relationships with women is not especially productive. It has since served as a personal reminder that we only live once and ought to take the risks that are well worth taking. From my perspective, my work with Dr. Meilman has enormously improved my sense of courage and confidence in confronting and making difficult choices and life decisions.

Finally the opportunity to read my own case history in such magnificent detail has been a wonderful gift. Reading my own words from the intake forms rushes me back to each point in time that we met. And the case study itself feels like a log or journal of my own personal growth; it is something whose value to me will only grow richer and deeper as I look back on it throughout the years. Thank you so much Phil!"

Sincerely,
Adam

QUESTIONS

1. *You referred to Adam's family, particularly the critical father and brother several times. Was that discussed at any length with Adam? Did he use the understanding (insight) into this dynamic as it played out in his current situations?*

Yes, in our discussions we drew a clear correlation between the criticism Adam had experienced in relation to his father and brother and his anxiety in his present relationships. That is why the suggestion, "It's not about you, it's about them," was so important. It spoke directly to the negative assumptions about himself that he had begun to project generally onto other people in his environment, in this case his friends. When he was able to separate himself out from the issues of others, he improved considerably.

2. *Adam's problems seemed to revolve around relationship difficulties. Did you consider recommending group therapy? Do you believe that this would have been appropriate or helpful in this situation?*

In retrospect, yes, perhaps Adam could have benefited from group therapy. However, there were several reasons we did not go that route.

First, Adam's initial presentation was fairly intense and he looked as though he needed some individual work with respect to adjustment issues and grief work with respect to the situation with his ex-girlfriend. Only after a while did it become apparent that his problems were connected with relationships more generally. By that time it was late in the semester, too late to join a group. A similar scenario occurred in Round 2. The remaining courses of therapy were very brief and seemed to be all that he needed, so group therapy was not considered at that point.

3. *Adam seemed to have problems being assertive in relationships. Did you consider any behavioral approaches such as assertiveness training? Why or why not?*

Although it is not otherwise reflected in the write up, we would occasionally talk over some specific language that he might use in talking with Abby and his male friends. On occasion we would role-play those conversations. These role-plays were important because assertive ways of approaching people represented new territory for Adam and he had a relative deficit of skills in this area. The role-playing very specifically and intentionally was introduced as a skill-building exercise.

4. *Can you discuss a bit how you set the stage for the intermittent nature of counseling with Adam? Do you typically give clients this option?*

I wish I could take full credit for the brief, intermittent approach. It seems consistent with contemporary approaches to psychotherapy. However, this was largely Adam's doing. He determined the starting and stopping points. If I set the stage at all, it was by adopting a direct problem-solving approach with respect to the presenting complaints rather than adopting an approach involving transference or so-called "depth" interpretations. My approach tended to be commonsense and practical, and I believe this shortened the course of treatment relative to the time frame that would have been needed for these other types of approaches.

Do I typically give clients this option? No, the approach I take depends more on what "feels right" for a particular client with whatever particular concerns they bring to the counseling setting.

5. *The quotations that you provide include some rather direct advice and interpretation. Do you see this as an important element in a "brief approach" to counseling?*

I could not say that direct advice and interpretation are essential elements in a brief approach to counseling. However, they can help. They were used here because the issues were so very clear. They made good sense given the circumstances and situation that Adam was presenting. Also, it is consistent with my style to "cut to the chase" when the issues are straightforward. The straightforward approach also provided a counterpoint to Adam's tendency at times to get overly cerebral and lose sight of what he actually needed to do.

REFERENCES

Fry, C.C. (1942). *Mental health in college.* New York: The Commonwealth Fund.

Grayson, P.A. (1989). The college psychotherapy client: An overview. In P.A. Grayson and K. Cauley (Eds.), *College psychotherapy.* New York: Guilford Press, 1989, pp. 8-28.

Grayson, P.A., & Meilman, P.W. (1999). *Beating the college blues.* (2nd ed.). New York: Facts on File, Inc.

Hanfmann, E. (1978). *Effective therapy for college students.* San Francisco: Jossey-Bass.

Margolis, G. (1989). Developmental opportunities. In P.A. Grayson and K. Cauley (Eds.), *College psychotherapy.* New York: Guilford Press, 1989, pp. 71-91.

Chapter 8:
Saying Goodbye Ten Years Later:
Resolving Delayed Bereavement

Jeff E. Brooks-Harris

SUMMARY. A male graduate student attended seven sessions of integrative counseling to resolve problematic emotions associated with delayed bereavement ten years after the suicide of a childhood friend. First, a cognitive approach tested and modified beliefs about healing. Second, the client experientially explored and resolved unexpressed emotions. Third, a narrative approach reconstructed new meaning about the death of the client's friend. *[Article copies available for a fee from The Haworth Document Delivery Service: 1-800-342-9678. E-mail address: <getinfo@ haworthpressinc.com> Website: <http://www.HaworthPress.com> © 2001 by The Haworth Press, Inc. All rights reserved.]*

KEYWORDS. Delayed bereavement, integration, experiential

In the ten years since I graduated with my PhD in Counseling Psychology, I have worked full-time as a psychologist at two different university counseling centers. I consider university students my specialty

---

Address correspondence to: Jeff E. Brooks-Harris, Counseling and Student Development Center, University of Hawaii at Manoa, 2600 Campus Road, SSC 312, Honolulu, HI 96822-2205.

[Haworth co-indexing entry note]: "Chapter 8: Saying Goodbye Ten Years Later: Resolving Delayed Bereavement." Brooks-Harris, Jeff E. Co-published simultaneously in *Journal of College Student Psychotherapy* (The Haworth Press, Inc.) Vol. 16, No. 1/2, 2001, pp. 119-134; and: *Case Book of Brief Psychotherapy with College Students* (ed: Stewart E. Cooper, James Archer, Jr., and Leighton C. Whitaker) The Haworth Press, Inc., 2002, pp. 119-134. Single or multiple copies of this article are available for a fee from The Haworth Document Delivery Service [1-800-342-9678, 9:00 a.m. - 5:00 p.m. (EST). E-mail address: getinfo@haworthpressinc.com].

and I enjoy working with the wide variety of concerns that young adults face. In addition to the normal range of depression and anxiety, I am attuned to the developmental challenges that accompany the transition from adolescence to adulthood. I watch for ways that my clients express their desire for separation and individuation and their search for personal identity. I have been particularly interested in gender and sexual orientation issues and have led counseling groups for men and for gay, lesbian, and bisexual students at both of the counseling centers where I have worked.

When providing counseling to students, I use an integrated approach drawing upon skills from diverse orientations including cognitive, behavioral, humanistic, psychodynamic, and multicultural psychotherapy. In my ongoing development as a psychologist, I have tried to acquire training from diverse sources in order to build a repertoire of adaptable skills. As an integrationist, I try to identify clinical markers that suggest that a particular approach or set of skills will be most helpful. I also engage in collaborative dialogue with clients describing the different ways we can view and approach their concerns and then make such decisions together. I find that I work particularly well with the interaction between thoughts and feelings, using cognitive understanding and emotional expression to encourage behavior change. My interest in experiential and cognitive integration has been augmented by recent continuing education experiences in Gestalt therapy and cognitive-behavior therapy.

Personally, I am a Euro-American, Protestant male in my late thirties. I am married with a young daughter. I know that most of my cultural demographics result in privilege rather than oppression. As a psychologist who works on a campus where Euro-Americans are a distinct minority, I try to remain aware of how cultural differences impact my ability to work with different students. I discuss these power dynamics with my clients in an attempt to "put my cards on the table" and to try to create a warm, open relationship. I base part of my therapeutic alliance on an informal interpersonal style that allows for self-disclosure and the use of humor. I enjoy my work a great deal and feel privileged that my clients trust me enough to reveal the most intimate and painful parts of their lives. As a psychologist, I hope I can help these students find more effective ways to think, feel, and act.

DESCRIPTION OF CLIENT

Mark was a single, heterosexual Euro-American male in his mid-twenties. He was a graduate student in the social sciences and had grown up in the Midwest. I had met Mark a few years earlier when he obtained three sessions of individual counseling before attending a men's group that I facilitated. He had participated in the group for about a year exploring issues related to emotional awareness, developing friendships with men, and romantic relationships with women. He had terminated from the group about a year before this course of individual counseling. Because of our successful work together in the past, Mark and I already had a warm and secure therapeutic alliance. Mark commented on his feelings of trust during our first session together.

PRESENTING PROBLEM

Mark entered counseling because of unresolved feelings of grief that had recently resurfaced. He was experiencing sadness, guilt, and fear about the death of his closest childhood friend ten years earlier when they were both teenagers. A few months before coming to counseling, on the tenth anniversary of William's suicide, Mark had heard a song that they both had liked and listened to together. Since then, Mark had been preoccupied with thoughts and feelings about Will's death. Two of his concerns were that he might have been able to prevent Will's death and that Will's parents might have blamed him for the suicide.

Mark was distracted from his schoolwork and other important activities. His sleep was disturbed by his preoccupation with fearful and guilty feelings. He had recently tried to reestablish contact with Will's father via e-mail. Specifically, Mark thought that the only way he could resolve his uncomfortable emotions was to spend concentrated time talking to Will's parents about the suicide to ensure that they did not blame him. Unfortunately, Will's father wrote to Mark that he didn't want to discuss Will's death but preferred to remember the happy times when Will and Mark were children together.

SOCIAL/CULTURAL HISTORY/ENVIRONMENTAL CONTEXT

Mark grew up in a rural area near a big city in the Midwestern region of the United States. His upbringing was Euro-American and culturally homogeneous. As a child and teenager, he participated in activities that reinforced values of doing the right thing and developing personal discipline. For example, he participated in Boy Scouts and attained the rank of Eagle. Despite the cultural homogeneity of his background,

Mark became interested in other cultural practices and became a black belt in Karate. He began studying Asian religions and embraced Buddhism. Additionally, he had traveled overseas and was pursuing international research. Mark was doing well in graduate school and had developed positive relationships with his professors. He presented himself as sincere, eager, hard-working, and earnest.

Assessment/Diagnosis (DSM-IV)

Axis I	V62.82	Bereavement
Axis II	V71.09	No diagnosis
Axis III	None	
Axis IV	None	
Axis V	GAF = 75	(current)

Most of the relevant variables in Mark's situation do not fit into a DSM-IV diagnosis. My assessment of important psychological variables like inaccurate thoughts and unexpressed emotions are included in the next section.

COUNSELING GOALS/TREATMENT PLAN

The counseling goals and treatment plan are organized around three emphases that also will be used to describe phases of the counseling process. First, Mark and I agreed to explore his thoughts about how to heal and whether he needed to talk to Will's parents in order to do so. From a cognitive perspective, his belief that he could heal only with the help of Will's parents was an inaccurate belief. We talked about ways that his thoughts could be identified, evaluated, and modified (Beck, 1995). Second, we agreed to create a safe place for Mark to revisit painful memories about Will's death and to express unresolved feelings. From an experiential perspective, I hypothesized that Mark's feelings of guilt and fear were reactive secondary emotions that might be interfering with more primary adaptive emotions like sadness and grief (Greenberg & Paivio, 1997). I talked to Mark about exploring his feelings in order to find more adaptive ways of emotionally reacting to his loss. Third, Mark and I agreed to try to understand the meaning of Will's life and death. From a narrative perspective, I hoped that Mark might learn to tell his story in a different way in order to a construct a new meaning about this pivotal event in his life (White & Epston, 1990). Together, these three counseling goals provided a helpful blueprint for our work together.

Mark entered counseling shortly before graduating with his master's degree. He was to leave the country on an international trip after graduation. We agreed to meet eight times before Mark left. I was not sure whether we would be able to reach a point of clear resolution, but I thought we could make considerable progress based on Mark's high motivation and readiness to work hard in counseling. Our need for efficiency was also aided by our previous work together that had resulted in trust and mutual rapport.

COUNSELING PROCESS

My counseling work with Mark also can be organized conceptually into three overlapping phases. First, I used a cognitive approach to help Mark recognize, test, and revise some of his inaccurate thoughts about how he could heal and resolve his grief. Second, I used an experiential approach to encourage Mark to become aware of, explore, and express his feelings about Will's life and death. Third, I used a narrative approach to help Mark tell his story in a new way and understand the meaning of these events in his life. I will use these three conceptualized phases of counseling to describe our work together in more detail.

Phase One: Cognitive

When Mark entered counseling, he was discouraged and felt unable to make progress on his own. Since the tenth anniversary of Will's death, a few months earlier, Mark had concluded that the best way to process and resolve his feelings would be to spend time with Will's parents sharing intense emotions about their common loss. When Will's father declined Mark's invitation to visit and explore this grief, Mark felt stuck. He did not know how to heal on his own without the aid of other people who loved Will and had felt the same bitter loss he had experienced a decade earlier. Mark's belief that he could heal only with the help of Will's parents was hindering him from finding another path.

At the end of the first session, I began to explore Mark's thoughts about his inability to heal without the help of Will's parents. In order to flesh out Mark's disappointment, I asked him to write an "unsent letter"

to Will's father to clarify his own thoughts and feelings without impos-
ing them on someone who might not respond in a helpful way. When we
reviewed this letter during our second session, it revealed an assumption that Will's parents would benefit from revisiting their painful loss
as much as Mark would. Mark viewed their preference not to discuss
Will's suicide as unhealthy avoidance. Using a cognitive approach, I
helped Mark identify specific thoughts (Beck, 1995), and make a distinction between personal thoughts like, "I would benefit from talking
about Will's death" from thoughts about others like, "Will's parents
would benefit from talking about their loss." When we tested these
thoughts for accuracy, Mark reported greater confidence in the accuracy of his thoughts about himself compared to his thoughts about others. The process of identifying and testing Mark's specific thoughts led
to an emotional shift. Instead of feeling angry with Will's father, Mark
began to feel disappointed. He was sad that he could not reconnect with
Will's parents and had to face his loss alone. Mark expressed that he
was afraid he would not be able to resolve his grief by himself. We concluded the second session by discussing the need for Mark to find a different way to resolve his feelings. I invited Mark to consider using our
time together as an alternative way to foster healing.

> T: As I listened to you read your letter to Will's Dad, I noticed
> something interesting. Three or four different times you wrote that
> you and Will's Dad could help each other.
>
> Mark: Yes. I think we really could.
>
> T: I'd like to take a look at your thoughts about this in a slightly
> different way. I'd like to try and test the accuracy of your thoughts.
> Is that something you'd be willing to look at?
>
> Mark: Sure.
>
> T: But, I'd like to modify your thoughts in one way if this fits for
> you. What if we separated your conclusions about yourself from
> those about Will's Dad?
>
> Mark: What do you mean?
>
> T: Well, what is your conclusion about how helpful it would be for
> you to talk to Will's Dad about the suicide?

Mark: I think it would be very, very helpful for me to talk to him.

T: And how sure are you that it would be helpful for you?

Mark: Absolutely sure. 100%!

T: Okay. How about for Will's Dad? What's your conclusion about the impact that talking about Will's death with you would have on him?

Mark: Well, I assume it would be helpful for him as well.

T: And, for that conclusion, how confident are you?

Mark: I don't know. I guess that's a trickier question. I guess I'm not as sure that he would benefit as much as I would.

T: So, you're 100% sure that you'd benefit from talking; but you're less than 100% sure that Will's Dad would benefit. Can you think of any reasons why it might not be as beneficial for Will's Dad as for you?

Mark: Well, I don't know. Maybe this just isn't the right time. Maybe he's already gotten over all of this and getting into it right now might not feel right.

T: I noticed a shift in your facial expression just then. What was that?

Mark: I guess I felt a little sad.

T: Sad?

Mark: Yeah. I feel disappointed that Will's Dad won't talk to me right now.

T: But in the letter you sounded pretty angry.

Mark: Yeah. I think I'm feeling less angry than when I wrote the letter.

T: Less anger but more sadness and disappointment?

Mark: Yes. Disappointment.

T: I think that's an important shift.

Phase Two: Experiential

The second phase of our work focused on the experiential process of helping Mark explore and express feelings he had been unable to reveal and resolve in the past. Although Mark openly wept during our first session, his tears were not directly associated with sadness or loss. His strongest emotions were fear that Will's parents might blame him for the suicide and guilt that he may have failed to prevent his friend's death. I hypothesized that guilt and fear might be blocking his grief and sadness. Primary adaptive emotions (like Mark's sadness and grief) are sometimes buried beneath secondary reactive emotions (like Mark's fear and guilt) (Greenberg & Paivio, 1997). My hope was that, by exploring his fears, we could clear a space for Mark's long-interrupted grief to emerge in a way that might lead to resolution.

During our third session, I asked Mark to tell me the story of growing up with his childhood friend. By starting with early, positive memories and moving slowly through the narrative, we allowed long-forgotten emotions to emerge. This session is an example of "systematic evocative unfolding" through which a client moves through an experience in slow motion with keen attention paid to emerging emotions (Greenberg, Rice, & Elliot, 1993). This exploration climaxed when Mark re-experienced strong feelings of fear and helplessness when he recalled the night Will first told him about his suicidal thoughts and gestures. Mark vividly recalled the conflict between wanting to keep Will's secret in order to preserve their friendship and the desire to tell someone about his concerns for Will's well-being. Months later, when Will did take his own life, Mark's deepest fear was realized and his guilt was sealed. Now as an adult, Mark could see the terrible double bind that he did not understand as a teenager. By carefully revisiting this painful and confusing event in Mark's life, he felt relief from expressing unresolved feelings and insight about why he had kept Will's awful secret.

The double-bind was revealed at a point when I was encouraging Mark to speak directly to Will as if he were in the room, telling him the things that he wished he could have told him before he died. In Gestalt therapy, this is called empty chair work because an empty chair is sometimes used to symbolize the absent person. Empty chair work is used to address "unfinished business" that interferes with an individual's ability to respond adaptively to current situations (Perls, Hefferline, & Goodman, 1951; Greenberg, Rice, & Elliot, 1993).

T: Are you scared that you betrayed Will?

Mark: I'm scared that I'd lose him. [Shifting to second person] Will, I'm afraid that if I tell someone else, you're not going to want to have a thing to do with me ever again. To betray a best friend, to tell someone else their deepest, darkest secrets, is something that best friends aren't supposed to do.

T: But I'm afraid that if I don't tell anyone . . .

Mark: I'm afraid if I don't tell anyone, you're actually going to do it and you're going to die and I'm going to lose you.

T: Say both parts again.

Mark: Will, I'm afraid that if I tell someone, I'm going to betray our friendship. I'm afraid that if I don't tell someone that I'm going to lose you; that you will die.

T: So, it's really a double bind.

Mark: I'm stuck.

T: If I tell someone, I'll lose you. If I don't tell anyone, I'll lose you.

Mark: Either way, I lose you Will!

T: What an awful choice to have to make.

Mark: I was stuck. [tears] I was stuck.

T: You didn't know what to do.

Mark: I didn't know what to do . . . [Sobbing][Pause] I'm alone.

T: You had this terrible secret; this terrible choice that you had to make; that you had to make alone and you don't know what to do and you can't tell anyone about it.

During our fifth session, Mark reviewed his memories of the weekend he spent with Will right before his suicide. This process of exploration resulted in Mark discovering feelings of anger at Will for leaving him and ending their friendship. Upon careful review, Mark also discovered subtle ways in which Will may have been trying to say good-bye and to affirm their friendship so that Mark would not blame himself after his suicide. The dynamic exploration of emotion and meaning helped Mark discover new aspects of the story that had been hidden all these years. During our sixth session, I helped Mark by conducting an empty-chair experiment (Perls, Hefferline, & Goodman, 1951; Greenberg, Rice, & Elliot, 1993) in which Mark reconstructed the conversation that he wished he could have had with Will before his death. Initially, he ventured to conclude his dialogue with Will by saying, "Take care." I encouraged him to take one step further and to say "Good-bye."

> Mark: I never would have thought that I would move through the rest of my life without you Will. [Pause] And even though I don't want you to die, your friendship will always be with me. But, I will move on. I've got my life to live and I will live it well, I guarantee you. And, I will have other friends. Not necessarily to replace you. You are Will. You will always be Will to me. But I will take your memory and move on and I will be fine. And, someday, when I'm very, very old and I die because of natural causes, or whatever, I'll be going to heaven and I'll look forward to seeing you there. But until that time, take care.

> T: Why don't you say good-bye?

> Mark: Say good-bye? Why didn't I say good-bye?

> T: No, I want you to try it. "Take care" is a little ambiguous. I want you to say it with a little more finality. "I don't want to see you go . . ."

> Mark: Will, I don't want to see you go but I've got to let you go. You've meant a lot to me. You always will. But now it's time for me to go. [Pause] Good-bye my most honored friend.

> T: Take a deep breath. [Pause] How are you doing?

Mark: It was hard to say good-bye.

T: So, it was easier to say, 'this is what you meant, this is why you're important,' but saying good-bye was harder.

Mark: Yeah. Just to say that to Will. "Good-bye." That was even Will's last word to me.

T: So, you're remembering him saying it in a more . . .

Mark: "Good-bye."

T: Which, at the time you may have wondered, 'Huh? That was a little dramatic.'

Mark: Yeah.

T: What was it like having the conversation that you all couldn't have had ten years ago?

Mark: Although our friendship was at that very, very deep level, we had never been able to articulate it. We even had difficulty showing it. It's one thing to tell other people, "Yes, he was my best friend." But, it's another thing to hear me say it to Will, how much he meant to me, and to hear him to say how much I meant to him.

At the conclusion of this session, I asked Mark to write an unsent letter to Will that would honor his dear friend. When Mark read this letter to me during our seventh and final session, it provided a summary of his feelings of sadness, anger, and fear. But, it also affirmed a friendship that had positively shaped Mark's life. By exploring and expressing all these tangled feelings, Mark was able to say good-bye and begin to let go.

Phase Three: Narrative

The third and final phase in Mark's work with me was learning to tell his story in a different way. Narrative therapy emphasizes the power of strengthening adaptive themes in clients' stories and letting go of less helpful themes (White & Epston, 1990). This third phase of psychotherapy overlapped with the second considerably. When exploring strong emotions, I find it essential to move back and forth between expressing feelings and reflecting on meaning. After Mark expressed strong feelings of fear and helplessness in the third session, the next session reflected on the meaning of these experiences and used Kubler-Ross's (1969) stages of grief to help Mark conceptualize his own loss. Thoughts like, "I could have saved Will if only I had . . . " were seen as a form of bargaining. Using a conceptual framework like the stages of grief is often helpful to let clients see their experience within a different framework.

The last two sessions also focused on telling the story in a different way with new meaning. Mark realized that he thought that saying, "My best friend committed suicide" was a contradiction as part of him felt that if he had been a good friend, Will would not have killed himself. By expressing his fears and then exploring their meaning, Mark could begin to affirm their friendship. During the final session, we talked about selecting a ritual action through which Mark could express the new meaning he saw in Will's death. Mark decided to place a small plaque at Will's gravesite and donate money to a suicide prevention group. These actions seemed like a positive expression of the new meaning that Mark had found by exploring Will's death and saying good-bye ten years later.

> T: So, I'm curious, Mark. Clearly, in other people's minds, they may have thought less of you knowing that your best friend committed suicide. Did you or do you feel that maybe it's true? Maybe there's something wrong with you.

> Mark: With remembering that I had left Will in the middle of the night that night had always been with me: Gosh, what was I thinking?

> T: I can see that that one's really haunting for a 15-year-old. What do you think of it as a 25-year-old?

> Mark: Oh, for crying out loud. You know. [pause] Kids do that. Even adults do that. You know. If a spouse starts snoring, I'm sure, sometimes, a spouse in the middle of the night might go sleep on the couch or something.

> T: It might be a little disappointing.

> Mark: Yeah. Disappointing. You know. And then another thing; this last week was one, between the last time we met and now, the

conversation with Will really sunk in. It took time to really penetrate and it did. I mean now I can say that clearly Will had this planned out. It was in no way did it have any reflection on me that particular evening going up there to sleep.

T: Particularly since that weekend seemed to be a goodbye weekend. He wasn't at that dark point of desperation. In some ways, as we've reconstructed it, it sounds like the desperation had lifted because he had a plan. You know?

Mark: Yeah.

OUTCOME/TERMINATION OF COUNSELING

Mark and I agreed that our counseling work together had been a success. Although we had originally agreed to meet eight times, there was a clear sense of closure during the sixth and seventh session and another appointment did not seem necessary. We concluded our work by reviewing the changes in Mark's thoughts and feelings about Will's suicide. Mark graduated a couple weeks after our last session and moved away. He sent me a postcard months later from the trip overseas and reported that he was doing well.

DISCUSSION

The counseling work that Mark and I did illustrates the dynamic interplay between thoughts and feelings that I often observe and try to facilitate. By cognitively examining Mark's beliefs about healing, his feelings toward Will's parents changed and he felt able to explore his feelings with me. As a result of emotional exploration and expression, he was free to let go of fear and guilt in a way that allowed for sadness to emerge and for grief to be resolved. In turn, this emotional change allowed Mark to think about Will in a new way that allowed him to move on in his life, saying good-bye in a new way. As a result of both cognitive and affective change, Mark was able to resume more adaptive behaviors as he continued to develop as an adult. I think the transcript segments are illustrative of the experiential work I frequently do. I like to use Gestalt experiments, such as empty chair work or two-chair dialogues, to provide clients with a new way to explore and express their feelings. Frequently, the result is a more adaptive emotional response than may have been possible at the time of the initial experience (Perls, Hefferline, & Goodman, 1951; Greenberg, Rice, & Elliot, 1993; Greenberg & Paivio, 1997).

When I think about the developmental aspects of this case, I recognize that traumatic events can arrest psychological development. During a crucial time in Mark's adolescence, he lost the most significant friend in his life. Because of the guilt and fear he felt at the time, he was not able to grieve in a healthy way. Much of Mark's emotional experience had been frozen and stored within his memory for ten years until they began to thaw on the anniversary of Will's death. I think that this event made it more difficult for Mark to make close friendships and may have led to the sense of interpersonal distance that I sometimes sensed with Mark. It is my hope that resolving some of the painful feelings from the past will free him to build closer friendships in the future.

Although our counseling was kept brief by Mark's impending graduation, there were other important factors as well. Because we had worked together in individual and group counseling in the past, there was already a sense of interpersonal trust and rapport. The brevity of counseling also was aided by an agreement to move through stages that I described to Mark and his willingness to complete specific between-session assignments like the two unsent letters described earlier.

QUESTIONS

1. *Was your ability to handle this case in seven sessions a result of having a prior therapeutic relationship with Mark? Can you speculate about how you would have proceeded if Mark were a new client?*

Yes, my ability to reach a point of resolution in seven sessions was definitely facilitated by our prior relationship. Without a previously established sense of trust, it would have been difficult to challenge Mark's inaccurate thoughts so early in the counseling process or to engage in intense emotional exploration. If Mark were a new client, I would have been more likely to begin with a narrative approach, allowing him to tell his story and looking for adaptive themes to focus on and explore. Listening to Mark's story and highlighting the positive themes that I heard would be a helpful way to establish a therapeutic relationship that would support cognitive challenges or experiential exploration.

2. *The counseling seems to be very focused on Mark's reaction to the tenth anniversary of his friend's suicide. Were other factors in his current life that may have contributed to his reaction explored? Had Mark had previous problems with guilt about the suicide? Had he experienced any problems with intimate relationships and the fear of loss?*

No, we did not explore many other factors that may have contributed to his grief reaction. In retrospect, I'm not sure if this is a positive example of maintaining a clear therapeutic focus or if, on the other hand, I may have failed to explore salient contextual features that would have facilitated Mark's development. Mark did describe previous struggles with guilt that he had thought about exploring in the past. He told me that he had considered discussing this issue when he was attending group counseling but that it had seemed like an "old issue from the past." It was the strong anniversary reaction that convinced Mark that he should not ignore this unfinished business. We did not directly explore the impact that his fear of loss may have had on intimate relationships. My thoughts about the relationship between Mark's unresolved grief and my impression of interpersonal distance represent unexplored hypotheses.

3. *Can you discuss a bit more why you think that the empty chair technique helped Mark give up his feelings of guilt and realize that he had been placed in a double bind?*

Emotionally reentering a place of great conflict gives you a second chance to look around and notice parts of the landscape that you may have overlooked before. From a Gestalt perspective, Mark's adolescent experience of guilt may represent an example of "introjection" in which an emotional conclusion is "swallowed whole" without careful "digestion." Reworking the experience in which a disturbing emotion was introjected allows a second chance for more adaptive emotional processing. Greenberg, Rice, and Elliot (1993, p. 245) describe the purpose of empty-chair work in this way: "having the person express unresolved feelings to the significant other in an empty chair will lead to arousal and completion of previously restricted affect expression towards the other."

4. *How do you think the approach you used might work with students from the other cultural groups that you counsel in Hawaii?*

Generally, I have found it more difficult to use experiential psychotherapy with Asians and Pacific Islanders in Hawaii. The idea of emotionally exploring the past seems to be more consistent with North American culture. In general, cognitive psychotherapy may be more consistent with some Asian cultural emphases on rationality. In contrast, a narrative approach may be more acceptable in Pacific Island cultures that often put an emphasis on "talking story" as a way of communicating and creating a common understanding.

5. *Can you say more about the narrative approach and techniques that you used in the two sessions in which Mark reconstructed the meaning of his friend's suicide?*

My use of a narrative approach with Mark centered on the recognition of storytelling as an essential aspect of counseling. During the last couple of sessions with Mark, I was encouraging him to tell his story in a new way; emphasizing different themes than were initially presented. When Mark first told me the story of Will's death, it was a story of loss, guilt, and fear. By the end of our work together, Mark was able to tell me the story of a loving friendship that death could not destroy. I was able to help Mark transform his story by carefully attending to the themes of love and friendship that were always in the story but that were being overshadowed by strong negative emotions. Strengthening these overlooked but adaptive features of a client's story is a key feature of a narrative approach.

REFERENCES

Beck, J. S. (1995). *Cognitive therapy: Basics and beyond.* New York: Guilford Press.

Greenberg, L. S., & Paivio, S. C. (1997). *Working with emotions in psychotherapy.* New York: Guilford Press.

Greenberg, L. S., Rice, L. N., & Elliot, R. (1993). *Facilitating emotional change: The moment-by-moment process.* New York: Guilford Press.

Kubler-Ross, E. (1969). *On death and dying.* New York: Macmillan.

Perls, F., Hefferline, R., & Goodman, P. (1951). *Gestalt therapy.* New York: Dell.

White, M., & Epston, D. (1990). *Narrative means to therapeutic ends.* New York: Norton.

Chapter 9:
Separation/Individuation
in a Cultural Context:
The Case of a Haitian-American Student

Lynda D. Field

SUMMARY. In the past decade there has been an increased awareness regarding the importance of providing culturally competent counseling services. Professionals must therefore take into account a client's cultural background when formulating the nature of the client's difficulties and during the intervention process. This chapter provides an example of how to incorporate a cultural perspective in addressing the developmental stage of separation and identity development in the college student population. A short-term model of treatment is utilized in the case of a young adult Haitian-American woman. *[Article copies available for a fee from The Haworth Document Delivery Service: 1-800-342-9678. E-mail address: <getinfo@haworthpressinc.com> Website: <http://www.HaworthPress. com> © 2001 by The Haworth Press, Inc. All rights reserved.]*

KEYWORDS. Multicultural competence, Haitian-American, short-term psychotherapy, college counseling

---

Address correspondence to: Lynda D. Field, Suffolk University, 148 Cambridge Street, Boston, MA 02114 (E-mail: lfield@acad.suffolk.edu).

[Haworth co-indexing entry note]: "Chapter 9: Separation/Individuation in a Cultural Context: The Case of a Haitian-American Student." Field, Lynda D. Co-published simultaneously in *Journal of College Student Psychotherapy* (The Haworth Press, Inc.) Vol. 16, No. 1/2, 2001, pp. 135-151; and: *Case Book of Brief Psychotherapy with College Students* (ed: Stewart E. Cooper, James Archer, Jr., and Leighton C. Whitaker) The Haworth Press, Inc., 2002, pp. 135-151. Single or multiple copies of this article are available for a fee from The Haworth Document Delivery Service [1-800-342-9678, 9:00 a.m. - 5:00 p.m. (EST). E-mail address: getinfo@haworthpressinc.com].

The past decade has seen a growing consensus that counseling practices must incorporate a multicultural framework in order to effectively assist those seeking our services (APA, 1993; Sue, Arredondo, & McDavis, 1992). The goal of this chapter is to provide an example of how to address the emotionally turbulent process of separation/individuation in a culturally competent manner for college students who come from non-dominant cultural backgrounds.

Like many professionals, my commitment to the utilization of multiculturally appropriate practices originates in my personal experiences. I am a first generation college student who left a poor, urban, Puerto Rican community to attend a university in the rural Midwest where most of the students were descendants of Scandinavian or other North European immigrants. When I left the community I was raised in to enter college, I had a culturally based manner of expressing myself that was often misinterpreted by the dominant culture. For instance, in my community people stood close to one another as they talked and expressed emotion frequently and strongly. But when I stood close to others in college my comfort with closeness was either interpreted as a threat or I was viewed as being sexually provocative. My open expression of emotions was also misinterpreted. It was during this time that I began to adopt a multicultural perspective and when I entered a doctoral program, I eagerly embraced the notion that one needed to be multiculturally competent in order to be a qualified psychologist. I have always sought to understand how a particular issue, theory, disorder, or test could be understood from various points of view. Over the past fourteen years, I have continued to build my multicultural perspective through my work with families and individuals from diverse cultural groups, and in various training and employment settings.

My professional work is guided by Sue, Arrendondo, and McDavis' (1992) theory of Multicultural Counseling Competencies (MCC). Sue and his associates hypothesize that cultural competencies develop when the counselor values cultural diversity and has *Beliefs, Knowledge,* and *Skills* that are consistent with this value. This approach allows a mental health professional to develop his or her own cultural self-awareness, an understanding of the client's cultural perspective, and the ability to develop and utilize interventions that are culturally sensitive. Having adopted this framework, I am conscious of how my physical appearance, culture, class, and life history impact my work with clients. Specifically, I am an olive skinned, second generation Puerto Rican woman who grew up listening to my relatives converse in Spanish while I replied in English because I wanted to be "an American." This resulted in my relatively good Spanish language comprehension skills but poor verbal communication skills, resulting in some disconnection from clients who are monolingual Spanish speaking or choose to speak only in Spanish.

My multicultural framework has been essential to my work in a small, private, urban university counseling center where a third of the student population (and thus the client population) are either ethnic minority or international students. Like most university counseling centers, ours has made a commitment to utilize short-term modes of treatment, consistent with our basic philosophy which views individuals presenting with difficulties from a health perspective. It is also consistent with the needs of our clients who tend to enter counseling only when in distress, and on average, will only use approximately five sessions to obtain the support and tools they need for adaptive functioning. In addition, our college student population tends to fit the client profile most likely to benefit from brief therapies. Empirical evaluations regarding the effectiveness of short-term psychotherapy show that those who benefit the most are those who enter therapy with a high level of problem awareness, commitment, and the ability to quickly form a therapist-client alliance (Koss & Shiang, 1994). Furthermore, our clients from non-western cultures seem to prefer the structure required in short-term psychotherapy. Clients from cultures that expect mental health professionals to behave like medical doctors, i.e., behave as experts in their field and provide active concrete assistance (McGoldrick, Giordano, & Pearce, 1996) feel more comfortable with the active role that short-term therapists must take, as well as the practice of quickly identifying a focus for treatment and setting observable goals.

As a counseling professional, I incorporate several frameworks into my general treatment approach. I am a relationally based therapist (Jordan, 1991) who utilizes basic helping skills (Egan, 1998) in order to quickly form an empathetically based alliance. These skills enable me to support my clients while facilitating their identification of obtainable treatment goals and movement toward those goals. While I establish a working alliance, I am constantly gathering data and making an assessment of my client's coping skills and the problems they are confronting. I then assist my clients by offering some psycho-education regarding factors that contribute to their stress (e.g., the impact of stress on one's ability to concentrate; or the impact of acculturation on one's family dynamics). Once we agree upon a focus for our treatment, I often incorporate cognitive-behavioral techniques to provide clients with the tools they need to reduce anxiety and depressive symptoms which are present in a vast majority of cases, even when the source of the distress is quite varied (e.g., history of sexual assault, family conflict, academic and financial pressures, or culture shock).

For most American students, entering college represents the beginning of a new developmental phase. They leave adolescence behind and take on the increased responsibility of young adulthood. Western culture views this as a time when the young adult achieves increased independence from the family while actively engaging in the process of developing a separate identity. This process of separation and individuation can be conflict and anxiety-filled, especially when the family does not support this process. The problems become even more complex if the student comes from an immigrant family and a culture that neither expects nor supports such individuation. Students will often turn to counseling during this process for assistance. The following case study illustrates how a multicultural perspective is essential in helping college students from varied cultures navigate this developmental transition of young adulthood.

HAITIAN CULTURE

This case involves a young woman student who is second-generation Haitian American. In order to do culturally competent work with her, I had to know some important information about the Haitian culture. Haiti is a country with a long history of violent oppression and struggle against corrupt regimes. Few families in Haiti have neither witnessed nor experienced violent political persecution. Complicating intragroup dynamics, there are conflicts between Haitians who value the language and physical appearance of the former French colonizers and Haitians who value their African heritage (Buchanan-Stafford, 1987). Like many immigrants in the U.S., Haitians are extremely hard workers who take great pride in their accomplishments and struggle to overcome feelings of shame and inferiority (Bibb & Casimir, 1996).

Due to the history of political oppression, Haitians have developed a strong mistrust for those outside of the family. At times, this mistrust may look like paranoia to a mental health professional unaware of the cultural history. First-generation Haitian Americans rarely seek mental health services because problems tend to be minimized, intellectualized, rationalized, believed to be in the hands of God, or seen as a result of voodoo (Bibb & Casimir, 1996). If they do enter therapy, they look to the therapist as an expert or authority figure, someone who can help solve the problems that lead them to seek treatment by being active, directive, empathic, and respectful (Gopual-McNicol, Benjamin-Dartigue, & Francios, 1998).

Parenting practices in Haitian families do not allow for a child's independence, separation, or self-expression (Bibb & Casimir, 1996). Conformity and obedience are expected and the community supports these expectations. This is important information to have while working with these students. In the U.S. and Canada, many Haitian families have been referred to social services because of the community's use of corporal punishment and parenting practices that are viewed as harsh and punitive by middle class U.S. and Canadian standards (Gopual-McNicol, Benjamin-Dartigue, & Francios, 1998). As in many immigrant families, there is often conflict between Haitian parents and their adolescent and young adult children who acculturate to the U.S. culture and seek independence and freedom. The young adult's need to assert a separate identity can result in mental health problems for all concerned.

BACKGROUND

Nina, a young Haitian woman in her third year of college at a small, private, relatively diverse urban university, came to see me shortly before her 20th birthday, more than halfway through the fall semester. Nina appeared distressed when she came into the university counseling center, and asked to see a therapist immediately because she was feeling desperate. Once in session, she explained that she had been studying pre-law at her mother's insistence, but could no longer tolerate following her mother's wishes. Nina longed to study dance and theater and had dreams of starting her own dance company, but her mother wanted her to enter a more traditionally respected profession, such as law or medicine. She experienced her mother as always having been very critical of her and not allowing her to grow up to be her own person. Whenever Nina attempted to assert her individuality, mother would complain about her behavior to extended family members who came to view her as a "bad child," which made her very unhappy. The year before, she found herself becoming increasingly depressed. She would frequently burst into tears and had difficulty concentrating. She noted that in the spring her grades dropped from a B to a C average, and she was fearful that her grades would drop even further in the current semester. Because of her obvious decline in performance, her mother had allowed her to consider transferring to another school but was adamant that Nina could only leave her home to attend another school if she would live in campus housing. For example, although she had gone with Nina to visit a prospective school in another state, she prematurely ended the visit upon learning that Nina would not be able to live on campus due to a shortage of dormitory space. Nina had felt particularly demoralized by this experience and entered the fall semester feeling helpless and depressed. She decided to seek help because she was fearful that she was "messing up" in her classes and would therefore fulfill her family's expectation that she had become a "bad" person who would be doomed to fail.

Nina's level of distress was verified by her responses to the College Adjustment Scale (CAS) which she completed as part of the standard intake process. The CAS is a multidimensional self-report questionnaire designed by Anton and Reed (1991) for use in college and university counseling centers. The authors report acceptable psychometric data to support its use and recent studies by Nafziger, Couillard, and Smith (1999) have supplied additional confirmatory data. Although the scale was originally developed with a White, U.S. student population lacking in ethnic diversity, Nafziger has included some diversity in his studies and the scale has been useful with our diverse student population. The CAS comprises of 108 items scored on nine scales: Anxiety, Depression, Suicidal Ideation, Substance Abuse, Self-Esteem, Interpersonal Problems, Family Problems, Academic Problems, and Career Problems. Nina's responses indicated that, compared to other college students, she was experiencing relatively severe family problems, career problems (99th percentile) and anxiety (98th). In addition, she reported a severe level of depressive symptoms (96th percentile) and self-esteem problems (97th percentile). Fortunately, her difficulties had not left her feeling desperate enough to contemplate suicide. She did not report significant suicidal thoughts on the CAS and denied feeling suicidal when queried in session. When I shared the CAS data with Nina, like many of my clients, she appeared to find this information validating of her emotional experience.

FAMILY HISTORY

Nina is her mother's only child. The two live together with her maternal grandmother in a multicultural urban center near the University. Nina's mother emigrated from Haiti with Nina's father before she was born and left her father when Nina was about two years old because he was physically abusive toward her. Nina has had no contact with her father since then. She described her mother as a hard working woman, who held both a full-time and a part-time job in order to pay for Nina's education, and put all of her hopes on her, because Nina is the first in the family to attend college.

Nina expressed fears about mother's mental health, saying her mother was "strange" because mother did not have friends, did not trust people who were not a part of her extended family, and in recent years had become very religious. Moreover, Nina experienced her mother as overly controlling. For example, she described how her mother had obtained a caller identification box in order to obtain the telephone numbers of all of Nina's friends. She then uses the phone numbers in order to track Nina down whenever she is not home.

GOAL SETTING AND COUNSELING PROCESS

After assisting Nina in telling her story and providing her with empathic support, I helped clarify her counseling goals. In addition to obtaining some emotional support and a reduction of her anxiety and depressive symptoms, Nina was seeking assistance transferring to another school. Nina's mother had repeatedly told Nina that she would be harming herself by transferring, as she would lose some college credits in the process. Nina felt guilty because mother was working so hard to pay for her college education, and did not want to extend her time in school. However, Nina was very unhappy living at home and attending her current school because it did not offer a dance major and had a very minor theater department. In her opinion, she was just wasting time and money. She thought that it would be better to transfer to a school that could meet her career needs as well as allow her to separate from her mother. Nina became tearful as she explained that her mother's continual criticisms of her left her feeling unsure of herself and depressed. An additional goal for counseling became finding some balance between Nina's desire to become more independent and pursue her own career interests and her need to please her mother in order not to experience herself as "bad."

In our first session, I talked with Nina about her conflicts with her mother and suggested that some of them stemmed from different cultural expectations. I noted that because Nina had been born and raised in the U.S., she had adopted many of the majority cultural values that include separation and relative independence from one's family as a youth emerging into young adulthood. I shared with Nina my experience in working with individuals from Haitian backgrounds, as well as other cultural groups, in which allegiance to the family is valued above individual choice. Nina became more relaxed and animated as she talked about the fact that many of her Haitian friends were experiencing similar conflicts with their families. As we began to explore this acculturation conflict, Nina appeared comforted by my suggestion that in coming to know and appreciate her mother's cultural framework, she might develop a different relationship with her mother, based on respect for the traditional Haitian perspective but unaccepting of the judgment that she is bad for having adopted an "American" cultural framework where independence is valued. Although verbatim transcripts are unavailable, the following is a reconstruction of part of the exchange between Nina and me regarding expectations for young adults in her culture.

> T: I asked you earlier about your ethnic background, how it's important to look at how the conflicts between you and your mother are related to this background. Tell me what you understand the expectations to be for young women in your culture.

> Nina: Well I'm supposed to be a good girl and listen to my mother. But she's crazy, she wants to control everything I do.

> T: It's been very distressing for you. So on the one hand your culture tells you to obey your mom and on the other hand you find this intolerable.

> Nina: Yes, and I feel like I have to just cut her out of my life if I want to make any decisions on my own.

> T: Is it helpful to know that your mother's behavior is similar to other mothers I have known who were born and raised in Haiti? Lots of families where the children are born and raised in the US experience conflicts when the children get to high school and college.

> Nina: I know what you mean, my other friends argue with their parents about some of these things too. But my mother is just so suspicious and distrustful she seems more crazy to me.

> T: Well, I know that many people in Haiti experienced or witnessed a great deal of violence due to the political upheavals. This leads to greater distrust and what we call suspiciousness. What do you know about your mother's life in Haiti?

This was the beginning of a rich and essential discussion regarding the role of Haitian history and culture on the current conflict between her and her mother. I went on to explore with Nina her knowledge regarding her mother's life in Haiti and the family's experience of the history of violent turmoil in the country. Nina shared with me that her mother had come from a large immediate family and that two of her siblings had been murdered during the political conflicts. She was unaware of her mother's personal exposure to the violence, but sensed that her mother had seen and experienced some violence. Then Nina and I discussed the impact of trauma on individuals and families. I suggested that some of her mother's behavior could be understood not only as part of the normal, strict parenting associated with Haitian culture, but also in terms of efforts to shield and protect Nina and herself from the violence she was all too familiar with. During this process, Nina began to see her mother's behavior as less "strange" and began to have more compassion for her.

At the end of this first session, Nina had clearly formed a positive working alliance. She appeared much more optimistic than when she entered my office. The following reconstruction demonstrates the use of between-session collaboratively agreed assignments to facilitate the counseling process (in terms of her primary goal).

> T: What do you think that you could do between sessions to help you come to a decision regarding transferring schools?
>
> Nina: I guess I need to find out what I need to do to transfer.
>
> T: What do you think you need to do to get that information?
>
> Nina: I could call the admissions offices or just go online to find out the process.
>
> T: Is it possible for you to make those calls before our next session?

Nina: Yeah, and I also want to call and find out about on-campus housing at the schools I want to go to.

T: Is there anything that could get in the way of making these calls?

Nina: I don't want my mother to overhear my phone calls because I haven't made a decision yet and I don't want her get angry with me.

T: It makes a lot of sense that you wouldn't want her to know until you've made a decision. What would you feel comfortable doing?

Nina: I could make the calls during my down time at work and I can also get on the Internet at school.

T: Sounds like you have a clear plan. I'll see you next week.

Nina returned the following week and appeared noticeably calmer and happier. She reported that talking with me had really helped her and made her feel hopeful. Not only did she feel accepted, understood, and supported, but she had been offered another way to view her mother, their relationship and a way to alter it. Nina shared that she had been receiving advice from her non-Haitian mentor at work, which left her in much distress. Her mentor had told her she must break away from her mother and that often becoming your own person means cutting off your relationship with your parents. The very thought of losing her mother and her extended family filled Nina with overwhelming feelings of anxiety and depression. After talking with me, Nina felt that she was gaining an ability to separate from her mother while not having to cut their strong connection. Nina then expressed fears that her mother would not be able to manage without her if she left home for the college of her choice. I explored with Nina her mother's migration to the U.S. This helped her to see how resourceful and competent her mother was, as evidenced by her ability to learn a new language, leave an abusive husband and take on sole financial responsibility for Nina and herself. Mother had obtained education and job training, and secured not only one good full-time job but also a lucrative part-time job. Reviewing this information, Nina gained confidence in her mother's ability to take care of herself. Nina then decided to take the next step of applying to other schools. Her homework for the following week was to request application materials and to apply for admission to those schools which offered on-campus housing.

By the third session, Nina reported an absence of depression and anxiety symptoms. She had achieved her goal by reaching a decision to apply to other schools and appeared to be empowered by this process. She was no longer suffering from difficulty concentrating and was once again motivated to learn in order to do well in her classes, so that she could transfer to another school. It so happened that our session fell on her 20th birthday. Nina described feeling exhilarated because during the weekend prior to our session she traveled away from home all by herself for the first time in her life. She had gone to visit friends in New York City, where she hoped to attend college. She had done this in spite of her mother's protestations and her grandmother's tears. In addition, she had completed her homework assignment and began applying to other colleges. Nina was excited by her increased ability to take on independence, even in the face of her mother's continuous punishing behavior. For example, her mother told her she would not give her a birthday present since she disobeyed her and went to New York City. Nina shared with me that all her life she had struggled with passivity, which negatively impacted her socially. At the various part-time jobs that Nina had worked, she did not stand up to people when they mistreated her. Nina expressed gratitude for the support she was receiving from me and the ways in which she felt empowered. She talked about how my understanding and acceptance of her mother's behavior within a cultural, socio-historical perspective gave her a way to continue to love and respect her mother as she moved toward greater independence and learned to hear her mother's punitive remarks as an effort to protect her and keep her close.

At this point we renegotiated our original goals, since Nina felt her symptoms were gone and she had made a decision to transfer schools. Nina decided she would like to meet at least once more in order to plan for her move to New York and to continue receiving support.

During our fourth and final session, Nina sought assistance in budgeting and thinking through the steps she would need to take in order to move to New York. She reported that her mother had agreed to allow her to attend school at one of the universities she had applied to, as long as she was going to live in the dorms. We discussed her coming to therapy for another week in order to continue support. Nina stated that she was very grateful for my assistance and would come. However, she did not return the following week, which did not surprise me because, clearly, she had accomplished her goals during the four sessions we had met. Although I thought I had given Nina complete autonomy in making the decision to continue meeting, I believe that her struggles to express her needs to authority figures prevented her from telling me that she no longer felt the need to come to counseling. Her words at the end of our final session suggested that she did not want to appear ungrateful, but that she was now feeling the need for independence not only from her mother, but also from her "supportive" counselor.

DISCUSSION

Nina was an ideal candidate for short-term therapy because of her high level of motivation to decrease her distress, her commitment to take actions that would help improve her situation, and her ability to quickly form a positive working alliance. I believe that my cultural sensitivity was essential to developing our alliance and meeting her treatment goals. From the very beginning, I integrated cultural concepts into my work with Nina. Although I viewed her depression and anxiety within a culturally bound framework (e.g., marked separation-individuation tension), it was only done after I made an assessment of her acculturation status and determined that in fact she was highly acculturated to the U.S. norms for young adult behavior. In making my assessment it became clear that much of Nina's distress was due to intergenerational acculturation conflicts (see Padilla, 1980). Although she had adopted the values and behaviors common to young adults in U.S. culture, her mother remained firmly rooted in the traditional Haitian culture. Although Nina's struggle to separate from her mother is characterized as "normative" within the dominant U.S. culture, within the Haitian culture Nina's actions were viewed as acts of disobedience. A key aspect of our work together was the examination of this acculturation conflict.

Once I conceptualized Nina's distress as acculturation conflict, my multicultural framework was evident throughout my work with her. For example, my *beliefs* led me to explore with Nina her understanding of her mother's actions within the Haitian culture. I was able to help Nina to see her mother's behavior as culturally appropriate because of the *knowledge* I had gained from my previous work with Haitian families and the efforts I had made to become culturally literate. In the past, I had known nothing about the culture and parenting practices of Haitian families. I obtained knowledge by contacting local health and social service agencies that provided culturally sensitive services to the community. In addition, I sought information from one of my favorite cultural references, the edited book by Monica McGoldrick and her associates, *Ethnicity and Family Therapy* (1996). In choosing to explore with Nina the cultural basis for her mother's behavior and to educate her regarding the acculturation conflicts that are typical of immigrant families, I demonstrated *skills* in multicultural counseling.

This culturally grounded method of working allowed me to readily structure our counseling sessions to conform to a brief therapy approach. Unlike long term psychotherapy, brief therapies develop a clear and specific focus for therapy which leads to the establishment of treatment goals (Budman & Gurman, 1988). In this case, the treatment goals were initially framed as a reduction in painful symptoms of depression and anxiety. However, it was clear that the only way to alleviate these symptoms was for Nina to come to a decision regarding her education and to develop some way to balance her mother's view of her behavior with her own view so that she could feel better about herself. This became the focus of our work. One of the key tenets of brief counseling is that the counselor must be active in helping the client to view things differently (Budman & Gurman, 1988). From the very first session, my multicultural approach led me to actively shift Nina's perspective of her own and her mother's behavior so that she gained a new appreciation and acceptance of each point of view. It is my belief that my ability to work within a cultural framework greatly facilitated our work together. Had I not had the knowledge of Nina's culture or had not framed her distress within a cultural context, effective treatment would have taken much longer or not occurred at all because Nina might have dropped out.

Once Nina was able to see her mother's behavior as culturally based she was able to better accept her mother's actions and to feel less hurt and distressed by them. Because I took an active approach using psycho-education, in contrast to long-term insight oriented approaches, Nina gained a new perspective within our first two sessions allowing her to then gain some emotional separation from her mother. Once she began to feel comfortable with the idea that both she and her mother could be entitled to their conflicting cultural views, Nina was able to make the decision regarding schools based on her own wishes and needs. My actions then helped Nina to actively pursue the information she needed in order to successfully transfer to another school.

Typical of brief therapies approaches (Steenbarger, 1992), I assigned homework in order to facilitate treatment. My assignment of homework between sessions served to keep Nina focused on her goal to make a decision and resulted in her feeling empowered to pursue her career interests. I believe that if I were working within a traditional long-term approach to psychotherapy I would not have chosen to assign the home-work. Nina would then have spent a great deal more time simply talking about her career interests, her current frustrations with her studies, and other issues, while not taking actions to actually change her situation.

Nina achieved the goals she set in four sessions. She had received re-lief from her distress by finding a way to be true to her own needs and separate from her mother, while maintaining a connection with her. If I were a long-term dynamic therapist, I may have expanded treatment by exploring the impact of Nina's traumatic family history on her sense of self, or addressed some of the other issues she raised such as her "pas-sive" behavior. Instead, my brief therapy approach kept me focused on the goals Nina had set, addressing her most immediate needs. While some may argue that it is the therapist's obligation to point out to clients other areas in which they may benefit from counseling assistance, for young adults who struggle to develop their own identity separate from parents they can be particularly sensitive to this paternalistic aspect of counseling. In this case after I attempted to go one session beyond the one in which Nina expressed the recognition that she had accomplished her original goals as well as the renegotiated goals, she did not return. Although the meaning of her failure to return is subject for debate, it is my opinion that it was Nina's way of making sure that her counselor stuck to their original contract and allowed her to separate when she was ready to do so.

QUESTIONS

1. *The change in Nina's understanding of her mother's thoughts, feelings, and behavior toward her seems to be the most significant "curative" factor in this case. This appears to have allowed Nina to become more independent and move further away from the Hai-tian cultural norms and toward the American norm, independence from parents. Was this discussed with Nina and how did she feel about giving up this part of her cultural heritage?*

Models of ethnic identity development, within the United States, generally posit a progressive series of stages in which, initially, the indi-vidual has not actively engaged in exploration of ethnic issues and is disinterested in ethnic issues. The individual at this stage typically has either a "diffuse identity" or a "foreclosed identity," meaning they ei-

ther have no clear identity or have prematurely chosen one based on either parental opinion or that of the dominant culture. In the second
stage, there is active exploration of one's ethnic identity and, in the final
stage, there is an internalization and integration of ethnic identity
(Phinney, 1990). Nina's ethnic identity development was at the very
first stage; she had internalized dominant American values and had not
actively explored her ethnic identity. Although the shift in her perspective on her mother's behavior eliminated Nina's distress, it did not lead
her to decide to follow mother's career dictates as "Haitian" and her
move toward independence as "non-Haitian," even though she understood that many of her Haitian-American peers were involved in similar
struggles with their parents. I did not think it would be helpful to point
out to Nina that, in deciding to pursue independence, she was "giving
up" a part of her cultural heritage. My expectation is that once Nina is
able to pursue her career interests and solidify that piece of her identity,
she will mature into the next stage of cultural identity development and
can then explore her Haitian identity.

   2. *How did you and Nina deal with the negative effect of Nina's new
       independence on her relationship with her mother? Was there any
       danger of them becoming estranged or of her mother no longer
       supporting her education?*

   When Nina entered counseling, the danger of estrangement appeared
to be at its highest. Although her mother had already recognized that she
had to allow Nina to pursue her own academic interests and agreed to
support her under certain conditions, she continued to criticize Nina and
expected her to be "obedient." It was her mother's criticism which Nina
found intolerable and left her believing that cutting her mother out of
her life might be the only way for her to manage the situation. When
Nina was able to see her mother's criticisms in cultural perspective, she
was able to depersonalize them. Where once Nina viewed mother's criticisms as "mean" behavior, she was subsequently able to hear them as a
culturally sanctioned way of showing caring and "good parenting."
This reframing of her mother's behavior helped Nina to ignore her
mother's words and appreciate that her mother cared for her. With this
greater comfort, Nina did begin to exert her independence in areas less
related to her career choice/academic pursuits which led to more criticism and punishing behaviors. She and I discussed the possibility of
mother cutting off her funding for her education and/or their relationship, but Nina felt confident that her mother would ultimately respect
her as a separate, grownup person.

3. *You mention that a rapid therapeutic alliance was formed and that Nina actively completed between session assignments. Speculate about these behaviors and how they may have been related to your serving as a transference object as an older female and person of color.*

Nina's ability to quickly engage in the counseling relationship was likely greatly facilitated by the fact that I am a woman of color who offered her unconditional support at a time when she felt very alone. It is harder to say whether she completed my homework assignments because of a positive transference (e.g., that she viewed me as the mother who supported her choices) or because culturally she had been socialized to obey authority figures (e.g., counselors). It may also have been that she enjoyed completing the assignments because I only gave her homework consistent with the goals she had set and in line with her specific interests.

4. *Can you speculate on how this case might have gone if Nina had been able to better understand the cultural context of her mother's behavior, but was still unable to act more independently?*

I have certainly seen cases like Nina's where the individual's fear of either being excommunicated from the family or causing a parent grief led them to comply with the family's wishes. In some cases the person endures chronic unhappiness, while in others, they give up their aspirations without too much damage to their sense of self. In Nina's case I think she would have remained in a state of crisis caught between her mother's demands and her own desires. Nina's history indicated that, under those conditions, her academic functioning deteriorated and then her mother allowed her greater freedom to pursue her own goals. It seemed clear that her mother was highly invested in Nina's educational process and her completion of a degree even if it had to be in an area other than business, law, or medicine.

REFERENCES

American Psychological Association (1993). Guidelines for providers of psychological services to ethnic, linguistic, and culturally diverse populations. *American Psychologist, 48*, 45-48.

Anton, W. D., & Reed, J.R. (1991). *College Adjustment Scale: Professional manual.* Odessa, FL: Psychological Assessment Resources.

Bibb, A., & Casimir, G. J. (1996). Haitian Families. In McGoldrick, M., Giordano, J. & Pearce, J.K. (Eds.), *Ethnicity and family therapy* (2nd ed., pp. 97-111). New York: Guilford Press.

Buchanan-Stafford, S. (1987). Language and identity: Haitians in New York City. In C. Sutton & E. Chaney (Eds.), *Caribbean life in New York City: Sociocultural dimensions* (pp. 203-205). New York: Center for Migration Studies.

Budman, S. H., & Gurman, A. S. (1988). *Theory and practice of brief therapy.* New York: Guilford Press.

Egan, G. (1998). *The skilled helper: A problem-management approach to helping.* Pacific Grove, CA: Brooks/Cole Publishing Company.

Gopual-McNicol, S. A., Benjamin-Dartigue, D., & Francios, E. (1998). Working with Haitian Canadian families. *International Journal for the Advancement of Counseling 20*, 231-242.

Jordan, J. V. (1991). The meaning of mutuality. In Jordan, J.V., Kaplan, A. G., Miller, J.B., Stiver, I.P., & Surrey, J.L. (Eds.), *Women's growth in connection: Writings from the Stone Center.* New York: Guilford Press.

Koss, M. P., & Shiang, J. (1994) Research on brief psychotherapy. In A. E. Bergin & S.L. Garfield (Eds.), *Handbook of psychotherapy and behavior change* (4th ed. pp. 664-700). New York: Wiley.

McGoldrick, M., Giordano, J., & Pearce, J.K. (Eds.) (1996). *Ethnicity & family therapy* (2nd ed). New York: Guilford Press.

Nafziger, M. A., Couillard, G. C., & Smith, T. B. (1999). Evaluating therapy outcome at a university counseling center with the College Adjustment Scales. *Journal of College Counseling, 9*, 3-13.

Padilla, A. M. (Ed.). (1980). *Acculturation: Theory models, and some new findings.* Boulder, CO: Westview.

Phinney, J.S. (1990). Ethnic identity in adolescence and adults: A review of research. *Psychological Bulletin, 108*, 499-514.

Steenbarger, B. (1992). Toward science-practice integration in brief counseling and therapy. *Counseling Psychologist, 2*, 403-450.

Sue, D. W., Arredondo, P., & McDavis, R. J. (1992). Multicultural counseling competencies and standards: A call to the profession. *Journal of Multicultural Counseling and Development, 20*, 644-688.

Chapter 10:
Saying Good-bye to the Guru:
Brief Intermittent Developmental Therapy
with a Young Adult
in a High Demand Group

Steve K. Dubrow-Eichel

SUMMARY. A young adult devotee of a High Demand Group ("cult") was engaged in brief intermittent developmental (BID) therapy, initially aimed at assisting him to critically assess his cult involvement. Over a five-year period, BID therapy helped him cope with two subsequent post-cult crises. Successfully negotiating these crises allowed further consolidation of his identity, and facilitated continued development of autonomy. *[Article copies available for a fee from The Haworth Document Delivery Service: 1-800-342-9678. E-mail address: <getinfo@haworthpressinc. com> Website: <http://www.HaworthPress.com> © 2001 by The Haworth Press, Inc. All rights reserved.]*

KEYWORDS. Cults, brief therapy, deprogramming, religion, exit counseling

---

Address correspondence to: Steve K. Dubrow-Eichel, Verree Psychology Group & RETIRN, 9877 Verree Road, Philadelphia, PA 19115 (E-mail: steve@vpsych.com).

[Haworth co-indexing entry note]: "Chapter 10: Saying Good-bye to the Guru: Brief Intermittent Developmental Therapy with a Young Adult in a High Demand Group." Dubrow-Eichel, Steve K. Co-published simultaneously in *Journal of College Student Psychotherapy* (The Haworth Press, Inc.) Vol. 16, No. 1/2, 2001, pp. 153-170; and: *Case Book of Brief Psychotherapy with College Students* (ed: Stewart E. Cooper, James Archer, Jr., and Leighton C. Whitaker) The Haworth Press, Inc., 2002, pp. 153-170. Single or multiple copies of this article are available for a fee from The Haworth Document Delivery Service [1-800-342-9678, 9:00 a.m. - 5:00 p.m. (EST). E-mail address: getinfo@haworthpressinc.com].

I am a counseling psychologist in independent practice in Philadelphia. Over the years, a major focus of my work has been adolescents and young adults struggling with a broad range of issues, including involvement in High Demand Groups (HDGs). "HDG" is a term applied to a sometimes slippery category of religious, political, therapeutic and marketing groups and movements that are often labeled "cults" by the media.

My introduction to the psychology of HDGs took place in 1975, when as an undergraduate researcher I allowed myself to be recruited into the Unification Church (the "Moonies"), a controversial HDG that was recruiting heavily on my campus. The most fascinating and disturbing component of my research was a participant-observation of their one-week indoctrination program. This experience, documented in the first chapter of a special issue of *Cultic Studies Journal* (Dubrow-Eichel, 1989b), eventually led to a clinical specialty working with young adults and families who have become involved with High Demand Groups (HDGs).

Since 1983, I have worked cooperatively with a network of mental health professionals and paraprofessional "exit counselors" called RETIRN, the Re-Entry Therapy, Information and Referral Network. RETIRN's stated purpose is to provide "counseling, forensic, consultation, information and referral services to individuals and families adversely affected by manipulative/coercive individuals, and totalistic/high demand groups or movements" (RETIRN, 1983). While I enjoy the challenge, complexity and uniqueness of this work, I am pained by the intensity, frustration and pressure brought by families and individuals who are typically desperate for a quick and/or simple resolution to a loved one's involvement in an HDG.

However, I don't blame them. A typical RETIRN referral involves a young adult, away at college or perhaps just graduated, who has either secretly become involved or (worse yet) has gradually become involved without disrupting his/her family relationships until it is "too late." Either way, by the time the family contacts us, their loved one is usually deeply involved and thoroughly convinced in the absolute and preeminent righteousness of the group's purpose. The member will typically refuse any direct request to talk to anyone they consider critical (or, worse yet, an apostate). Most HDGs are vehemently opposed to psychologists and psychotherapists.

The case I present describes the use of "brief intermittent developmental" (BID) therapy, an integrative treatment modality that combines developmentally-based psychotherapy (Greenspan, 1997) with time-limited intermittent therapy (Kreilkamp, 1989) and motivational interviewing (Miller & Rollnick, 1991). The central principle of developmentally-based psychotherapy is to "build on the patient's natural inclinations and interests to try to harness a number of core developmental processes at the same time" (Greenspan, 1997, p. 8). The developmental processes we want to mobilize involve age-appropriate ego functions, such as autonomy, decision-making, and affect and impulse regulation. Time-limited intermittent therapy relies on relatively focused and structured sessions that emphasize taking action. Developing insight is viewed as a by-product of taking action. This approach also relies on developmental theory, with the various stages of therapy viewed as a developmental process itself. In my experience, Kreilkamp's (1989) description of his approach fits in markedly well with the "stages of change" model developed by Prochaska and his collegues (Prochaska & DiClemente, 1982, 1984; Prochaska, 1999) as a transtheoretical approach to therapy.

PHASE 1: PARENTAL INTERVENTION

Mr. and Mrs. Bader initially contacted me in the mid 90s. Their 16 year old son, David, had become involved in a local group that seemed cultic, and he had just informed them that he would be leaving for an ashram in India in a few months. The Baders, like many parents who contact me, knew of their son's involvement for almost a year, but they initially viewed it as benign, and even as beneficial. David's grades had improved somewhat, he had cut his long hair, and he seemed "calmer." They knew little about David's group and rejected the opinions of some friends as an overreaction. As months passed, however, they began to notice what seemed like radical personality changes. Some of these changes seemed superficially positive; David stopped listening to heavy metal rock music, and he became more concerned with hygiene. Moreover, he seemed more energetic in spite of his new, rigid vegetarian diet. Other changes caused great concern. For example, David spent a great deal of time on his own chanting Hindu phrases. He became irritable and judgmental; he constantly preached to his family, and criticized them for being materialistic. Although his grades improved, David's thinking became more rigid. He seemed distant, "spaced out," and, oddly, "too content." And David began to manipulate and lie; when he claimed to be visiting friends, he was in fact spending time at the local temple or ashram affiliated with his group. In fact, David was completely neglecting his old friends, preferring to spend all his free time in the company of group members, whom he referred to as his "adopted family." David also lied about money. The Baders were an upper-middle class family and David received a liberal weekly allowance in addition to having all his other material needs met by his family. At this time, however, it gradually became clear that David was giving most or even all of his money to his group.

The Baders did what a great many families do in this situation: They took matters into their own hands, confronted David, made new rules, and demanded an honest accounting of his time and money. The Baders found a book about David's group and began confronting him about them. Family gatherings became highly argumentative and typically ended with David retreating to another room in the house where he would begin chanting, sometimes for hours on end. As David's parents put it to me: "There was just no getting through to him." At one point, David became so incensed that he picked up a chair and threw it through a window. The Baders called the police. David became enraged and destroyed some furniture before running from the home. Police on routine patrol encountered him a few blocks away, acting suspiciously. When they confronted him, David refused to talk to them and chanted continuously instead.

David's parents eventually found out their son was being held by the police. Upon the recommendation of a police sergeant, they agreed to arrange for a one-week stay at a local psychiatric hospital. David reluctantly agreed with the plan. At the hospital, David initially refused to participate in group or milieu therapy. In meeting with his individual therapist, David agreed to participate on the condition that the hospital allow him to obtain his group-sanctioned prayer beads and books. The hospital, naively believing that facilitating David's "spiritual growth" would help him in his therapy, convinced the Baders to bring their son's books and beads to the hospital. David did not live up to his end of the bargain. Once David had his beads and books, he remained in his room for the remainder of the week, reading and chanting.

Following his release from the hospital, David was angrier than ever. He refused to even talk with his parents, and he openly defied them by spending every spare moment at his group's meeting house just outside Philadelphia. He began staying overnight (something he had never done before) and he began to refuse to attend his school.

It was at this point that the Baders contacted me. Over the course of three sessions in two weeks (Phase 1), I obtained a family history and began to educate the Baders about their son's group and HDGs in general. My goal was to first diminish their panic, since actions taken out of panic typically make matters worse. By discussing their son's behavior in the broader context of HDGs, the Baders were reassured that for now there was still a considerable amount of hope. In many HDG cases, for example, parents do not know where their children are or have no way to contact them. I also explained why "deprogramming" was not an option in this situation. My own research (Dubrow-Eichel, 1989a, 1989b) dispelled many popular misconceptions about deprogramming, and by the early 1990s this heavy-handed intervention had been replaced by a gentler, more appropriate yet equally effective intervention called "exit counseling." I strongly advised against attempting a forced deprogramming. Yet, it was clear that some sort of action needed to be taken. Therefore, I referred the Baders to a "cult aware" attorney who might assist them; David was, after all, still legally a minor and they were his guardians.

> Mr. Bader: We've had it with David. This group is ruining his life and ruining ours, and we're deeply worried about him. Isn't there something we can do? What about deprogramming?

> T: You're deeply upset, and that's to be expected. Your primary reason for being here is to explore your options and develop a plan. I'm not sure what deprogramming means to you. If you're talking about the kind of process involving holding David against his will, I don't advise it. I also don't work with any so-called deprogrammers.

> Mrs. Bader: Then what do we do? Just leave him in his group? If he goes to India, it will be too late to do anything.

> T: Folks, the best thing to do right now is to look at these events as objectively as possible, to evaluate options as objectively as possible. It will be helpful to distinguish between your understandably intense feelings and any actions that might be taken. Now first of all, let's not forget that David is still legally a minor. And that means as his parents, you do have certain rights.

> Mr. Bader: Okay, I know that. But what do we do?

> T: First, find out what your legal options are.

> Mrs. Bader: You mean talk with a lawyer? But this is all so strange, and I don't think a lawyer would really understand.

T: Well, if you need a referral to an attorney, there is one we work with fairly routinely. She's very tuned into these groups and these issues, and she's an expert on domestic law.

The attorney hired by the Baders wrote a letter to the leader (guru) of the HDG reminding him that David was a minor and urging a cessation of contact between David and his group. Upon receiving the letter, the local leader of the HDG made it clear that David would not be welcome until he turned 18. David was initially quite angry. The Baders had been coached in how to effectively listen to their son's anger while still firmly maintaining their stance regarding David's group and his planned trip to India.

Our next step was to get David involved in counseling. The Baders presented me to their son as a psychologist who also had expertise in group dynamics and social coercion. As per my recommendation, the word "cult" was not used. David was very interested in meeting with me, and so we began Phase 2 of treatment.

DIAGNOSTIC/DEVELOPMENTAL FORMULATION

When I first met David, he presented as a thin, 16-year-old, white male adolescent with blonde buzz-cut hair. He seemed oriented in all spheres and showed no gross signs of cognitive impairment. David was the youngest of four siblings; his three older sisters were all adults, living on their own. His father owned a construction business and was proud of his Ivy League undergraduate education. His mother worked at home, part-time, typing medical transcripts. The marriage was presented as conflictual: David's father struggled on and off with drinking; his mother was a devout born-again Christian who greatly disapproved of her husband's behavior but felt duty-bound to remain in the marriage while praying for her husband to change.

Prior to his adolescence, David enjoyed a very close relationship with his father. Eight years separated him from his youngest sister, and he had very few memories of growing up with his two other older sisters, both of whom left home at age 18 while David was still a youngster. David performed well in elementary school where he attended classes for the mentally gifted. He played tennis and learned guitar and drums.

Adolescence hit David hard. When he was 12, his parents separated for almost a year. David remained with his mother but longed for his father. At age 13, David began showing signs of psychosocial disturbance. He developed a severe case of acne that contributed to his being very shy and reclusive. He began experimenting with alcohol and hallucinogens (LSD, mushrooms and marijuana). He was often truant from school and his grades dropped considerably. By age 14, David was in open rebellion. He began to dress in "punk" or "gothic" clothing, wore his hair in a punk spike fashion, and withdrew considerably from his family. I later learned that he was introduced to sex in a somewhat coercive/traumatic manner (in which he was the victim), while high on alcohol and psychedelic mushrooms. It was an experience that would later be repeated under similar circumstances and that caused David considerable guilt and self-loathing.

By the time I became involved with the Baders, David had met the criteria for Oppositional-Defiant Disorder. But that diagnosis only scratched the surface of this young man. He was clearly using his group as a means of defending against considerable internal and external turmoil. His chanting, for example, served to suppress his feelings and thought. Chanting for hours can become a means of denying and dissociating from difficult feelings, thoughts and impulses (Dubrow-Eichel & Dubrow-Eichel 1985; Goldberg & Goldberg, 1982; Persinger, Carrey & Suess, 1980; Zeitlin, 1985). Devoting himself for hours on end to studying esoteric religious texts prevented him from learning more mundane school subjects. Involvement with the group also served to provide a potent sense of community with other devotees and quick answers to difficult existential questions, while the guru of the group provided David with an idealized father substitute.

PHASE 2: INITIAL INTERVENTION WITH HDG MEMBER

Although the number of young clients who come to counseling with HDG-related issues is relatively small, the process involved in counseling them is in many ways similar to addictions counseling (Dubrow-Eichel, 1989a). Most of these clients come to counseling with ambivalence about the counseling process itself; they often perceive the problem as involving acceptance on the part of significant others in their lives. Although most HDG members harbor suppressed doubts (Galanter, 1999; Hassan, 1988) and may even have developed a "doubled self" or pseudoidentity (Lifton, 1986), when they do come for counseling they are typically (and understandably) suspicious. An early exchange be tween David and me illustrates this early suspiciousness and also illustrates early rapport building and an incitement to be curious.

T: Do you know why you're here?

David: You're going to try to talk me out of The Society.

T: Do you know that for a fact?

David: Well, I think that's a pretty safe bet!

T: So you have a belief about what I'm going to do.

David: Yes.

T: That's interesting to me. How sure are you about your beliefs about me and why you're here?

David: What do you mean?

T: Well, we only just met.

David: Yeah, Okay.

T: We don't really know each other.

David: Okay that's true.

T: What we know about each other is based either on what we've heard about each other, or our immediate first impressions.

David: Yeah, Okay.

T: Those impressions may be accurate, they may be inaccurate, they may be some combination of accurate and inaccurate.

David: Okay.

T: How do you determine if your impressions are accurate?

David: Over time, I guess.

T: Yes, me too. We usually have beliefs about things before we have complete facts. Are you willing to test your hypotheses with me over time?

David: I don't know. Maybe.

T: I'll take that as a conditional "yes" and that's good enough for me.

David: Okay, fine then. What do we talk about?

T: Whatever you want to talk about.

David was now a little curious. We began talking about his life, his values both before and during his involvement with his group. As we talked, I listened carefully to what seemed to be connected to David's core beliefs and values, the ones he had prior to becoming involved with an HDG. From my point of view, David was in the "precontemplative" (Prochaska, 1999) stage of therapy, and my primary goal was to spark an interest and motivate David to engage in the counseling process (Miller & Rollnick, 1991). In subsequent sessions, as David expressed more uncertainties about his group and its leader, I became somewhat more directly challenging. The following exchange, which occurred in the fifth session, is a good example:

T: David, at one point you said one of the things that attracted you to this group was a sense of great loyalty among the members. You said devotees would die for each other, if necessary.

David: Yeah, so?

T: David, why hasn't your group leader contacted you?

David: Because there's a stupid court order telling him not to.

T: So why not disregard the court order?

David: Then my leader might get arrested.

T: Maybe. Let's assume he would. So what? A little bit of jail time doesn't seem that bad if you're committed to die for each other.

[Pause during which David seems to be thinking hard.]

David: If my guru were in jail, then he wouldn't be able to spread the word to nonbelievers.

T: David, I'm going to ask you to listen carefully to me for just a moment. David, my primary purpose is to get at the truth of your group and your involvement in your group. If, after you have time to think things through, you still want to be in this group, then that's your prerogative. When you're 18, you can pretty much do what you want to do anyway.

David: So what's your point?

T: David, you said your guru would not want to go to jail because it might keep him from recruiting new members. Did I hear you correctly?

David: Yes.

T: So then recruiting other members is more important to your guru than sticking by you.

David: [Long pause.] Hmmm.

T: I'm not trying to bash your guru. I'm just kind of repeating back to you what you apparently already know. Your guru has told you repeatedly that you are more important to him than anything, yet that apparently isn't so. Recruiting new members is more important to him than you.

David: [Long pause.] Yeah, I guess I never thought of it that way. But why should I expect him to violate the law?

T: Oh, but I'm not saying it's right to violate the court order. I'm just saying that what your guru told doesn't seem entirely true, when push came to shove. Your guru and your group claim to be true and honest at all times. How does your guru's actions reflect on this?

We continued to meet on a somewhat sporadic basis with appointments ranging from a week apart to a month apart. Allowing the HDG member to exercise considerable control over the frequency of sessions is important because it emphasizes the noncoercive nature of counseling and is conducive to the development of autonomy in the young adult (Dubrow-Eichel & Dubrow-Eichel, 1988). Over the following 13 sessions, David's critical reasoning abilities seemed to grow. He questioned many things including the research and theoretical basis of counseling. Over this period of time, David decided to remain apart from his group and its leader, but he continued to find worth in some of the group's scriptural writings and religious rituals. I encouraged David to continue to explore these on an intellectual as well as an experiential level and David agreed. At his 17th session, we decided a "sabbatical" was appropriate, and the following session was our last meeting for two years.

PHASE 3: FIRST POST-HDG CRISIS

David contacted me after this hiatus from treatment to discuss a number of issues. In the year since I'd last seen him, he graduated from high school and then decided to work and pursue his music rather than attend college. He was still practicing some of the rituals he'd learned in his HDG. David was feeling extremely guilty about his sexuality. In our previous work, he would only discuss sexuality in abstract, theoretical terms. Now he admitted that he was "plagued" with sexual impulses, primarily toward women but occasionally toward men. In addition, he was worried that he masturbated excessively. His call to me followed an incident in which a middle-aged man made a sexual advance toward him while they were in a health club sauna. David reacted with panic, fearing that he was "sending out gay vibes." Concurrently, David had begun dating a young woman and the relationship had become sexual.

David's sexual concerns were not highly remarkable, and were typical of many young adults. However, his involvement in an HDG colored his personal struggle. The tendency of HDG involvement to delay normal development has been described by several researchers (cf. Dubrow-Eichel & Dubrow-Eichel, 1988; K. Schwartz, 1986; L. Schwartz, 1983; and Schwartz & Kaslow, 1981). In David's case, his HDG had been highly condemning of sexual impulses and any desires that might be described as "materialistic." Thus, his continued religious practice and belief structure caused him ongoing guilt and shame. David seemed to need permission to discontinue his rituals and to reexamine his belief structure. Yet he was also highly ambivalent about becoming "dependent" upon a therapist. I therefore concentrated on suggesting how he might find other sources of information against which he could evaluate the beliefs and practices that were causing him guilt. I couched my suggestions as invitations to "experiment":

David: I don't know . . . I mean, I've read that everybody does it [masturbates] but scripture says it's a form of self-pollution. And I always feel bad about myself after I do it.

T: So one of the issues seems to be, is your negative feeling due to the masturbation itself, or is it a result of your belief system. Your negative feelings certainly seem to reinforce the belief system.

David: Not only that, but then when I don't do it, I seem to think about sex even more. It's so screwed up [laughs] . . . so to speak.

T: Are you aware of any spiritual people or belief systems that do not condemn sexuality or do not view it as demonic and evil?

David: Are there any?

T: I invite you to find out. How might you do that?

David: I know this theology student who comes into the restaurant a lot, and I have a friend who knows some pretty cool ministers. I think they're ministers, but I'm not sure.

T: Would you be willing to try an experiment?

David: Sure.

T: And remember, experiments always have some kind of result. Do you remember doing experiments in bio or chem class in high school?

David: Yeah, sure.

T: Did you label a result "good" or "bad"?

David: No, not really. A result was a result. It always led to knowing something, even if it didn't come out the way you wanted.

T: Exactly. And I invite you to view the results of this experiment in the same way.

David: I can do that. What's the experiment?

T: I invite you to talk to three different "spiritual" or "religious" people about their beliefs about sexuality. Or you can check it out in books instead, if you prefer.

David: Yeah, I can definitely do that.

Over the course of the next seven sessions, David discovered that there are broad ranges of beliefs about the role of sexuality in a spiritually involved person. He was surprised to find that some religions consider sexuality one means toward enlightenment (e.g., tantric Buddhism). David ultimately decided to put his spiritual practices and beliefs "on hold" pending further investigations.

With this concern reasonably resolved, David began to experience his sexual relationship with his new girlfriend in a positive way. He was able to see himself as perhaps tending toward bisexuality with the freedom to choose to act or not act on those impulses.

PHASE 4: SECOND POST-HDG CRISIS AND MAINTENANCE OF GAINS

I next heard from David two years later. He was very dissatisfied with his current employment as a waiter, a job he found both boring and financially unrewarding. Sessions during this phase of Brief Intermittent Developmental therapy were therefore concerned primarily with his career interests and college. David was clearly struggling with his rebellious attitudes toward "traditional" learning environments (i.e., college). But he disliked his current work and realized that a college degree might be the best means toward a more agreeable career, yet wondered if he was being too "materialistic." Again, this decision was colored by his HDG belief system, which labeled his career concerns as "an attachment" and "an ego-based illusion" that would impede his enlightenment. After examining his feelings in the contexts of both his HDG involvement and his "true self," David decided he would apply to college for the next semester. He no longer seemed to be struggling with concerns about being "dependent" on therapy. He clearly asked for, and received, concrete guidance on how to apply to college.

CONCLUSION

In the five-year period between my initial contact with David's parents and my last session with him, I saw an adolescent progressively developing his potential. When we first met, David was a rigid ascetic. His HDG involvement served the dual purpose of circumventing difficult developmental conflicts and rebelling against his parents and, more broadly, a "materialistic society." It remained unclear whether David "really" would have proceeded to live in an Indian ashram. However, because of the real possibility of David leaving the country, his parents were faced with an immediate crisis that demanded thoughtful action. With brief but intensive coaching on how to interact with their son, the Baders were able to convince David to attend counseling. Once in my office, it was my goal to appeal to David's underlying curiosity and desire to find the truth. By combining a dialectical counseling approach (that borrowed liberally from motivational interviewing) with specific knowledge of cultic groups and a very non-coercive approach, I was able to pique David's interest enough to get him to return for subsequent sessions. Had I employed a more open-ended and "traditional" long-term treatment paradigm, it is doubtful that David would have continued beyond that first session.

I am becoming more and more convinced that for many people, brief intermittent developmental therapy yields results that are at least as beneficial as ongoing long-term therapy. I have tried to present an example of Brief Intermittent Developmental therapy as it is applied to a somewhat unusual case: that of an adolescent deeply involved with a High Demand Group (HDG) or "cult." In my experience, the BID therapy approach is uniquely suited for working with former HDG members. It closely resembles a developmental process, as the changes made by the client typically begin as assimilations (a first-order change) but may ultimately involve accommodation (a second-order change). The client-therapist relationship shifts slowly toward an increasingly collaborative one. Gains made in the first two phases of therapy are maintained and strengthened as the client progresses through fairly predictable post-HDG developmental crises and toward increased personal efficacy and autonomy and a more coherent and robust identity.

I have found the BID approach to be at least as effective as long-term therapy for the same or similar problems in clients with the same or similar demographics, a finding consistent with research on brief intermittent approaches to therapy as a whole (Roth & Fonagy, 1996).

QUESTIONS

1. *How do you distinguish between a youngster getting involved with a high demand group (cult) and one who is merely exploring religions/groups that are very unusual and/or quite different in values from their parents?*

Differentiating between a young adult on a religious/spiritual exploration and one who is becoming involved in an HDG can be problematic. I look for (1) evidence that the group possesses characteristics of an HDG, and (2) evidence of a cultic relationship between the client and the group. First, keep in mind that HDGs are not exclusively religious groups. Certain kinds of political movements, psychotherapy groups and marketing programs can also be described as "cultic." High Demand Groups usually demonstrate characteristics that include many or most of the following: dependence on a leader or small group of leaders who are perceived as significantly superior to any other leader, and who are not accountable to membership; suppression of dissent; an organized program of indoctrination that typically relies on manipulation of moods and states of awareness; use of deception in recruiting and/or maintaining membership; and an "us versus them" mentality toward nonmembers; a belief that their doctrine contains indisputable truth; and the employment of guilt and shame to suppress doubt.

I look for sudden and radical personality change in the client as the primary clue for HDG involvement, which almost always involves the following: denigration of the pre-cult personality (e.g., as "evil" or "demonic"); radical changes in behavior, beliefs, activities, friends; alienation from family; and a radical increase in secrecy, lying and deceptiveness.

2. *You made an interesting point in comparing clients like David to substance abusers who are forced to seek counseling and who are in the precomtemplation stage. Such referrals often don't work and the student stays in the precontemplation stage. What has been your experience in dealing with youngsters with whom you*

can't make any headway initially? In such cases would you ever recommend the more radical deprogramming approach?

As in addictions-related interventions, in my experience, a sizable number of HDG-related interventions also do not INITIALLY "work," so we often seem to be just "planting the seed" for future interventions.

I do not recommend the radical deprogramming approach for four reasons: First, years of experience have shown that this approach is not more effective in the long-run than "voluntary" approaches, and deprogramming in and of itself can be so traumatic that it causes harm; Second, when it is unsuccessful, deprogramming can result in a complete alienation between the HDG member and the individuals who planned the deprogramming (usually family); Third, because deprogramming can involve holding the HDG member against his/her will, the coercers can be subject to criminal prosecution; Fourth, given the first two reasons, the vast majority of paraprofessional interventionists with expertise in HDGs have publicly agreed not to conduct deprogrammings. These paraprofessionals, who refer to themselves as "exit counselors" and/or "thought reform consultants," have promulgated a code of ethics that bans forced deprogramming. And since all the interventionists I trust do not engage in deprogramming, I would be highly suspicious of anyone who would.

3. *Can you make any generalizations about the youngsters and/or families who are prone to be attracted to high demand groups?*

Generally, "state" rather than "trait" makes an individual susceptible to HDG recruitment. Research indicates that these "state" characteristics usually involve temporary vulnerabilities, such as loss of a loved one or a job (or anything that can cause temporary mild depression), a change in social status, a move to a new residence, or any transition (e.g., the transition from high school to college, or college to the work world or graduate school). We know that HDG recruitment is not related to: low intelligence or weak intellect; serious emotional disturbance; or gullibility or some other form of being "weak-willed." In fact, HDGs tend to attract individuals who are idealistic and idea-oriented (and thus usually have above-average intelligence), and they are usually intolerant of individuals with mental illness (they tend to drain the group's resources and are poor fund-raisers and recruiters).

The "formula" for HDG involvement involves "bad luck": being in a transitory vulnerable state (as opposed to having "cult-ready" personality traits) that creates a "window of opportunity" for cult recruitment, and then having the misfortune of encountering a cult recruiter.

4. *Was there any discussion/treatment specifically for the sexual abuse that you mentioned that David experienced? It sounded as if his pursuing a more cognitive approach of learning about how different religions view sexuality was the most important factor in freeing him to have a healthy sexual relationship with his girlfriend.*

In my opinion, David's sexual victimization has certainly played both a conscious and an unconscious role in some of his sexual behaviors, feelings and attitudes. Although he has achieved an intellectual awareness of the possible harmful effects of this early sexual experience, he has not (yet) been amenable to the kind of therapeutic work that is necessary for processing this experience on a more affective level. I expect that David will eventually return for additional therapy (a basic tenet of the BID approach), and we have identified his sexual victimization as one focus for future therapeutic work.

REFERENCES

Dubrow-Eichel, S. (1989a). *Deprogramming: An investigation of change processes and shifts in attention and verbal interactions.* Doctoral dissertation, University of Pennsylvania, Philadelphia.

Dubrow-Eichel, S. (1989b). Deprogramming: A case study. Part I: Personal observations of the group process [Special issue]. *Cultic Studies Journal, 6(2).*

Dubrow-Eichel, S., & Dubrow-Eichel, L. (1988). Trouble in paradise: Some observations on psychotherapy with new agers. *Cultic Studies Journal, 5,* 177-192.

Galanter, M. (1999). *Cults: Faith, healing, and coercion (2nd Ed.).* New York: Oxford University Press.

Goldberg, L., & Goldberg, W. (1982). Group work with former cultists. *Social Work, 27,* 165-170.

Greenspan, S. I. (1997). *Developmentally based psychotherapy.* Madison, WI: International Universities Press.

Hassan, S. (1988). *Combating cult mind control.* Rochester, VT: Park Street Press.

Kreilkamp, T. (1989). *Time-limited, intermittent therapy with children and families.* New York: Brunner/Mazel.

Langone, M. (Ed.) (1993). *Recovery from cults: Help for victims of psychological and spiritual abuse.* New York: Norton.

Lifton, R. (1986). *The nazi doctors: Medical killing and the psychology of genocide.* New York: Basic Books

Miller, W. R., & Rollnick, S. (1991). *Motivational interviewing: Preparing people to change addictive behavior.* New York: Guilford Press, 1991.

Persinger, M., Carrey, N., & Suess, L. (1980). *TM and cult mania.* North Quincy, MA: Christopher Publishing.

Prochaska, J. O. (1999, June). The process of behavior change: From individual patients to entire populations. *Clinician's Research Digest, 17* (6), Supplemental Bulletin 20.

Prochaska, J. O., & DiClemente, C. C. (1982). Transtheoretical therapy: Toward a more integrative model of change. *Psychotherapy: Theory, Research, and Practice, 19,* 276-288.

Prochaska, J. O., & DiClemente, C. C. (1984). *The transtheoretical approach: Crossing the traditional boundaries of therapy.* Homewood, IL: Dow Jones-Irvin.

RETIRN: The Re-Entry Therapy, Information & Referral Network (1983). *For those who question.* [Brochure]. Philadelphia, PA: Author.

Roth, A., & Fonagy, P. (1996). *What works for whom? A critical review of psychotherapy research.* New York: Guilford.

Schwartz, K. (1986). The meaning of cults in treatment of late adolescent issues. *Adolescent Psychiatry, 13,* 188-200.

Schwartz, L. (1983). Family therapists and families of cult members. *International Journal of Family Therapy, 5,* 168-178.

Schwartz, L., & Kaslow, F. (1981). The cult phenomenon: Historical, sociological, and familial factors contributing to their development and appeal. *Marriage & Family Review, 4,* 3-30.

Zeitlin, H. (1985). Cult induction: Hypnotic communication patterns in contemporary cults. In Zeig, J. (Ed.), *Ericksonian Psychotherapy.* New York: Brunner/Mazel, pp. 379-400.

Chapter 11:
Brief Therapy with a Grieving Grad Student

J. Eugene Knott
Tu A. Ngo

SUMMARY. This chapter examines the confluence of bereavement, cultural competence, and incest as experienced in the brief treatment of a Cambodian-born clinical psychology graduate student. Paradigms for end-setting in short-term therapy, approaches to grieving, the complications of culturally different values and a history of sexual abuse by the deceased are described.*[Article copies available for a fee from The Haworth Document Delivery Service: 1-800-342-9678. E-mail address: <getinfo@ haworthpressinc.com> Website: <http://www.HaworthPress.com> © 2002 by The Haworth Press, Inc. All rights reserved.]*

KEYWORDS. Bereavement, cultural competence, short-term treatment

I (Knott) have been intrigued by the variables at work in time-limited therapy since graduate school where I discovered the work of people like Sifneos, Mann, and Castelnuovo-Tedesco. The model of brief bereavement therapy I use is a product of considerable experimentation

Address correspondence to: J. Eugene Knott, Human Development & Family Studies, University of Rhode Island, 220B Quinn Hall, Kingston, RI 02881 (E-mail: gknott@uri.edu).

[Haworth co-indexing entry note]: "Chapter 11: Brief Therapy with a Grieving Grad Student." Knott, J. Eugene, and Tu A. Ngo. Co-published simultaneously in *Journal of College Student Psychotherapy* (The Haworth Press, Inc.) Vol. 16, No. 3/4, 2002, pp. 171-189; and: *Case Book of Brief Psychotherapy with College Students* (ed: Stewart E. Cooper, James Archer, Jr., and Leighton C. Whitaker) The Haworth Press, Inc., 2002, pp. 171-189. Single or multiple copies of this article are available for a fee from The Haworth Document Delivery Service [1-800-342-9678, 9:00 a.m. - 5:00 p.m. (EST). E-mail address: getinfo@haworthpressinc.com].

and discussions with counseling center colleagues at many other schools over the years. I have been involved with issues of bereavement and mourning for over 30 years, having published my first article in 1970 on college student suicides. In the mid-70s, I joined with a number of friends from other locations and disciplines to create the Association for Death Education and Counseling, an international group that will celebrate its 25th anniversary conference in Toronto in the spring of 2001.

Thus, my work with grieving adults and students has carried over into my writing and research, as well as to my private practice, where I am somewhat specialized in that most of my clients are either couples, bereaved individuals, other clinical providers, and many who fit more than one of those categories. A more recent interest, dating to the last 15 years for me as a presenter, has been the matter of cultural competence. I have had the opportunity to work with higher ed institutions, hospitals, prison staffs, and many private sector organizations to assist them with issues of needed respect for the diversity within their work settings. This, too, has been a feature of my private practice clientele increasingly in the past decade, and will only continue to grow in frequency and need as the clinical population itself diversifies further.

I (Ngo) have been interested in family violence since undergraduate psychology days, when I also volunteered at a battered women's shelter. The limitations of a case manager role–wanting to have more impact and gain more direct influence–led directly to pursuit of a doctorate in the helping professions. My first graduate program was in Public Health, where I sought to learn program design, implementation and evaluation. This was also the period when I became heavily involved with Asian populations, touching close to home, since I am a refugee from Vietnam. My need for more clinical skills led to my current doctoral program.

The following chapter presents a case of brief therapy with a young woman graduate student, herself a clinician-in-training. Treatment entailed a confluence of time-limited treatment, bereavement, a pair of conflicted relationships, and a challenge to cultural competence to help the Asian-born client. We begin here with an examination of the conceptual and clinical frameworks for treatment, then present background details about the client and her family of origin, and finally end with a session-by-session summary account, including a follow-up assessment.

BRIEF PSYCHOTHERAPY

While the now sizable literature on short-term and brief therapies ranges over a wide span of time-focused objectives, and lists single session to 20+ meetings as fitting the rubric, the model used by the senior author since the early 70s has been based in a particular eclectic framework. The following section details the three major elements of that approach, and offers a foundation for understanding how and why this particular case might fit a brief framework despite the complicated and traditionally open-ended or time-unlimited outlook it might present to most therapists.

Temporal Aspects

Three categories apply here: length, frequency, and duration. Length refers to the amount of time spent with the client in each session. In this model, that is a pliable variable. We met mostly in 50-minute sessions, but also had one 90, three 75, and two 30-minute meetings. The length chosen is often a function mainly of needs of the moment for processing narrative, yet occasionally is dictated by the status of the client's progress on some aspect of our therapeutic work. So, usually brief sessions reflect relative stability, and longer ones bespeak a need to work through more difficult aspects of the presenting and emerging problems. Frequency refers to the interval between sessions. The model recognizes that bereavement in particular will have what some (Stroebe, 1994) call an oscillating character, i.e., the griever will move back and forth between issues related to the loss on the one hand, and to the demands of everyday living on the other. Regular intervals between meetings are not only unnecessary but are unlikely to fit well the client's need to be seen. Thus, there were times when more than one or two weeks passed appropriately between scheduled and rescheduled appointments. Finally, duration calls for attention to the overall time expected to complete the therapy, and that, too, is a fluid feature of the model, allowing for early expectations to be shared, then adjusted as needs dictate over time. In fact, early statements of expectation for a relatively brief course of treatment are frequently cited features of a good short-term approach to therapy, helping to consolidate aspects of the client's outlook on care, self-efficacy, and motivation (Burlingame and Fuhriman, 1987).

Process Keys

A second category for consideration in this brief treatment paradigm addresses pivotal process keys. The major one sees treatment as a collaborative or joint problem-solving scenario, with a clear focus and a lot of client self-determination in consultation with the therapist. Another key is the nature of the concern, ideally recent onset and moderate severity, avoiding personality or psychotic disorder, or chronic and long-term genesis. The complication revealed later in treatment might not have seemed to match this ideal, but therapy was already underway and an alliance had been established. More critically, she had dealt with the abuse when in therapy twice before, and in therapy was very able to work through the established goals for our meetings. Goal-setting also provides criteria for weighing aptness of the brief treatment model, including an outcome that is specific, limited, feasible, and assessable. Thus, temporal as well as behavioral and cognitive end-setting characterize the approach. A final variable here is that of homework (although it's rarely referred to as such), a deliberate attempt to optimize the time-limited nature of the therapy by using the time between sessions to pursue treatment-related goals and objectives with small progressive assignments.

PHASES OF THE MODEL

There are six integrated and not always sequential phases, i.e., they look more like a helix or spiral than any linear unidirectional procedural model. In descriptive terms, they are:

- Exposition: unveiling the reasons for help-seeking, the nature of the problem from the client's vantage point, and the stories that comprise their take on the scenario
- Diagnosis: perhaps too medical a term for the joint process of arriving somewhat reductively at what is defined as the core problem, its roots, and the apparent path to its solution or amelioration
- Contracting: arriving at mutual consent on a set of change goals and time expectations, with explicit reference to the homework and time variation options likely to be used
- Implementation: the process of actually undertaking the series of agreements and actions devised over the course of treatment

- Evaluation: an ongoing overt and mutual assessment of progress and needed alterations to the contract
- Termination: a mutually agreed to ending of formal sessions, usually according to contract, with summary evaluation and further referral as appropriate.

BACKGROUND

"Monique," then in her late 20s, was referred for therapy by the second author after an intake appointment in the campus counseling center. The therapist, a former director of that agency, had moved to a faculty position, was in part-time private practice, and frequently saw referrals for assistance with grief work. Thus, it was felt to be an appropriate referral by all parties, including the client's private health insurer. She was referred explicitly for assistance with bereavement following her brother's recent death from cancer.

At the time of the initial appointment, Monique was on extended leave from her graduate program beginning in the middle of the semester a year before, to become the care provider for her older brother, a colon cancer patient. He had died a month before she sought therapy. At intake, she expressed her desire to come to terms with his illness and her loss, especially since she had played such a key role in his care as he was dying. She also wanted to successfully re-engage in school, finish her doctorate, and gain clarity about her relationship with the rest of her family, particularly her mother. Over the course of her caregiving, she had struggled with various other issues, including a complicated relationship with her mother, the influences of two different cultures, and past sexual abuses perpetrated by this brother.

Monique is the fourth of five children born to married parents. At the age of 7, she, her three older brothers, her younger sister and her mother came to the United States as refugees from an Asian country. Her father had remained behind to manage the family business, with plans to meet with his family at a later date. But he was captured and placed in prison. After many failed attempts to escape the communist regime, he finally reunited with his family. She described a life of luxury and high socioeconomic status in her country of origin, which not only helped to expedite their exodus, but eased their resettlement in the U.S., although they still had many obstacles to overcome. As the only refugees in their new residential area, the isolation from other family and a social support network reinforced a strong bond between the siblings, as they had to rely on each other while growing up in a new country.

According to Monique, the parents' traditional arranged marriage was miserable for both parties from the start and included violence, infidelity, and lack of love. A few months after the father reunited with the family, the parents' pre-existing irreconcilable differences led to their separation. The children stayed with the mother while the father went on his own. The separation may have been fueled by the differing degrees of the parents' acculturation. Though the parents were living together at the time of our therapy, there had been many years of living apart, and divorce had been avoided only because of cultural pressures to value and preserve the family. Their son's loss led to additional stressors which apparently brought them to a breaking point and they ultimately divorced seven months after the start of Monique's therapy.

Monique's mother was a central figure mentioned in practically every session. She described her mother as a fiercely independent woman who singly raised her five children and saw them all through college in a foreign country where she spoke minimal English. The mother was limited to an 8th grade education in her own country as a direct result of the war there. Monique depicted her mother is a strong and hard-working woman who took great pride in her children, instilling a sense of duty toward the family and the value of education as a means to excel and be successful in life. The children were greatly pressured to perform well in school. Mother felt that the only thing that could not be taken away was education, the direct and sole means for the family to regain their prior status. After venturing into two small businesses after resettlement, she exemplified this value when she went back to school in her 50s after a 30-year hiatus, and earned a degree. All five children graduated with bachelors' degrees, four have master's degrees and three of them are pursuing doctoral degrees. All the while, each helped one another financially, giving evidence of the strong cultural influences of collectivism in this family.

At the time of the brother's diagnosis, he was living in the Midwest. He endured the early phases of what quickly became an untreatable and terminal malignancy (cancer of the colon). Monique was the first to be notified of her brother's condition, the first to offer her time and to devote her care to his well-being. However, her decision to do so was met with internal resistance. The cultural values instilled in her now posed a dilemma. As the eldest daughter, the birth order played an important role in family and cultural expectations, adding to her sense of duty to be a primary caregiver for her brother. Thus, she experienced cognitive dissonance about whether she should remain in school to tend to her own goals (individualism) and honor her mother's emphasis on education (loyalty) or take care of her brother to fulfill her duty to her family and her need to belong to her collective (collectivism). On the other hand, the core to her personality was a nurturing trait evident in other family situations. As the brother's health deteriorated rapidly and treatment became more aggressive, he was moved to New England so that the client and other family members could more easily provide for his care. The mother, who was living in the South, quit her job as computer programmer and relocated to the Northeast to assist in the caregiving.

TREATMENT

The therapy comprised 14 sessions spanning 8 months, including intervals for travel she frequently undertook for family occasions and to be with friends. A more detailed session-by-session narrative of the progress of treatment will follow presentation of the major dynamics and focal issues of treatment beginning with a description of uniquely complicating variables in this case.

COMPLICATIONS TO MOURNING

As noted earlier, at the time Monique was referred by the intake counselor at her campus counseling center, she was on a leave of absence to catch up on school work accumulated over the two years when she provided for her older brother during his fatal illness. Her brother had died just one month before she presented for treatment. In the fifth session, she disclosed that her brother had sexually victimized her during junior high school. Although she had addressed her sexual abuse history in previous therapy with other therapists, this history now complicated her bereavement. The intimate care she gave during his deterioration was difficult in itself, as it would have been for any caregiver, and was made even more difficult by the existing perpetrator-victim dynamic. She was forced to face and resolve an old issue in a new situation with the roles reversed in that he had become powerless. Not only was there no ready opportunity to confront his wrongdoing, but she felt she could not get angry at a dying man, thus forcing the matter to be left unresolved. Still, her deliberate choice to be there for him was a powerful way of coming to terms with the ordeal of abuse because it was opportune to play out a situation in which he was vulnerable and she was in control. The process was all the more empowering for her because it gave her control over her reactions, and allowed her some choice in how she would try to resolve her ambivalent feelings (Rando, 1999). Also, she was able to avoid two potentially negative outcomes: she was relieved of having to identify the perpetrator of her victimization, and she did not have to break cultural taboos by disclosing the abuse to her family. To Monique's knowledge, her mother remained unaware of the incest.

Further complicating the period of care giving was an ongoing conflicted relationship with her mother. Like her daughter, mother had left her job to be a caregiver. The dynamics between the client and her mother had posed many mutual challenges since their immigration to the United States. The friction between them was caused primarily by the conflicting role expectations mother and daughter had for each other, resulting mostly from their differing levels and rates of acculturation. For example, Monique was often accused by mother of being too westernized, while mother was accused by Monique of being too traditional. While the daughter was yearning for a more egalitarian relationship with her mother, the mother felt that her daughter lacked the honor and respect owed to her authority as the parent. In addition, their discordant acculturation experiences posed conflict for the type of care they thought best for the brother. Monique put much effort into researching the full gamut of treatment options available for her brother and was cognizant of her bias toward more scientifically based ones, as she was trained in a Western scientific approach while her mother had a strong preference for the Eastern approaches. Although Monique's brother ultimately made his own decision about treatment choice, mother not only objected to the client's presentation of treatment options to her brother, but blamed her for the unsuccessful treatment outcomes and her brother's failing health. Further, their patriarchal culture, which valued males over females, challenged Monique. As she became acculturated much more quickly than her mother, she felt devalued and unloved by her mother.

In addition, there was the underlying issue of mother's lack of protection against the sexual abuse. As is common in such cases, Monique was more angry with her mother than her brother for the abuse (Courtois, 1995). Worse, each time her mother questioned her intent or quality of caregiving, Monique's feelings were minimized and she felt invalidated. Unbeknownst to her mother, each of those attacks felt like a revictimization in terms of Monique's earlier incest trauma. Yet, she did not feel that she could ever disclose the past to her mother. Given the importance of the gender hierarchy which valued males over females, Monique did not trust that her mother would believe her story or support her. As hard as it often is to disclose such a history in our culture, it seemed harder in her culture to disclose and to expect support and understanding. Though she and her mother had come to some limited understanding and rapprochement of their differences by the time of her brother's illness, their peace depended mainly on their geographic distance as mother resided in the South and Monique had moved to the Northeast. Therefore, the sudden change in proximity forced them once again to deal with their difficult relationship, this time in the context of an already loaded and tense situation.

In the current case, with Monique becoming a therapist herself, it was a simultaneous learning metaprocess and a therapeutic alliance. She came to use the time variables aptly and creatively, offering suggestions throughout for modification of sessions within the bounds of the brief treatment model. The contract became a 14-session process, and, as noted above, used all three temporal variables flexibly and well.

With a bereavement problem, brief treatment is often a very fitting template. Only a small minority of grievers ever seek professional help, and when they do, it's usually because of a poor or nonexistent social support system or a traumatic complication from the relationship or the manner of dying, or a combination (Rando, 1999). While the grief process following death is never really short-term, the intensity and nature of mourning in particular are most intensely troubling within the first year in most cases. Thus, this case was a good conjunction of approach, problem, client, and provider in terms of characteristics each brought to treatment.

COURSE OF GRIEF

This model for viewing the process of grieving as a therapist recognizes that there is no single schema with empirical or widespread support. I look at the three time categories relative to onset of bereavement: the awareness of loss as Immediate (usually days at most); Intermediate (weeks to many months or even sometimes growing into a year or more); and Ultimate, a fitting label for what becomes a lifetime of living with the loss via memory. Associated with each, in turn, are the dominant states of early *Awareness,* yielding to *Adaptation* after the crisis period of realizing the physical loss has passed, and finally to a state of

Accommodation, a general label for the still unique way each griever comes to live with the loss in a less intense, frequent, and intrusive kind of encounter that characterizes the rest of life.

Further, the terms used throughout are often treated synonymously, although they refer to different dynamics. Bereavement is viewed here as the perception of loss. Grief is the constellation of responses to bereavement, comprising somatic and psychosocial aspects, and somewhat unique to the particular griever, yet also common in some ways to most bereaved people's responses. Finally, the term mourning is seen as grief gone public! That is, mourning is either the invitation to or allowance for sharing emotionally with others; it involves both private and public acts, as well as personally meaningful and culturally endorsed expressions and rituals.

A useful intervention for helping a bereaved person progress beyond the shock of the Immediate period, and the subsequent struggle to adapt to the deceased person's absence, is a trio of leading and focused questions adapted from Schneider (1994): What's been lost?; What remains?; and What's possible? These often recirculating questions can lead to useful perspectives for finding meaning and perhaps some acceptance in attempts to grieve privately and mourn publicly in beneficial ways. The first question addresses the reality that the psyche can only gradually embrace the impact of a death loss, doing so mostly by coming to terms with the secondary losses that accompany the loss of the actual physical person. It involves a thorough and repeated examination over time of the many role relationships and symbolic attachments the survivor had with the now dead loved one. The latter two questions refer to exploring what resources and viewpoints comprise the here and now of survivorship, to help the survivor to grapple with how to get on without the deceased. Rando (1993) argues that such a circumstance as Monique presented initially is not truly complicated mourning, as the accommodation of grief was not thwarted in any way. But the incest posed the question of how she could reconcile that with her other memories of and positive regard for her brother. Such meaning reconstruction usually requires a narrative, social constructivist approach to make sense of the loss, their unique co-histories, ultimately constructing a perspective to reside with about the dead person and the relationship (Neimeyer, 2000). This question is a frequently cited means to accommodate to a specific death loss, and it provided the main vehicle for Monique's grieving during treatment (Parkes, 1988; Attig, 1996).

CULTURAL COMPETENCE

Culturally competent caregiving in therapy requires recognition of and respect for the differences that clients bring to the treatment, taking into account an enormous number and range of variables and experiences. Awareness of differing cultural and familial customs, practices, beliefs and value systems is one of the most common and noteworthy aspects of the pervasively needed sensitivity. The great differences between the cultural experience of provider and client challenge every therapy dyad (Sue and Sue, 1990). Knowledge of the client's culture, which may require outside help or additional information, has become more necessary to ensuring competent care. In this case, a consultant was found to offer advice and understanding about some of the more salient and obvious elements of Monique's history and heritage as an Asian-born woman, fortunately the referring intake counselor from the university's counseling agency. The consultant provided invaluable information to help direct the therapist to understand Monique's origins and respond to her needs for grief and mourning. Key examples included the beliefs about family cohesion and values, and the roles of parents in the continuing lives of their children, even into adulthood.

THE THERAPY

The initial session held in late January was an abbreviated meeting (30 minutes) as there was a misunderstanding between us about the appointment time. Thus, the session was used simply to get some background information and hear her goals for therapy, using the model explained above. I asked her to come back prepared to tell me what a successful therapy for her in this case would feel like. We set a second meeting for two weeks later in accord with mutual availability.

She introduced the roles and significance of her mother for the first time in the second meeting, which went 75 minutes. Monique again related the story of her brother's illness and detailed somewhat his final hours, ending by noting her mother's reluctance to leave the bedside, and she introduced the significance of her often difficult relationship with her mother. A reconstructed excerpt from that session shows some of the dimensions of that difficult dynamic.

Monique: My mother is like no other. In many ways I have the utmost respect and admiration for her. She brought me out of a war-torn country and in turn, gave me the opportunities many others do not have, not even ones in this country. For that I'm eternally grateful. I am who I am today because of her. But that's a bittersweet statement because, on the other hand, she can cause me so much misery. Although she has inspired the many great qualities in my siblings and me that I'm proud to have, she also possesses others that are undesirable. She can be extremely negative and downright depressing.

T: So . . . you both appreciate her and find her a challenge.

Monique: Yeah, for example, I wonder what the world must have been like for her to grow up during two wars in our country. She lost her mother at 16 and had to then assume the maternal role for her six younger siblings. That could not have been easy. In essence, she has lost out on the unconditional love and encouragement that she needed and never had a role model to show her how to provide this. Given that, she hasn't done such a bad job . . . (pause) . . . But because of that her world is colored with so much loss, so much hurt and despair. This has made her fiercely independent, self-reliant, and strong. But also as a result, she is bitter, suspicious, and even paranoid. She trusts no one, not even herself. This has made it very hard for me to relate to her not just as a mother, but also as a person. It seems that her defense mechanisms are so deep-seated that there is little room to explore the ideal qualities for a healthier relationship between us.

T: It sounds like you really do want to see things improve between you despite all the struggles you two have.

Monique: Yes, but I'm not sure how that can happen.

The third session, two weeks later, was 50 minutes long. Monique was almost continually tearful as she began to relate to the secondary losses that accompanied his death, citing his significance in her life as an older brother, and recounting her pride in him and his abilities as a professional. An often telling characteristic of early grief present this session was her constant reference to the deceased brother in present tense terms. She offered several examples of how close they were in the past, as she spoke of the many things she'll not experience again with him gone. (Some asides about their mother were also noted in this session.) The next meeting was set for a week later.

In the fourth meeting, Monique spoke more of the goals for our sessions, of dealing with her mother's bothersomeness in her life, and her recent insomnia. She also sought my assessment of her progress (How am I doing?). We talked of her sadness at her brother's death at such an age, and she ended by telling me of a long-planned trip that would preclude another meeting for a month. We checked in with each other to insure that would be okay, and made an appointment for four weeks later. For that month's homework, I asked her to think about what other (secondary) losses she felt she sustained as a result of his death. My notes for this session, which ran 50 minutes, ended thus: "Wondering where her relationship with him got conflicted?, as there appeared to be a mixed presentation of nonverbals and statements while describing him."

A month later we met for 75 minutes. Monique began with a brief recounting of her trip, followed by a short discussion about anti-depressant medications (SSRIs in particular) and whether I thought they might be of some use to her. The question was more a curious one than a request from a needy depressed person, which I said I had not seen in our meetings to date. But by the end of this session, I was wondering aloud if she might benefit from pharmacological intervention should she share any major disclosure. In response to my wondering about possible conflict with her brother, she haltingly disclosed a two year history of somewhat regular sexual assault by him when she was in middle school and he was finishing high school. This also led to a short exchange about the role of her mother in her past and present life. We scheduled the next meeting for 50 minutes five days hence.

In our sixth meeting Monique led early discussion to her academic situation, talking of her motivation to return to full-time student status and finish her program. When I suggested she seemed not to want to talk about the relationship with her brother, she politely and tactfully shifted that talk to a consideration of some of the secondary losses she was feeling as a result of his death, including long-distance phone conversations, his commiseration about their mother, and his future absence from shared celebrations and holidays. The exchange below briefly notes our dialogue at this point. We were finally examining her recall of his abuses of her as we ran out of time, and she seemed relieved to have the reprieve.

T: It appears that you are reluctant to get back to the matter of your brother's sexual abuse of you in grade school.

Monique: Well, it's not something I like to talk about!

T: At all? With anyone? Ever?

Monique: Certainly not outside of my earlier therapy in college. And maybe with a few close friends.

T: Do you want to talk about it here?

Monique: I'm not sure . . . I suppose so . . . I probably should.

T: Has it been more difficult to think about since his cancer and death?

Monique: Only somewhat. Maybe in that we never did talk about it since he left home when I was entering high school. And we didn't actually talk about it before. No one in the family knows . . . I don't think?!

T: And now you two never will?

Monique: I couldn't do it while he was lying there dying!

The seventh meeting, scheduled for a week later, was re-set due to her delay in returning to the state from a short out-of-town trip, finally taking place for 50 minutes two weeks later instead of the one week as originally planned. It centered on further addressing what Monique needed for herself in relation to her brother, and included questions about whether his death equated with escape, as well the issue of forgiveness. It ended with conversation about how she felt about him as a person at this time.

Our eighth session for 90 minutes was a week later. It was an especially good one for her with clarification of some sources of feelings of guilt and shame, emotional conflict with her mother and within herself. She was clearer than ever this time about her goals for the balance of treatment and what she needed to accomplish them. She reported beginning a course of Zoloft from a physician friend just the day before, so we talked briefly at the end of the session about the medication and its side-effect profile.

Our ninth session, two weeks later, contrasted with the productivity of the previous one. Monique spent the first 40 (of 50) minutes studiously avoiding–dancing I suggested to her–finally stating that she had been very nervous anticipating the session, and had almost cancelled it. She was relieved to have been able to not deal with her past this evening. We talked at the close about the course of grieving, about how she might still be sorting out what she was grieving over, and that perhaps for whom was not so clear either. She reported feeling a bit better but also said she felt disappointed at the mostly unremarkable effects at this stage of SSRI (Zoloft) treatment. However, her behavior in the interview might have indicated that the medication was having more of an impact than she was disclosing.

The tenth meeting was a 75-minute session two weeks later. Monique briefly mentioned feeling okay about how things were left with her brother and their history and wanted to talk mostly of her family, her parents' relationship, and prospects for improving relations with her mother. At this point, she truly seemed reconciled both to her brother's death and the fatal status of the incest history, vowing again that she was not ever likely to relate it to anyone else in the family, especially her parents. I introduced the likelihood that her sister had also been abused. Monique had thought of this before and had concluded that her sister had not been sexually abused by this brother; she upheld her belief and did not wish to bring up the possibility with her sister.

In our eleventh session, a 30-minute meeting, she talked about the medication and what else was needed to accomplish her therapy goals. She was mostly future-focused, on school, an upcoming family wedding, and the prospect of meeting a promising potential date in the forefront of her thinking.

Our twelfth session was 50-minutes a month later after she had been away for most of the interval. She spoke of the wedding, her mother and father, and their plans to divorce (finally) and, for the second straight session, seemed to be dealing mostly with Schneider's (1994) question about what seemed possible for her near future.

Meeting 13, a week later, was another 50-minute session and had all the earmarks of a penultimate session. She reported feeling great, better than ever in recent memory, Monique attributed it to a combination of talk, pharmaceutical therapy, and a seemingly reliable improvement in how her mother and siblings were treating her of late. She characterized their behavior as more respectful, caring, and acknowledging of her maturity and independence than in the past. We set another meeting for two weeks later and began to talk of terminating treatment with a "doorknob disclosure" by her of an interest in talking about her relationships with men and how the sexual abuse has affected these relationships.

That session was delayed another week as she called apologetically from an hour away, just an hour before the scheduled appointment, to report a car breakdown. When we met for a final 50-minute session, we talked briefly about her past and future male relationships, then quickly moved from that topic at her query as to whether this was a good point to end. She said she felt very good about herself, her accommodation of grief over her brother's loss, and the childhood incest, and even about her mother's regard and treatment of her these days. I felt that the grief work was mostly done for now, and she was functioning at the best level in all our time together. So, termination seemed both appropriate and timely. We agreed to stop here, mutually evaluating the worth of the work and describing the changes we noted relative to our therapy goals at the outset.

EPILOGUE

At termination, Monique appeared to be doing well in regard to the issues for which she entered therapy. It is evident that the personal growth that occurred during the process of her complicated grief is being maintained. Our sessions provided a safe and supportive place for her to discern the differences between parts of her which are clearly influenced by her culture and other parts which clearly are her own personality traits. Monique realized that the differences were often subtle because her identity is inclusive of all her influences and all those differing parts of her. Our interaction was the process through which she finally accepted grieving her brother's death, and resigned herself to a history of sexual abuse by her brother and the difficult relationship with her mother, and lastly, her identification with two cultures. She recognized that she is a participant in a life-long process which will continue to challenge her beliefs and affect her actions. Monique expected that the individual vs. the collective values dynamics will constantly play a role in her decisions as she will likely always struggle more than most people with the question of whether to meet her own needs or the needs of others.

One year after termination Monique returned for two sessions to address a dilemma involving another sibling. She was once again faced with compromising her schoolwork by taking an additional year to complete her program in order to allow her to help her sister. During one of those final encounters, she said that the cycle of healing begun during the course of therapy had continued to help foster her self-awareness and a sense of identity within the two cultures she lives in simultaneously. She said the meaning she has found was both profound and pervasive throughout her daily life.

Meanwhile, the family continued to acknowledge the loss of one of their members and to recognize their unity. Foreseeing the third anniversary of her brother's death, the mother asked the surviving siblings to meet for a first memorial reunion to be celebrated on two dates–one representing the Western Gregorian calendar, and the other four days earlier representing the Eastern lunar calendar.

QUESTIONS

1. *Can you discuss your rationale for determining the different session lengths?*

The primary reasons for the lengths of the sessions–aside from the first late arrival–were the nature of the sessions anticipated focus, and the client's emotional state. As noted above (first paragraph under Temporal Aspects), the model calls for flexible time allocations, and I often saw Monique last in the day, or intentionally left space between her's and the next appointment to accommodate that need; thus, the four extraordinarily long sessions. The one other abbreviated session was a mutual decision to end at thirty minutes, after discussing briefly the anti-depressant's impact and side effects, as she was feeling good at that time, and her focus was very much on the immediate future trip.

2. *The client avoided discussion of the sexual abuse by her brother during the sixth session. It looks as if the only time she processed this was in the seventh session. She went on to other issues in session 8. She seems to have dealt with the effects of this abuse on her grieving process very quickly.*

We actually did talk more about it, in the ninth and tenth sessions particularly. While I feared this issue would be a real impediment to her healing, it did not prove to be so for a pair of related reasons. The main one was that Monique had dealt with this topic more specifically with satisfactory outcome at least twice before in past therapy experiences. She also mentioned that she did not disclose the abuse there for some time either. The only sticking point for her at the time we met was the now terminated option to ever confront him and have a discussion about it as adults. She quickly showed her pragmatic side, and seemed readily resigned to that in light of his death. Further, all her affective cues showed a calm firmness about her renewed decision not to risk harming his memory and possibly her relationships with other family members by raising it with any of them. In that seventh session, I did talk about the prospect that her sister might have also been a victim, but she weighed that against the possible negatives she saw to raising it (mostly backlash from relatives, with whom she still had a living relationship), and again decided not to talk at all within the family about the abuse. Perhaps she was also trying by that decision to secure the more positive or favorable reminiscences she seemed to want to nurture about her brother in her own memory.

3. *You mentioned that you received consultation regarding the client's cultural background. Can you discuss how this worked? Was the client aware of it?*

That proved rather fortunate and simple at the same time, as the referring party was from similar ethnic and geographic origins, and Monique signed a release at the time of the referral for consultation regarding the case. We spoke throughout the treatment period about the specific ethnic issues involved, with her knowledge, particularly regarding her mother and the place of children in the family's cultural belief system.

4. *You mentioned the issue of forgiveness as a topic in session 7. Was the client able to forgive her brother and was this critical in helping her through the grieving process?*

Perhaps I did seem to give that short shrift in the session seven description. However, that was but a brief topic in our therapy, as Monique remarked openly and rather certainly about having forgiven him during the last few minutes of his life. She made a point to tell me of this thought at his bedside when the medical team was announcing his time of death. She said that without forgiveness she didn't feel she'd be able to move on, and she really wanted to. It's apparent to me that through forgiving him she greatly facilitated finding some easier peace with his loss and her grieving.

5. *How did the client-counselor relationship affect the brevity in this case? Can you comment on how the relationship developed, considering the cultural differences between you and her?*

Early on, Monique stated that she had considered looking for an Asian therapist, but realized that finding a respectful good listener with willingness to learn was more important! I also believe that her own training background aided our building a connection quickly and well, just as her own prior medical experience helped her negotiate that cultural world during her brother's illness. Also, given the way I work in this model, the client knows up front how we will proceed regarding matters of time and co-ownership of the treatment and its nuances. Monique often asked me both appropriate process and even good metaprocess questions (the query behind the answer to why) throughout our time together. It was truly a good working alliance characterized by give-and-take transactions.

REFERENCES

Attig, T. (1996). *How we grieve.* New York: Oxford University Press

Burlingame, G. M., & Fuhriman, A. (1987). Conceptualizing short-term treatment: A comparative review. *The Counseling Psychologist, 15,* 557-595.

Courtois, C. A. Assessment and Diagnosis. In Classen, C. (Ed.) (1995). *Treating women molested in childhood.* San Francisco: Jossey-Bass.

Niemeyer, R. A. (2000). *Lessons of loss: A guide to coping.* Keystone Hts, FL: PsychoEducational Resources.

Parkes, C. M. (1988). Bereavement as a psycho-social transition. *Journal of Social Issues, 44*: 53-65.

Rando, T. A. (1993). *Treatment of complicated mourning.* Champaign, IL: Research Press.

Rando, T. A. (1999). *Clinical dimensions of anticipatory mourning.* Champaign, IL: Research Press.

Schneider, J. M. (1994). *Finding my way.* Colfax, WI: Seasons Press.

Stroebe, M. S. (1994). Coping with bereavement: A review of the grief work hypothesis. *Omega, 26*: 19-42.

Sue, D. W., & Sue, D. (1990). *Counseling the culturally different: Theory and practice.* New York: Wiley.

Chapter 12:
A Runner's Journey

Dennis Heitzmann

SUMMARY. This case study illustrates the value of intermittent, brief psychotherapy applied over an extended period of time. The client, an undergraduate student athlete, presented with issues related to her athletic performance, claiming to "have lost my focus and desire." Underlying that concern, however, were a host of other clinical concerns, including unresolved grief, family issues, individuation, and eating disordered behavior. The following case study traces the course of treatment while demonstrating the value of a staged pattern of therapeutic encounters. *[Article copies available for a fee from The Haworth Document Delivery Service: 1-800-342-9678. E-mail address: <getinfo@haworthpressinc.com> Website: <http://www.HaworthPress.com> © 2002 by The Haworth Press, Inc. All rights reserved.]*

KEYWORDS. Brief therapy, intermittent psychotherapy, sports psychology, eating disorders

During my initial semester as a student at Loyola University in Chicago I aced a psychology midterm exam. As a first generation college student I knew nothing about psychology but figured that 50 out of 50

Address correspondence to: Dennis Heitzmann, Center for Counseling and Psychological Services, Penn State University, 217 Ritenour Building, Penn State University, University Park, PA 16802-4601 (Email: deh8@psu.edu).

[Haworth co-indexing entry note]: "Chapter 12: A Runner's Journey." Heitzmann, Dennis. Co-published simultaneously in *Journal of College Student Psychotherapy* (The Haworth Press, Inc.) Vol. 16, No. 3/4, 2002, pp. 191-207; and: *Case Book of Brief Psychotherapy with College Students* (ed: Stewart E. Cooper, James Archer, Jr., and Leighton C. Whitaker) The Haworth Press, Inc., 2002, pp. 191-207. Single or multiple copies of this article are available for a fee from The Haworth Document Delivery Service [1-800-342-9678, 9:00 a.m. - 5:00 p.m. (EST). E-mail address: getinfo@haworthpressinc.com].

on any test must portend success. As a result, English Literature was relegated to the minor study and Psychology became the major. It proved to be a good fit.

For one whose family tradition emphasized the practical, the academic side of psychology proved to be more difficult to inculcate. I studied it and taught it at the graduate level, but theories of psychotherapy did not become really meaningful to me until years after I had gone into practice. In re-reading the literature from a more experienced practitioner's perspective, I discovered that what I did as a therapist coincided rather neatly with the cognitively based approaches with which I had become familiar. At present I am confident that theory is embedded in my practice without consciously being aware of it in the therapeutic moment. On the other hand, I continue to believe that my exposure to literature and creative writing has as much to do with my understanding and skill as a psychotherapist as did any psychology coursework. Perhaps that is why Moustakas and Wheelis, while relatively unknown, to me share the limelight with the "names" in our profession. Perhaps that is why reading Conrad, Merton, J. M. Coetzee, Alice Walker, Neruda, Gunther, and lately Anna Quindlen energize and inspire me. How could one not be forever deepened by radiantly human fiction such as *Charly, Of Mice and Men, The Heart Is a Lonely Hunter, Cry, the Beloved Country,* and *A Tree Grows in Brooklyn*, to name just a few.

Finally, I have had no ambivalence about my interest in sports and in working with student athletes. Athletics played an important part of my early development and remains my acceptable way to sublimate aggressive impulses! An avid racquetball player and inveterate runner, I cannot imagine life without sweat or the feeling of exhilaration in the aftermath of a long (now) slow run. Naturally then, I am drawn toward working with student athletes, one of whom is the focus of the case study which follows.

INTRODUCTION

Years ago, as incoming president of the American Psychological Association, Nicholas Cummings foretold the future of psychotherapy by espousing what was then known as "intermittent psychotherapy throughout the life cycle" (Cummings, 1988). In essence, Cummings posited that psychotherapy is best applied to the greatest number of consumers by adopting a "therapy as needed" approach, recognizing that most consumers would profit from an occasional limited course of therapy to do focused work on significant but circumscribed problems.

What seemed to make sense at the time as reasonable treatment has become the norm in today's managed care market place, where the emphasis on "effective" is modified by "cost efficient." Fortuitously, this rationale for treatment is particularly cogent in view of the limitations placed upon our current college mental health practice by economic constraints and staffing limitations. Moreover, in working with university students it is also fair to say that many have neither need nor desire for lengthy uninterrupted treatment designed to evoke a "cure" or fundamental personality change. In the main, what is more likely to succeed in this population is the approach embraced by most university mental health facilities: that is, brief treatment followed (if necessary) by intermittent contacts designed to resolve circumscribed problems efficiently and/or to reinforce or extend moderate personal change, growth (or correction) and development. The course of treatment with the current client, Ariana, follows this modality and may serve as one example of how brief treatment applied intermittently throughout the course of an extended period of one's life may yield positive and enduring results.

THE RUNNER

On a flat road runs the well-train'd runner,
He is lean and sinewy with muscular legs,
He is thinly clothed, he leans forward as he runs,
With lightly closed fists and arms partially rais'd.

–Walt Whitman, *Leaves of Grass*

DIAGNOSIS AND BACKGROUND

On the surface, and using standard clinical parlance, Ariana at first contact presented the following profile:

AXIS I: 309.0 Adjustment Disorder with Depressed Mood

AXIS II: 799.9 Diagnosis Deferred

AXIS III: No Attending Physical Problems

AXIS IV: Problems with Primary Support Group/Other
           Psychosocial and Environmental Problems

AXIS V: Current Function, 65 Highest in last year, 75

Ariana was referred to me by the university's athletic team physician, the usual gatekeeper for student athletes in psychological distress who would profit from consultation with the university's Center for Counseling and Psychological Services. Her intake self report indicated significant depression and sadness, guilt, feeling self critical or worthless, with attendant weight/body image problems. Her self description to an open ended question revealed a narrowness and singularity of identity as a student athlete that would prove to be the key focal point for brief intermittent treatment: "As an athlete I feel that I have lost my focus and desire. I would like to regain that." Affirmative responses on the Beck Depression Inventory indicated sadness, discouragement, anhedonia, guilt, self-loathing and believing "that I look ugly." Ariana was referred to me after intake, where it became clear after a few meetings that her preliminary diagnosis needed to be revised to 300.4 Dysthymic Disorder on AXIS IA and 307.1 Bulimia Nervosa on AXIS IB. But she was more than that.

Beyond that clinical profile was a hurting young woman with a desperate need to find herself. Not unlike other student athletes with whom I have worked, Ariana was personally defined by her sport, fixed on determining her worth by the speed with which her legs would carry her around a track or across a meadow. Whereas running in and of itself is a healthy, well researched method for optimizing one's physical and emotional well-being, at the extreme it may serve as a way to run from one's self as well as real problems in living. As a distance runner Ariana was expected to put in long hours of running, still curiously referred to as "practice" though really more an exercise in endurance, diligence, time and energy. For competitive runners, the running formula translates not only to conditioning but also to a pursuit of the lean body, whippet-like, raw and sinewy. At the extreme, and for an unfortunate few, it becomes a neurotic pursuit of thinness, with a loss of essential body fat to dangerous limits, jeopardizing not only one's health but also one's very life. For the latter group there is a misguided, oversimplified formula: if loss of weight leaves less to move, it stands to reason that less weight equals more speed. Ariana took a long time to fully disclose the pervasive quality of her eating disorder. Coupled with that was the absence of an awareness of whom she was outside of being an athlete. In metaphorical terms, Ariana the runner, in the course of brief therapy, found a way to continue to run relentlessly, diligently, but with a new purpose, until she found herself.

TREATMENT RATIONALE

The eating disorder literature consistently emphasizes that eating disorder clients suffer from low self-esteem (Heatherton, T. F., & Baumeister, R. F., 1991; Hirschmann, J. R., & Munter, C. H., 1997; Polivy, J., Heatherton, T. F., & Herman, C. P., 1988). When an individual perceives herself to be efficacious in tasks or situations that she values highly, she generally feels a sense of competence and thus experiences a more positive level of self-esteem. However, repeated failed efforts to control behavior only reinforce a bulimic's perceived inadequacies. To an athlete in particular, ineffectiveness in any sphere keeps one trapped in a cycle of effort followed by failure, followed by the lowering of one's self-esteem.

In Ariana's case, the emergence of her bulimic behavior was symptomatic of a person feeling flawed, unworthy and unable to cope with her larger self in an uncontrolled world outside of the athletic arena. The initial goal in working with her was to reduce symptoms while laying the groundwork for a revised view of her core identity. Whereas Fairburn's (1985) cognitive behavioral treatment was pursued to alleviate eating disordered behavior, integral to the sessions and intertwined with the cognitive behavioral treatment was an effort designed to give Ariana an opportunity to foster the development of her emergent self.

IDENTIFYING INFORMATION

Ariana was a 19-year-old, single, white, female sophomore majoring in nutrition with a current grade point average of 2.85. She was a long-distance runner on the university's track and cross-country teams. In addition to the team physician, she was seeing the university's sports psychologist to deal with performance related issues. Since Ariana was considering withdrawing from school and returning home, she was referred to psychological services to deal with her emotional and depressive symptoms, before she made a decision about withdrawal. She had not told anyone of her bulimic behavior.

BEHAVIORAL OBSERVATIONS

Ariana was dressed in sports attire with her hair pulled back tightly into a ponytail. She seemed moderately anxious throughout the intake interview but was able to establish and maintain rapport throughout the session. She averted her eyes through most of the session and displayed little emotion. Though not particularly expressive, she did expand on her answers when encouraged to do so.

PRESENTING CONCERNS

Ariana acknowledged that she was very depressed at the time (Beck Depression Inventory total score = 28). She described herself as unattractive, even ugly, and was discouraged with her performance on the cross-country team. While recounting her history, she focused on her running career, which began about age ten when she began to train and compete. She was viewed as a premiere runner, and in her freshman year in college she competed internationally as a member of an elite team. Unfortunately, an injury to her foot that spring precipitated an emotional slide and depression. She became discouraged when her injury kept her from practicing and took away a lot of her energy for competition. As a result she would not be going to the national competitions in her sophomore year, and she felt she was in a rut. She was able to indicate that dissatisfaction with running was "not all that was going on with me" but did not choose to elaborate. Ariana alluded vaguely to the possibility of having an eating disorder when stressed. She talked of eating "an extra bagel or an extra bowl of cereal, which makes me further depressed and angry." She was trying to lose five pounds in the belief that she would then be able to run faster. Her then current weight was 115 at a height of 5'6". It was clear from her statements that running cross-country has been her mainstay and primary focus, and several times she described the cross-country team as "my family." Since she was on a full scholarship for four years, she felt some pressure to perform in cross-country and track, though her parents told her she could quit running if she wanted to, and they will find a way to pay for college, but it did not appear that Ariana took their offer very seriously. She had friends on the team but had difficulty sharing deeper feelings with them in accordance with her general difficulty of opening up to others and letting go of control.

FAMILY HISTORY

Ariana, the youngest child in a large family, had an older brother who died when she was 12 years old, "from a fall from a tree or perhaps there was a piece of machinery involved." Her lack of certainty about this important detail suggested family quietness around the events of his death, a family dynamic that appeared to prevail in response to tragedy or emotional issues. She recalled feeling she had to be strong for her parents, and as a result she believed that she did not work through her brother's death adequately. When people at school would mention her brother's name, Ariana would ignore them and work very hard not to think about him because memories of him made her very unhappy. Avoidance of feelings seemed to be paramount with Ariana as her way of staying in control so as to manage her rigorous activities, limited time and heavy load of athletics and academics. She described her family as a family of runners but added that she was running because she wanted to, not because she ever felt any pressure from her family. Of her many siblings, she is the only one who stayed with competitive running.

CLINICAL IMPRESSIONS

Clearly, Ariana was still experiencing pain subconsequent to the death of her brother and questions remained about whether she ever truly mourned his loss and put it into proper perspective. She seemed protective of her family and was intent on leaving the impression that her family life was happy and intact. Ariana appeared to equate "strong" with not showing emotion or crying and not sharing what was truly going on in her life. She relied on her running as a rallying point for determining who she was and her purpose in life. Thus, as a result of her athletic injury, she had considerable difficulty dealing with flagging self-esteem and distorted self-image, reflected in part by her excessive focus on perceived negative aspects of her body. In the absence of a firm basic source of self-esteem and self-image, she seemed open to looking deeper within herself but was wary and perhaps frightened of the affective side of her personality. She seemed quite lost in her depression at the time of our therapy and lacked insight into her depressed feelings.

DISPOSITION/TREATMENT PLAN

The focal points for Ariana's brief treatment would be to: (1) review emotional issues relative to her brother's death; (2) focus on the role running has played in her life and how its absence affects her self-esteem; (3) help her learn to be more expressive emotionally; (4) examine control issues; and (5) rule out an eating disorder. Topics covered in the early sessions of our initial work made it clear that Ariana would be likely to limit herself to dealing with discrete issues to be addressed in accord with her timetable. This expectation fit well with what ultimately became an intermittent course of treatment of circumscribed issues in the context of a developmentally based treatment plan.

PHASE ONE

Ariana was feeling the need to withdraw from school temporarily to reorient herself, reduce her stress and come to terms with her future. However, what she described as a happy, optimally functioning family was actually a family beset by several important conflicts. Though the family functioned well in general, there were discordant themes involving Ariana, her parents and others in the family. Consequently, it was important that the family dynamic to which she was returning be addressed so that her return home would be therapeutically useful and supportive of her goals. She opted not to discuss her problems with eating and remained unprepared to deal with them. After six sessions, Ariana withdrew from school and returned home where she expected to work and take classes in the evening. Prior to her departure we were able to explore the meaning of her brother's death and the family's failure to deal with it. We set an agenda for her to pursue while at home.

> Ariana: I feel as though I'm just getting started and already I'm leaving. I'm afraid that any progress I've made won't last until I return to school.
>
> T: Maybe there is some work for you to do at home that you wouldn't have been able to do here anyway.
>
> Ariana: You mean with my family?
>
> T: Yes. All of that unfinished business that you spoke of. You tell me that there are other things that you would like to work on eventually but it seems like you're telling me that this is the first order of business. Perhaps by dealing with those issues while you're home could be the platform to launch you into our next stage when you return.

Ariana: I'll think about it. I know it needs to be done but I don't know if I have the courage. Maybe it's just easier to leave it alone.

While at home, Ariana was able to address her brother's death directly with members of her family. It soon became apparent that others in the family also had continued to suffer silently in the wake of his death. Ariana felt good about the fact that she was able to bring these issues to the surface and was convinced that others, as well as she, had profited from discussing openly their sadness and anger over the loss of their son/brother. She remained at home for seven months working independently on issues related to her family, self-image and future.

PHASE TWO

On returning to the university in the fall, Ariana reported that our earlier work, combined with her independent efforts while at home, enabled her to bring covert family matters to the surface for all to see. The ensuing discussions helped the family to heal old wounds and collectively grieve the loss of her brother. She claimed that she was now "ready to leave the family," in a symbolic sense, having resolved key issues with them. She did admit, though, that some depression remained at varying levels while she was away from school, and that she remained unresolved in regard to her future and "who I am." At this juncture, however, what emerged in treatment was her sense of loss and depression over her failure to manage intercollegiate running and academic work. Moreover, competitive running and body image remained major concerns for her.

Early in this sequence, Ariana acknowledged for the first time that she had been anorectic with occasional episodes of bulimia. This admission was difficult and guilt producing for her, and she backed away from discussing it further. Furthermore, a stress fracture developed in her tibia and had curtailed her running. She claimed that, as a result, she put on twenty pounds over her weight the previous year and felt "fat and out of shape." She wanted to get back into running but realized that she could not do it to the extreme that she pursued previously. Ariana felt pressure from her coach who expected her to resume her running regimen quickly because, as her coach put it, "you are so mentally strong." She was intent on not returning too quickly, but needed to develop a rationale before she broached the issue with her coach.

At this juncture, Ariana began to discuss the possibility that she may have value as a person apart from being an athlete. She was motivated for treatment and evidenced little reticence, a change from her first course of treatment. The goal for this phase of treatment was to facilitate her efforts to solidify her healthy distancing from family while promoting her efforts to redefine herself as a person apart from athletics. As we focused on Ariana's efforts to resolve issues with her parents, she realized they played a more influential role in her development and current pursuits than she had thought. She was able to think more independently, pursue issues of conflict with her parents in a reasonable way, discuss her circumstances candidly with her coach, and lay out the long-term plans which reflected her agenda rather than the expectations of others for her.

By the end of this course of treatment (14 sessions), she began to experience greater ego strength, individuality and self-direction than at any other time in her life. Ariana continued to view herself as an athlete (which she was!) but recognized that this was too narrow and shallow a self-descriptor. She was now seeking out others who "relate to me as a person, not only as an athlete." One sister, in particular, gave consistent messages that she valued her more broadly.

> Ariana: You know I really got to know Kelly much better than ever before while I was at home. She seemed to pay much attention to me and always made me feel comfortable around her.
>
> T: And what was it that she did that allowed you to feel more comfortable?
>
> Ariana: Well, I know I said that I got to know her a lot better but maybe it was that she allowed herself to get to know me a lot better.
>
> T: That's an interesting twist Ariana. What does that mean to you?
>
> Ariana: Well, she just let me be me when I was with her. No strings attached, no expectations to be a certain way or do certain things . . . and she never really brought up my running (or failure at running!). She seemed more interested in all the rest of who I was and that was important to me.

T: Maybe Kelly saw that you were much, much more than that and wanted you to know what she really saw in you . . .

Our sessions were structured to crystallize the focal points in her current treatment, teasing out salient issues, strategizing methods for making change, and reinforcing her renewed view of herself. Concerns about her eating habits remained as a background issue since Ariana was not ready to address them with any intensity through this segment of treatment. It was becoming clear, however, that it was "on her agenda" and that in due time she would take on the effort required to modify her eating disordered behaviors. At the end of this second course of brief treatment, Ariana was content to exercise her newfound view of herself outside of treatment. We agreed that when she was ready, we would proceed with issues related to her eating disorder.

PHASE THREE

Bolstered by her earlier successes, Ariana did indeed return in the spring semester. She was now prepared to take on what she had been avoiding: her eating disordered behaviors. Interestingly enough, despite Ariana's difficulty in broaching her body image/eating disorder, the self image issues with which she had grappled heretofore served as a platform for what proved to be an expeditious effort to resolve her problems with eating. Nonetheless, her efforts to modify her eating disordered behavior moved along an upward slope with numerous setbacks typical in the treatment of eating disordered individuals. With much shame and guilt, she spoke of her longstanding history of body image problems going as far back as age 16 when she became obsessed with running and restricted eating. In a diary note to herself (which she shared with me) Ariana, as a 16-year-old high school junior, wrote the following:

> It was the summer before my freshman year (high school) when I realized I needed to lose weight. Of course, to many people being 5'6" and 125 lbs is not fat but to me it was. When winter came I really began to train. For a while I wouldn't eat all day. Then after I went running I would eat many peanut butter crackers. Eventually I made myself sick from this. I soon began a new diet. I would eat one half of an English muffin in the morning and one rice cake with very little peanut butter on it. Dinner would be approximately 200 to 300 calories or less. Most of the time I wouldn't eat dinner

and that is how I lost so much weight. For a while I was between 100 to 108 lbs at 5'6"–I felt good about my self . . . I even fit into a pair of 28" Guess Jeans. I loved those jeans. One day my jeans got stolen from my locker. I know that the cause of me gaining weight is not because my jeans were stolen but it seems as though my attitude, figure and everything else went downhill from there. I want, really want and need to lose weight.

Her desperation and restrictive focus obscured the many other issues that were spinning out of control in her life beginning at an early age. As a result of her earlier gains in treatment, and encouraged by her success, Ariana came to terms with some of the other compelling issues and experienced a better sense of control over her life, gaining the courage to pursue the correction of disordered eating patterns. She responded well to the cognitive behavioral treatment plan for bulimia originally outlined by Fairburn (1985). This plan included: (1) disrupting habit patterns; (2) introducing a pattern of regular eating; (3) providing information about physical consequences; (4) understanding the "function" of binge eating and self induced vomiting; and (5) enlisting the cooperation of friends and relatives. We made efforts to identify and modify thoughts, beliefs and values that had originally established and ultimately perpetuated the eating problem. Ariana began reducing her compulsion to exercise artificial control through disordered eating habits as she began to exert legitimate control over her many life challenges. By the end of treatment, she was able to go for lengthy periods of time without binge/purge episodes but recognized that she may have continuing challenges related to eating. The third phase of treatment lasted 12 sessions.

CONCLUSION OF THE THERAPY

After a lengthy hiatus from treatment Ariana returned for a few sessions prior to completing her studies. Approaching graduation after a protracted academic experience, she had secured a responsible, entry level position in medical sales, a fiancée with whom she was planning marriage, freedom from her anorectic and bulimic behaviors, and a sense of optimism about the future. She was pleased to have been named "Intern of the Year" by her academic college. She spoke of her new relationship with her parents as a "really loving relationship." Despite her success, however, she also expressed some uncertainty and mild trepidation about the future. She recognized that concerns around eating might continue for the foreseeable future and possibly for the rest of her life. Moreover, her insecurities and ability to value herself remain challenges. The intensity, focus and organizing qualities of her life as a premiere runner had not yet been completely replaced by anything she had found in her current life. While recognizing that broadening her view of herself is inherently good for living a full life, she still felt a sense of loss for what had been, what could have been, and what might have been a simpler though flawed formula for living her life. I reminded her that she will always be justified in laying claim to being an athlete but she now had a healthy view of its place in her life. She continued to run, not for time but for expression of self. What she learned in our brief series of sessions is that she has the capacity to live her life independently though she can always avail herself of professional counseling to streamline her processes of change and development in a more efficient manner. Having had a productive experience in this therapy, she may choose to engage in counseling in the future to continue the process of self-evaluation, insight and change.

DISCUSSION

Decades ago, psychiatrist Allen Wheelis (1970) spoke simply of emotional pain and the factors influencing change. His words remain influential in my practice. One passage may fit Ariana's plight at the beginning of therapy:

> Sometimes we suffer desperately, would do anything, try anything, but are lost, find no way. We cast about, distract ourselves, search, but find no connection between the misery we feel and the way we live. The pain comes from nowhere, gives no clue. Nothing has meaning; we become depressed. What to do? How to live? Something is wrong but we cannot imagine another way of living which would free us. (p. 138)

Wheelis admonishes us all to consider that the only appropriate goal for the therapist is to assist. At best, our goal as therapists should be to facilitate slight, subtle, often unnoticeable changes in action and behavior. Many clients report they are challenged to convey to friends and families what they have learned in therapy. What were the main insights? How does it work? Clients may not be able to produce an adequate answer, but they know at some more fundamental level that they are better able to thrive and not merely survive, to feel the emergence of the self they were meant to be. Most often change occurs over time through diligent and arduous effort. In therapy, it needs to be continually clear that the client is responsible for any change and fittingly so. It is the client who does the work and struggles with the dissonance slowly and often painfully. It is the client whose cumulative insights, efforts to change behavior, and force of will bring about the change.

I continue to be impressed by the young Arianas of my practice. If I have performed well in my efforts to facilitate change, I know that they have been better. Slowly, inexorably, and remarkably these young charges restore and renew not only themselves but their therapists as well with the immutable understanding that therapy works. Counseling, this "tech free" exchange, is a simple bringing together of two individuals with vested interests which can yield important changes in the revival (and often discovery!) of spirit and belief in one's self. The relationship remains the core of our "soft science." It contributed, I would like to believe, in no small way to the new view of herself that Ariana shared in the form of a framed manuscript bearing her original writing, that was delivered to me at the end of our work together. Elegant in its simplicity, meaningful to both of us, it read:

A RUNNER'S JOURNEY

Out in a world which seems so free
I search so far and near.
I've found a world that seems to be
Both full of courage and fear.
To be the best, that is my goal
What else is there to be?
Yet with this thought I lose my soul
For all eternity.
At first these feelings pull me through
This life I try to live.
I want a change, something new
So that I am able to give.
It won't be easy, but I must take
A road which seems to wind.
I'll take a chance, my heart may break
But strength is what I'll find.

In the end I'll love myself
And those who have stood by.
I'll always know that in this life
I must run before I fly!

QUESTIONS

1. *What was your rationale for focusing on family issues during the first phase of counseling?*

In order to open up Ariana to her feelings, it was important to address a number of unresolved issues, buried deeply within, that had gone unexpressed. In finding words for her pain and bringing deeply imbedded issues and feelings to the surface, Ariana became cognizant of the fact that it is safe and freeing to be emotionally expressive as an alternative to dealing with issues silently and alone. Accomplishing this provided the propellant to pursuing other agenda.

2. *This appeared to be an instance when leaving school was a beneficial experience. Did you encourage/support this decision?*

Yes, it was fairly clear from the beginning that Ariana was determined to leave to "get a fresh start." I chose to bridge to that desire rather than to resist it. It was important however that we send her away with an agenda to work on–family–so that upon her return the way was clear to address issues related to her identity and eating disorder.

3. *Individuation and identity development appear to be significant aspects of this case. There is little mention of the role that peer and romantic relationships played in identity development. Were these a factor?*

Yes, in particular since her primary peer group was her running cohorts, it played an enormous role of importance in the treatment. It was critical that Ariana develop contacts and establish relationships outside of her primary group as a way of establishing a more complete and rounded view of herself. This was often met with some confusion and occasionally even open hostility among her teammates, but the positive results of her efforts to extend her relationships outweighed the occasional loss or reduction of friendship from her original peer group. Romantic relationships were challenging to her but meaningful in that they allowed her an opportunity to express feeling states both positive and negative that were important to consider and assimilate in therapy. What was important was that she was truly feeling deeply and broadly for the first time in her life.

4. *How would you characterize your counseling approach in this case?*

My counseling orientation in working with Ariana would be best described as a hybrid of theoretical models. Fundamentally, my work with Ariana could be described as broadly psychodynamic. I like what Pinsker, Rosenthal and McCullough (1991) espoused, and it seemed to apply most closely to Ariana's therapeutic focus: change stems from learning and from identification with an accepting therapist. Change occurs not merely by discovering reasons for the existence of the behavior or feelings but rather as a consequence of better self-esteem and improved adaptive skills. Poor self-esteem is associated with helplessness and unwillingness to try new behaviors. Thus, efforts to form a healthy identity were operant throughout all phases of treatment. Second, elements of a cognitive behavioral approach were present in all phases of treatment and most directly applied when the eating disordered behavior was the focus of treatment. Third, since this treatment extended over four distinct phases of brief therapy, I reiterate the importance of Nicholas Cummings' considerations at the beginning of this chapter: intermittent psychotherapy works best, and indeed, is more enduring with certain clients. These clients' readiness to proceed and accept the responsibility for working towards change is critical. Finally, I would like to add the rather radical notion that, irrespective of one's claim to theoretical orientation, I believe that the most important thing one can offer a client is himself. To be truly present, to be complementary to any efforts pursued by the client, to be aligned with one's client is central to the stimulation of change and development. Suffice it say that when there was doubt as to method or manner, I typically went with my instincts informed by an understanding of theory. The very best, most effective therapists I have known have been persons first and theoreticians/technicians specialists second.

REFERENCES

Cummings, N. A. (1988). Emergence of the mental health complex: Adaptive and maladaptive responses. *Professional Psychology: Research and Practice*, *19*, 308-315.

Fairburn, C. G. (1985). Cognitive behavioral treatment for bulimia. In Garner, D. M. & Garfinkel, P. E. (eds.) *Handbook of psychotherapy for anorexia nervosa and bulimia* (pp. 160-192). New York: The Guilford Press.

Heatherton, T. F., & Baumeister, R. F. (1991). Binge eating as escape from self-aware-ness. *Psychological Bulletin,* 110 (pp. 86-108).

Hirschmann, J. R., & Munter, C. H. (1997). *When women stop hating their bodies.* New York: Fawcett Columbine.

Pinsker, H., Rosenthal, R., & McCullough, L. (1991). Dynamic supportive psycho-therapy. In P. Crits-Christoph & J. Barber (eds.), *Handbook of short-term dynamic psychotherapy* (pp. 220-247). New York: Basic Books.

Polivy, J., Heatherton, T. F., & Herman, C.P. (1988). Self-esteem, restraint, and eating behavior. *Journal of Abnormal Psychology, 97* (pp. 354-356).

Wheelis, A. (1970). *The Desert.* New York: Basic Books.

Chapter 13:
"I Am Trapped Inside
of Something That I Am Not":
The Case of Mary

Edward A. Delgado-Romero

SUMMARY. This case study illustrates a brief therapy experience of 15 sessions with developmental aspects. The client initially presented with vague problems and ambivalence toward beginning therapy. As the therapeutic relationship developed the client was able to work through issues regarding independence and individuation from her family of origin. Transcripts are provided. *[Article copies available for a fee from The Haworth Document Delivery Service: 1-800-342-9678. E-mail address: <getinfo@haworthpressinc.com> Website: <http://www.HaworthPress.com> © 2002 by The Haworth Press, Inc. All rights reserved.]*

KEYWORDS. Independence, individuation, development

I enjoy hearing and telling stories and, as a therapist, helping clients repair the stories of their lives. My story in psychology began with my

Address correspondence to: Edward A. Delgado-Romero, Counseling Center, PO Box 114100, Gainesville, FL 32611-4100 (Email: delgado@counsel.ufl.edu).

[Haworth co-indexing entry note]: "Chapter 13: 'I Am Trapped Inside of Something That I Am Not': The Case of Mary." Delgado-Romero, Edward A. Co-published simultaneously in *Journal of College Student Psychotherapy* (The Haworth Press, Inc.) Vol. 16, No. 3/4, 2002, pp. 209-224; and: *Case Book of Brief Psychotherapy with College Students* (ed: Stewart E. Cooper, James Archer, Jr., and Leighton C. Whitaker) The Haworth Press, Inc., 2002, pp. 209-224. Single or multiple copies of this article are available for a fee from The Haworth Document Delivery Service [1-800-342-9678, 9:00 a.m. - 5:00 p.m. (EST). E-mail address: getinfo@haworthpressinc.com].

experiences as a first generation American. My parents immigrated to the United States from Colombia, South America in 1965 and I was born in New York in 1966. I constantly struggled for a way to deal with the pressures of acculturation, the need for cultural pride and the reality of racism both from society (overt) and from within (internal) (Delgado-Romero, 1999). Creative writing and psychology courses helped me make sense of my experiences and I decided to become a psychologist. My first ventures into psychology were at an Attention Deficit Clinic and an inpatient Adolescent Sex Offenders Unit. Although I grew from these experiences, their emphasis on pathology took its toll on my spirit.

I was drawn to counseling psychology because of its emphasis on normal developmental issues and focus on the university population. College was a challenging time for me, and I could relate to the hope, excitement, pressure and challenges of the university population. I began my practicum training at the counseling center of the University of Notre Dame and have remained at college counseling centers ever since.

Theoretically, I describe myself as "eclectic." I find that I use the language and techniques of psychodynamic theory, object relations, interpersonal theory, and family systems theory in conceptualizing cases. The work of Teyber (1992) and his synthesis of the above-mentioned theoretical orientations with his Interpersonal Process Approach most accurately represent the theoretical approach I take. In graduate school, I also discovered narrative therapy (Howard, 1996; Parry & Doan, 1994) and multicultural therapy (see Sue & Sue, 1999). Both of these approaches helped me understand and work with clients from a perspective that felt natural. The work of Kaufman (1996) in the treatment of shame-based syndromes was an important influence on my work for the case discussed here, which represents one of my favorite therapy experiences. I learned a great deal about therapy and myself during the time I worked with Mary.

DESCRIPTION OF CLIENT

Mary was a 20-year-old Caucasian female senior majoring in psychology, self-referred. She was soft spoken, appeared younger than her age, dressed very casually, and wore braces. Mary placed great importance on being perceived as "nice." We met for 15 sessions.

PRESENTING PROBLEM

Mary identified her concerns as depression, with tiredness and lack of motivation to work. She had been having "gruesome" nightmares, in which she would die. This was the impetus for her to come into counseling. Mary hinted at issues with men and father figures and voiced a preference to work with a male counselor. Her initial presentation was very vague. The quotation that is the title of this case write up, "I am stuck inside of something that I am not," was the way she described her issues during session 9.

SOCIAL/CULTURAL HISTORY/ENVIRONMENTAL CONTEXT

Mary was an only child. She described having an "ideal" childhood until her family moved abroad when she was seven. In addition to having to deal with the culture shock of moving to a new country, Mary experienced significant family turmoil. Her mother found another woman's clothing in the house and asked Mary if the clothing belonged to her. Thus, it was discovered that her father was having an affair. Mary felt protective of her mother and became estranged from her father. Feeling guilty for turning Mary against her father, Mary's mother soon confessed that she too had previously had an affair. Mary felt confused, betrayed and dependent. Then, upon their return to the United States, when she was 12, Mary and her mother were victims of a robbery, and her mother experienced a significant extended illness and became depressed. At the same time her father withdrew emotionally from the family and began drinking. Mary then began a relationship with a man who became abusive.

ASSESSMENT/DIAGNOSIS

My assessment was that Mary had ruminative depression rooted in an internalized history of enmeshed family interactions. Her family inhibited emancipation by discouraging developmentally appropriate steps towards independence and autonomy. Therefore, Mary internalized these enmeshed templates of self-other relational units (the models she had for relationships) and had been unable to fully establish an independent, developmentally appropriate identity. She inhabited a world that was a vortex of obsessions and confusion about her identity, her past, her relationships and her future. Her unproductive rumination about her problems sapped her energy. Furthermore, she had difficulty utilizing her internal resources and controlling displaced anger. Her fear of abandonment and emancipation manifested itself in academic problems, relationship problems and depression.

COUNSELING GOALS/TREATMENT PLAN

Two main goals emerged through the assessment: first to help Mary become the source of her own self-esteem and establish a secure identity, with the ability to establish new, affirming self-other relationships. Second, to recapitulate and resolve ineffective and painful self-other relational patterns through a therapeutic and emotionally corrective relationship accommodating the polarities of separateness and relatedness. We accomplished this principally through identifying and working through challenges that arose in our counselor/client relationship.

COUNSELING PROCESS

My first objective was to help Mary clarify her problems. I had a clear sense in the initial sessions in December that Mary did not want to get started on her issues; that she would feel better if she could wait until the next semester to begin. Rather than push her to engage in issues, I fostered and supported her autonomy, giving her permission to address issues when she felt ready, a stance that contributed to building the therapeutic alliance. The following passage illustrates this process:

> T: It depends, if you want to deal with the present, then we'll deal with the present; if you want to deal with the past, then we'll deal with the past.
>
> Mary: Okay, and like how, I guess, I don't know you to answer this, I am going to a psychologist so this is silly, so I don't see how anyone can help me (laughs). You know? What are things that would help?
>
> T: What do you think?
>
> Mary: I have no idea.

T: No idea?

Mary: No clue, I know that there is something or else I wouldn't be here. (laughs). I think I need to deal with it sometime. You know, where before I was like this doesn't bother me. I think it's because it's kinda hard to help someone if you don't know them. You know? (laughs) um, does it take a while?

T: Yeah, it's an interaction, with some people we hit the ground running, with some people it takes a long time.

Mary: Okay.

T: Well, we only have the semester framework anyway. . . .

Mary: Well, maybe something you might need to know about me is that I tend to talk about my problems and ramble on but, generally, if I don't know somebody I talk about my problems in a way that is disconnected from my feelings, sometimes? It might be hard for you to tell how I really feel. I know I will have to tell you, but usually I let it all spill out to my Mom, it's harder for me, do you know what I mean, or I won't say what's on my mind.

T: What I hear you saying is that you have a tendency to kinda disconnect, that you can verbally say what you are feeling, but the feeling might not be there, and that's one of the things that you want both of us to watch.

Mary: Yeah, exactly because it takes me a little while to really warm up to people, to feel comfortable to do that. I guess.

T: Me too.

Mary: Okay. (laughs)

T: Some people are just like that, and for some people it takes a while, what I see us doing is negotiating, what's okay . . . what we are going to do.

Mary: Okay, it's probably better if we get started next semester don't you think? I feel like it would be (laugh). I am interested in my past, first . . .

T: I really think that people know when they are ready, I think if we were sitting here talking in October, and you said "well, maybe next semester," then I might say, " you know . . . "

Mary: (laughs).

T: But since it is almost finals week and stuff, and one of the things you came in saying is "I want to keep my mind clear for right now, and focus on this [finals]." I don't think we are collaborating to avoid the issue, I think what we are saying is that we are trying to negotiate a relationship so we can get started next semester and not feel like we have to do the "dance" again next semester.

Mary: Yeah, that's how I feel, it would be too broken up if we got started.

T: I respect that.

Mary: But I'm glad I came here, kind of like just coming helps, you know what I mean?

T: Yeah.

Even though I respect the ability of my clients to decide when they are ready to work on their issues, I second guessed myself during the break and wondered if Mary would return to counseling. She did return and was ready to work intensely. She began to clarify the underlying conflict, most of her energy centered on unresolved issues that stemmed from the move abroad. Alone and betrayed by her father's affair in a foreign country, Mary and her mother formed a cross-generational alliance that resulted in Mary becoming *parentified*; a role reversal occurred in which Mary met her mother's emotional needs rather than mother responding to Mary's needs, and they formed an alliance against her father. Mary was left feeling "special," yet profoundly inadequate. A strong bond was created with her mother at a developmental stage when Mary would normally have been moving toward independence.

This bond prevented Mary from exploring the local culture, as she feared the world outside of her family. Her fear remained with her even on her return to the United States, and she often looked selectively at events to confirm that the world outside of her family was dangerous. Because I had grown up the son of immigrants in a foreign country, I could certainly empathize with Mary's fear about the outside world. I, too, had been cautioned against joining the world outside of the family and consequently had conflicts over individuation, acculturation and autonomy.

When Mary's mother, perhaps fueled by her own guilt over Mary's intense anger at her father, told Mary of her own affair, Mary once again felt betrayed; she could not trust either parent. In response to this loss of trust and her "ideal family," Mary began to block out feelings of needing or wanting in order to avoid the pain of possible further loss. The subsequent robbery and mother's illness added the dynamic of losses feeling uncontrollable. Mary's defenses became more rigid as she felt increasingly helpless. She attempted to manage her anxiety through denial, substance use and passivity until the anxiety over her impending graduation (another emancipation conflict) began to amplify her fear that autonomy leads to abandonment. Perhaps as a consequence, Mary began to have "gruesome" nightmares centered on her death.

In therapy I encouraged her to locate, connect with and express her feelings, especially the angry ones toward her mother. Mary feared her own anger, and believed that if she expressed it she might explode in a fury of hither to repressed feeling and be abandoned. In an attempt to compensate for her angry feelings, Mary tried hard to be "nice," often through being stereotypically feminine, taking care of others through a denial of the self. Her niceness, however, was not always reciprocated, and others could not sense her pain in the same intuitive manner that she could sense their pain. As her anger escalated Mary became consumed with ruminative worrying in an attempt to control her feelings via an emotional paralysis. That is, she prevented herself from experiencing her emotions by unproductive worrying. I served to help Mary establish and utilize a safe and unconditional holding environment in which she could express these feelings without fear of my abandoning her.

However, Mary often looked to me as an "expert" who could fix her problems and she tried to prompt me to take responsibility for her actions and feelings, assuming autonomy would lead to abandonment, her central fear and "generic conflict." The generic conflict is what Teyber (1992) described as the main conflict that the client tries to resolve in successive relationships. The goal of therapy is to uncover, re-enact and work through this conflict. Instead of trying to save her, or making her defensive by shaming her for her needs and fears, I responded with process comments and encouraged a collaborative relationship. By responding in this new and safe way, I helped Mary resolve rather than reenact the original conflict in her family.

Mary described the "turning point" in her therapy as the day she re-vealed the secret of her abusive relationship. Due to her fear of aban-donment and betrayal, Mary had carefully chosen her romantic partner based almost exclusively on his loyalty. Therefore she gravitated to an individual whom she described as "suicidal but fiercely loyal." He eventually became violent with her. Mary's reaction was to sever all ties with him, but she began to gradually re-establish that relationship dur-ing the course of counseling, trying to stay "in control" of her ex-boy-friend. Mary was able to admit that her fear of revealing the secret of the abusive relationship was that I would force her to leave him, that my re-lationship with her was conditional on her compliance and that, again, "independence would lead to abandonment." This was another reenactment of the generic conflict. Here is a transcript that illustrates this process:

> Mary: . . . it's not good. I don't want to get back into him thinking I'm his girlfriend, so I want him to know the truth about every-thing, I don't want to feel trapped in my lies, because that's a very uncomfortable place to be
>
> T: Yes, sounds uncomfortable
>
> Mary: Feels really horrible, so I don't know . . . what do you think? (laughs)
>
> T: I'm not sure what you want me to tell you. Because I'm not sure how much it would be helpful to tell you that you are dysfunc-tional [a term she had used earlier in the session] or not, I'm here with you, I'm not really standing in judgment of you, so it's real hard for me to feel this um, push to like "tell me I'm okay" because I really don't feel like I'm in that position.
>
> Mary: Okay, if you thought I was being pretty destructive to my-self, would you step in and say "hey," or is that for me to find out? (laughs)
>
> T: Good question, so you are asking what's our relationship like. If you told me that you were in danger, or that you had gotten your-self in danger and were being self-destructive, or a victim of vio-lence, then I would reflect that and be real concerned, *real* concerned for you and I would let you know. Right now it seems

like you are making decisions and you are handling it, right now it looks like everything is going okay, seems real manageable, so I respect that. If you are asking me if I truly felt, from what you told me, that you were in danger would I say something, would I act alarmed? Yeah, I would.

Mary: Even if I couldn't see it?

T: Yeah, you are the one who tells me things, I don't have any special insight other than what you are telling me, so if you tell me, I'll say "This is what you are telling me." How did that feel about what I just said?

Mary: How did that feel?

T: Yeah, because you are asking directly, I'm not being real direct in terms of giving you a judgment of good or bad

Mary: I guess I'm confused, but I think I feel, I guess it makes me feel a little more confident about my decision . . .

T: What are you confused about?

Mary: Well, I guess, if it was an abusive relationship or it has the potential to be, I guess I don't understand why? Because in my eyes it is okay, what is going on right now.

T: Yes

Mary: I don't understand how it could be okay for me to have some sort of relationship with him, because, all you usually hear is "stay away," I guess I want to know if it's okay, if it is possible to learn to be functional together in a friendship? I don't know, I guess it surprises me that if, well, my mom and my friend Angie, they more reflect me, like you are doing actually.

T: Yes

Mary: I guess it surprises me that a counselor . . . that's why I was afraid to tell you all this, because I was afraid that a counselor would say, "Nope, stay away." Maybe not say it like that, and I would be open to that, but I'm surprised. . . .

T: Do you want me to tell you to stay away from him?

Mary: No (laughs), not at all.

T: Do you want me to tell you that what you are doing is okay?

Mary: Well, that would be nice (both laugh), I know it's hard for you because you only see what I tell you.

T: Yes

Mary: It's kinda hard to say if actions are right or wrong, but, I wonder what you think, you probably don't know enough to . . . don't know.

T: Yeah, I'm reflecting what you are giving me, there's some confusion. There are some really cool things about him [the ex-boyfriend] and then some of what draws you to him, you have a really good conceptualization that that is maybe not so healthy, and so that's what I'm getting from you, you're right, I don't have a special test to know if you are "messed up" [her term].

Mary: Do you think it's okay to. . . .

T: (laughs) Do I think it's okay?

Mary: (laughs) Like what I'm doing now, do you think that's okay, if things are functional now, this moment in time, do you think that's okay? (laughs)

T: I mean you are laughing, I'm wondering what that laughing is about when you ask me that question?

Mary: Because I know that you . . . , not that you don't want to give advice, but that you think that I'm the judge of my own actions, that I can decide basically? You are here to guide me and help me through that, so I don't think that you will answer when I ask you if what I am doing is okay.

T: Right

Mary: That's why I'm laughing. But it is a possibility! (laughs)

T: So you'd want to know anyway, so there is that *wanting to know*.

Mary: Yeah.

T: Yeah, I respect that, I mean you really want to know, get some sort of official opinion that you are messed up or that you are completely okay.

Mary: I guess there is no definitive answer.

My countertransference and caretaking of Mary surfaced in subtle ways. During supervision I had maintained that I was objective about the ex-boyfriend, yet it became obvious that I was not neutral and in fact had decided that he was a negative person. Mary picked up on my judgment, became confused and responded by asking me to be more directive. After processing the issue in supervision, I was able to interact without conveying any negative messages about the ex-boyfriend, and Mary responded by being more self-directed. Instead of conceptualizing Mary's dynamics independently of the counseling relationship, I was able through supervision to understand the reciprocal nature of our interactions.

A particularly cathartic experience in therapy occurred when we explored the extent to which Mary believed she was responsible for being abandoned. She had carried around a sadness and fear that she might be responsible for the problems in her life. Specifically, when mother discovered the clothing of the "other woman," she asked Mary if it was her clothing; Mary admitted to me that, intellectually, she understood that her mother *knew* the clothing was not hers. Yet Mary felt implicated in and responsible for her father's affair, and felt she could have "fixed" or prevented the marital problems if she had lied at that moment. Adding to the overwhelming sense of responsibility, she soon learned of her mother's affair. As an only child, Mary questioned her worth and ability to keep her parents together. Voicing this fear during therapy became a highly emotionally charged, productive catharsis. She had given voice to one of her deepest fears and had become able to express emotions that had been suppressed or repressed for years.

Addressing this aspect of self-blame is a difficult task in therapy. On the one hand, her unrelenting self-criticism and blame fueled her ruminative depression, but this "responsibility" also made her "special." Mary often felt like being responsible is *who she is,* and to give that up would lead to a destruction of the self. Therefore, I helped Mary organize her inner world by supporting and guiding her as she expressed and released her feelings and developed her cognitive abilities. In therapy it was my role to be nurturing, supportive and patient, yet also confronting and assertive. Thus I modeled unconditional assertive caring, which it seemed Mary began to internalize, allowing her to find and develop a core sense of herself as a person.

I saw my role as the "idealized parent" in this relationship, in that I provided the emotional connection that her mother provided and represented what Mary called the "masculine" (assertive, logical) characteristic that father withheld from her. She wanted me to solve her problems for her, yet would resent me and feel further invalidated if I did. Instead of solving her problems or being caught up in Mary's idealization of me, I worked with her to explore her reasons for not wanting to look within herself. When she was ready to look within herself, I was there to support, accept and validate her.

OUTCOME AND TERMINATION OF COUNSELING

We finished therapy as the semester ended. In our last sessions Mary found out that her parents were going to move abroad again for business, in an attempt to fix their relationship. They were literally returning to the "scene of the crime." Mary was invited to come with them, but she would have had to give up her last semester at school and her graduation. She worried about what would happen to her parents if they were left alone, yet felt some relief that they were trying to solve their problems without her. She reported that she was initially angry, then depressed, but at our last session announced that she had spent the weekend helping her parents pack their belongings. Mary had accepted their moving and had accepted her independence and autonomy. Although her parents were leaving the country, she did not feel abandoned.

DISCUSSION

I chose to present this case because the developmental issues were so striking. Becoming an individual while maintaining contact with family is a typical challenge for college students. For Mary the reality of approaching graduation, participating in an abusive relationship, and her parents' decision to live abroad again caused her to become confused and doubt her ability to cope with the consequences of autonomy. This case illustrated how a client can re-enact that conflict within the therapy relationship, and how therapy can provide a corrective experience through careful attention to the nature of the work alliance.

The brevity of this therapy relationship was due to several factors: pragmatic; intentional; and creative. Pragmatically, we had a semester framework to work with, and considering semester break and holidays, 15 weekly sessions fit naturally. I believe that university students are used to the intensity of the semester schedule, and are used to working within this framework.

I like to model an egalitarian decision-making model and to be clear about what I can and can't negotiate from the beginning of therapy. I set the expectation that therapy will occur over a specific time period and we negotiate how to spend that time. Further I make it a point to remind the client of the time frame we are working with at each appointment. I find that for many clients these reminders help them use their time intentionally.

Finally, Mary and I were aided by her willingness to be creative outside of therapy as well as in sessions. On my part, I agreed to expand the scope of our sessions to include her dreams, writings, poetry and drawings. For example, Mary drew me a picture of her family that was laden with psychological imagery, depicted herself as totally contained within her father and mother and with some lines of her mother intruding into Mary. Mother had a noticeable smile and the paper was worn with erasures around the smile; she explained "I drew my mother's face three times, I couldn't get her to look happy and dominant at the same time." I believe that Mary's willingness to share her creative expressions of her feelings helped move the therapy at an accelerated pace and illustrated how using the client's specific strengths and assets can be helpful.

QUESTIONS

1. *You mentioned that you identified with Mary as someone who had conflicts over individuation because of family dynamics. Did you share this information with Mary? How did it affect countertransference issues?*

I did not directly share this information with Mary. I value moderate self-disclosure as a valuable component in therapy, yet I decided against directly sharing this connection with Mary because I felt that she might feel that she had to take care of me rather than herself. Initially, she tended to overly defer to me as an "expert" and I was concerned that she might continue to focus on my experience rather than hers. In terms of countertransference, I was careful to monitor my feelings and expectations of how to handle the issue of individuation and individuality. I had dealt with my conflicts by leaving home and using school as a way to create psychological and physical space between my family and myself. I did not want to unduly influence Mary and imply that she should solve her problems in the same way. I find that therapeutic self-disclosure is an art I am still working on.

2. *Can you elaborate some on how Mary's drive toward autonomy led to her abandonment schema? Specifically, how did the events described with her parents lead her to conclude that, if she became independent, she would be abandoned?*

Mary's world was her parents; she was their only child and they raised her for her first seven years in a foreign land. These circumstances brought the family closer together, but not always in a healthy way. Problems between the parents were played out in their relationship with Mary, and she often felt she had to choose between her parents. When proof of an affair was discovered, Mary felt implicated and blamed, and feared that she might be abandoned. She formed an intense relationship with her mother that was based on anger toward her father, the classic family triangle. Mary believed that if she were independent or neutral, she would be abandoned. During this crisis Mary felt that she had very few choices and at that time in her life she may have been right. However, as things progressed and balance was restored to the family, Mary's mother realized that she had erred in allying with Mary (especially since Mary could not understand the subtleties of adult relationships). To correct the balance, she admitted her own affair. Mary found herself completely dependent, betrayed and powerless. Any anger that would have normally emerged was repressed when her mother became ill and the victim of a crime. Mary learned that she was an integral part of her family structure, but only in a dependent and childish role. If she were to assert her independence or display her anger, she would be abandoned. This belief also permeated her adult relationships, including her counseling relationship.

3. *You seem to describe a fairly "client centered" stance, deciding not to take much control of the direction of the sessions. Is this an accurate perception? If so, how would you deal with a client who does not decide to use their limited number of sessions in a useful way?*

Yes, that is an accurate perception. I find that many times decisions in counseling are a "leap of faith" in the client. Most clients respond positively to being treated as adults. However, there are clients who are not able or willing to be responsible for themselves. I find that I am good about confronting this issue and offering choices to clients on how to use the therapy time. I process what occurs in therapy and ask for feedback to see if therapy is being useful. Some clients do not use their time in counseling productively, yet will insist that the time was well spent. In these cases I have to examine my expectations for the client to make sure I am not forcing the pace of therapy. If I am fairly certain that my expectations are accurate, then I confront the client again. The client has to decide when they are ready to work. One thing that I have learned is that life offers many chances to deal with issues, and a given therapy session is just one opportunity. There will be others.

4. *In working with adults the therapist often finds him or her self viewed as an idealized parent. Do you see this as a kind of corrective parenting experience that allows the young adult client to move forward with identity development?*

Yes, I think the role of an idealized parent is a very powerful one. However, I think therapists have to be careful with this role because it is so gratifying. Frankly stated, it feels wonderful to be seen as "ideal" and I have to be careful not to foster dependence in order to maintain the parent/child relationship. I am looking to help the client develop into adulthood and aim to nurture and support individuation and independence. The idealized parent embodies the hopes, aspirations and dreams of adulthood and can help the client develop as an adult.

5. *You mentioned that creative activities were helpful in moving the therapy along. Did you suggest these activities and are they an important part of your therapy approach?*

I like to set up an accepting environment with the client and invite them to participate in creative ways. So I look for ways that clients express themselves and welcome them to share these proclivities in therapy. The activities *per se* are not a focus of my therapy, but the permission to use creative means of self-expression is an essential part of my therapy approach.

REFERENCES

Delgado-Romero, E. A. (1999). The face of racism. *Journal of Counseling and Development, 77* (1), 23-25.

Howard, G. S. (1996). *Understanding human nature: An owners manual.* Notre Dame, IN: Academic Press.

Kaufman, G. (1996). *The psychology of shame: Theory and treatment of shame-based syndromes.* New York, NY: Springer Publishing Company.

Parry, A., & Doan, R.E. (1994). *Story re-visions: Narrative therapy in the postmodern world.* New York: The Guilford Press.

Sue, D. W., & Sue, D. (1999). *Counseling the culturally different: Theory and practice.* (3rd ed.) New York: John Wiley & Sons, Inc.

Teyber, E. (1992). *Interpersonal process in psychotherapy: A guide for clinical training.* Pacific Grove, CA: Brooks/Cole.

Chapter 14:
Shoulder to Shoulder:
A Single Session Success Story

Paula Phillips

SUMMARY. This single session conversation demonstrates a post-modern approach to counseling. Using constructionist concepts, the therapist and student collaborated to create a common language. Through this shared meaning making, the therapist witnessed the student retrieve a preferred story of her life. Furthermore, the retelling of this story has helped others to find their own forgotten narratives. *[Article copies available for a fee from The Haworth Document Delivery Service: 1-800-342-9678. E-mail address: <getinfo@haworthpressinc.com> Website: <http://www.HaworthPress.com> © 2002 by The Haworth Press, Inc. All rights reserved.]*

KEYWORDS. Single session, narrative therapy, constructionist

When I am in a counseling relationship, I have often found that it is necessary to create a common language in order to help clients create a change in the stories of their lives. We all weave experiences and constructed meanings into narratives about ourselves. Often we privilege

Address correspondence to: Paula Phillips, Counseling & Human Development Center, Franklin Pierce College, Granite Hall, Rindge, NH 03461 (E-mail: phillipa@monad.net).

[Haworth co-indexing entry note]: "Chapter 14: Shoulder to Shoulder: A Single Session Success Story." Phillips, Paula. Co-published simultaneously in *Journal of College Student Psychotherapy* (The Haworth Press, Inc.) Vol. 16, No. 3/4, 2002, pp. 225-237; and: *Case Book of Brief Psychotherapy with College Students* (ed: Stewart E. Cooper, James Archer, Jr., and Leighton C. Whitaker) The Haworth Press, Inc., 2002, pp. 225-237. Single or multiple copies of this article are available for a fee from The Haworth Document Delivery Service [1-800-342-9678, 9:00 a.m. - 5:00 p.m. (EST). E-mail address: getinfo@haworthpressinc.com].

certain stories about ourselves, neglecting or forgetting many others. My role as counselor is to help people revisit and retrieve self-affirming narratives. I think of it as accompanying people as they explore the metaphoric attic where their experiences are stored.

I have often been curious about the meaning one assigns to events and experiences. I find that conversing with and listening to clients through metaphor an effective way to find common meaning. I invite people to draw on their experiences through artwork or music. Occasionally, I write a haiku, based on the person's imagery, as a summary of our work together. My picture of counseling was inspired from a PBS suffragette documentary titled, "Shoulder to Shoulder." This haiku reflects my conceptualization of the helping process:

> *Shoulder to shoulder/Ear to ear, sounding such strength/*
> *Re-storying self*

Early on, I was attracted to Alfred Adler's ideas. His citing of the need for power and competence as the driving force in human development "spoke" to my own conceptualization of how we develop as people. I consider Adler to be a forerunner of postmodern approaches, especially Narrative therapy. David Epston and Michael White (Epston & White, 1993) have also had a profound effect on how I think and speak about a person's struggles. As a result of their influence, my therapeutic stance has become one of collaboration in teaming against problems. Having the person externalize her/his difficulties becomes an essential part of the therapy and this is illustrated through my use of capitalization throughout this case discussion. To clarify, I try not to be duped by the Problem to believe that the person and the Problem are one in the same. It is important to distinguish the Problem from the person. Naming the Problem (for example, Self-Doubt or Nastiness) allows the person and therapist to join against the Problem. By siding with the person, tremendous respect is shown for the courage in facing one's struggle.

Issues of power and agency have also been of particular interest to me, most likely a reflection of being a middle-aged female who has grappled with how power is obtained and used. As a result, empowering people to stand up against difficulties is a core goal of mine. Sometimes Disempowerment can disguise itself as Aggression. I try not to be distracted from noticing the vulnerability of ostensibly strong persons, especially abusive ones. Epston and White (1992 & 1994) cite the inequitable use of power as the constant, central issue of people's lives. Further, their view is that personal struggles are a reflection of systemic subjugation. Since Isolation is the greatest ally of Disempowerment, Epston and White encourage people to enlist others to become part of their team. By forming a network of people to serve as both witnesses and cohorts, resistance to Problems is fortified.

Finally, O'Hanlon, Weiner-Davis (1989) as well as other Solution-Focused therapists have developed tools that I find useful to deconstruct problem-saturated stories. By focusing on future solutions, rather than past, repeated failed attempts, people can create a success story. Furthermore, unique ideas can lead to unique outcomes. I endeavor to help people envision a preferred future by developing a detailed "roadmap" to the desired outcome. This map's legend may include: how one knows when the goal is reached; what evidence will appear when the solution is nearer; who will notice the difference; and what will be different for her or him when the solution shows up.

SANDY'S NARRATIVE

Sandy was a 19-year-old second semester sophomore at a small residential college in rural New England. She had a grade point average of C+ and was involved in several co-curricular activities. She had quite a few friends in her residence hall and was very close to her roommate. Sandy was the only child of divorced parents. Her parents had a civil relationship, though they did not interact more than necessary. She liked her father's partner; her mother had not had another romantic relationship. She spent time with both parents over the past fifteen years and had lived with each, depending on her choice. In more recent times, most of her time was spent in her mother's house. The area in which she lived was near a high crime area and there was frequent gang-related violence, including drive-by shootings. Sandy, however, was not unduly frightened. She felt confident and secure, especially at home.

In addition to Sandy and her mother, there was another woman living in the house. Her mother had often opened their home to women who needed a safe place to stay and could eventually contribute to paying the rent. Sandy expressed deep admiration for her mother's strength and generosity.

Sandy had a boyfriend of nine months who was living at his home. He had enlisted in the military and planned to leave for basic training during the summer. She described him as being caring, but not expressive about his feelings.

THE PRESENTING ISSUE

Sandy called on a Thursday and requested to be seen as soon as possible. Since an intern was the only person available for the next two days, I requested he shift his lunch by a half hour to meet with her. He was a bit annoyed, but agreed to do so, albeit reluctantly. Because of his and my respective schedules of appointments, we did not touch base for the rest of the day. The next day, I was out of the office at a workshop. On Monday Sandy was scheduled to see me. Since the intern did not work on Mondays, I had no knowledge of the reason for the transfer or the issue Sandy wanted to discuss. Occasionally students changed from one to another counselor because of gender preference, area of expertise or comfort level with certain issues. I assumed one of these criteria was present. The only information the administrative assistant had was that it was the intern's suggestion that Sandy meet with me.

Sandy had always lived on the West Coast and thus had experienced several earthquakes. She reported never having had any sustained symptoms of anxiety after the quakes. To illustrate this, she described a time when she was four years old. Sandy stayed at her father's condo after an earthquake had dislodged them from their home for several weeks. Although initially unsettling, Sandy did not detect lingering uneasiness or fear about earthquakes.

Sandy's reaction was quite different after an earthquake that had occurred two months prior to our appointment. Since then, she had been unable to sleep through the night, especially around 4 a.m., when the tremors had started. This insomnia was occurring even though she was a coast away from home and earthquakes, and Anxiety was increasingly taking over her life. She reported being tearful, "crabby" and unhappy. Her roommate also noticed that Anxiety and its cohorts, Self-Doubt and Sleeplessness, had shaken Sandy from her equilibrium. Though she was initially concerned about Sandy as a person, her roommate had been tricked by Anxiety into resenting and blaming Sandy for its symptoms.

From Sandy's description of the problem, I could not ascertain the intern's rationale for transferring her to me. When I inquired about why the transfer had taken place, Sandy explained that the intern had told her that he had no expertise in surviving earthquakes and thus referred her to me. As a result, by the time she saw me, she was even less hopeful and defined herself in a problem-saturated manner. The encounter with the intern entrenched the idea that her problem was very complex and could not be readily resolved.

NAMING THE PROBLEM (A.K.A. DIAGNOSIS)

The counseling center where I work refrains from using DSM-IV codes to label people. This approach is consistent with my collaborative stance. We assign an A-Z code that names the concerns the person presents. Sandy's concerns were Insomnia, Mood and Stress.

CO-CREATED COUNSELING GOALS

Sandy's goals were to reclaim sleep and to regain equilibrium in mood.

PLAN

In the following single session example, I took a narrative, solution-focused stance. By standing with Sandy, I assisted her in standing up against Anxiety.

PROCESS

In the initial part of our single session meeting, I was curious about Sandy's perception, or in narrative terms, her predominant story, of herself. What was most apparent and distressing to Sandy was the contradiction in her current narrative from that of her past 18 years. She had always seen herself as a positive, confident person, not susceptible to fear. However, for the past couple of months, Anxiety had locked her in a sleepless, hypercritical and tearful box. She resisted attributing her current state to the earthquake, yet could not find any other attribution. I thought it was important to assist Sandy in tracking down the meaning of this experience, as well as to focus on an empowering narrative.

> T: You talk about having experienced other earthquakes and not having Anxiety linger about; I wonder what was unique about this one?
>
> Sandy: I don't know. The others happened when I was much younger. I haven't been able to sleep since it happened. At first I would just wake up around 4 when the first tremors started. In the past couple of weeks, I keep waking up all night. I feel frightened, but

not about an earthquake. I don't know what's the matter with me. I'm much moodier and snapping at everyone. My roommate is worried, but is also getting annoyed. She thinks I should just get over it.

[She doesn't seem to equate the earthquake with her uneasiness.]

T: You mentioned that you were at home with your Mom and her roommate when it happened. Can you describe the sequence of events?

Sandy: I was asleep and my mom woke us up. The house was shaking a lot and we had to leave in our nightgowns. There was a lot of damage to the house and there was concern about additional aftershocks, so we couldn't go back for a few days. (She starts tearing up at this point.) I feel stupid getting so upset. . . I never cry for no good reason.

[Her house, not the quake, seems to evoke strong feelings. When she made reference to her house, her confidence seemed to have been shaken by Anxiety.]

T: It must be difficult to stop self-criticism from creeping in when you don't know the meaning of your experience.

Sandy: It doesn't make sense for me to be like this. I'm the one who's always even-tempered; all my friends come to me to figure out their problems. Now, I can't even help myself. I have been through several earthquakes when I was younger, so why is it bothering me so much?

T: If it's okay with you, I'd like to switch topics. I'd like you to think about where you feel safe and peaceful. Please take a few moments to imagine being safe, confident and peaceful.

[I want to have her side step the fear by re-placing herself into a safe memory. I want her to remember other narratives of her life.]

T: (After a few moments) Can you describe where you were?

Sandy: Well, in my mother's house . . .

T: You mentioned that other women have lived there and felt the same way. It truly was a safe house.

[I'm trying to check if we have common meaning for "house."]

> Sandy: Yeah, I guess so. I never thought of it that way. I like that . . . a safe house.
>
> T: Is there any other place where you feel secure?

[Since the house no longer represents a story of safety, I'm trying to help her remember another source of self-comfort and confidence.]

> Sandy: The beach.
>
> T: I'd like you to imagine that you're at the beach. (After a few moments, I resume.) Can you tell me which of your senses you were most aware of?

[This is a self-affirming self-hypnotic technique as described by Lankton, 1993.]

> Sandy: (Smiles) Touch. I like the feel of the sand and the coolness of the ocean.
>
> T: So it's both texture and temperature that is most reassuring. Are there other aspects of the beach that are reassuring to you?
>
> Sandy: I also like the sounds of the waves and the birds.
>
> T: As you were telling me about the beach, I noticed that you had pushed away Anxiety and seemed calm.

[There was a noticeable difference in her face and positioning in the chair.]

> Sandy: Yeah, I do feel better. The beach is so relaxing; I can get away from it all when I go there.
>
> T: See those seashells on the table? I'd like to invite you to take one with you, so you can "feel" the beach and take its security with you.

[I intentionally use language, in this case "feel," that reflects her pre-dominant method of processing information.]

Sandy: Really? I have a shell collection at home. (She examines them and chooses one.) Is it okay to take this one?

T: Yes. Do you have any New Age music of ocean sounds?

Sandy: No, but I think my roommate does.

T: Tonight, I'd like you to hold the shell, listen to the music and imagine yourself at the beach.

[I want her to have agency in warding off insomnia by placing herself at the beach.]

Sandy: Okay.

T: I'm wondering whether you think it'd be possible to sleep through the night one time before we see each other next week.

[I'm working with possibilities that I think would be achievable. Because of how well she was able to regain strength by the previous imagery, I think she would be able to loosen the grip Anxiety has on her sleep. This is what M.Weiner-Davis would identify as solution-focused goal setting.]

Sandy: I definitely think so. In fact, I think I'll be able to sleep tonight.

T: I'm not sure if that's possible, but I do think you might be able to sleep through at least one night.

[It is important for Sandy to have a success story rather than another occurrence of an anxiety-saturated narrative. I intentionally suggest a lower threshold than I think is possible for her.]

OUTCOME

At our follow-up appointment, Sandy came in very upbeat. As she had predicted, she slept through the night of our first meeting and every night after. She not only used the shell, but also had remembered she had a vial of ocean water and held it against her face. The coolness helped her to imagine herself at the beach–strong and serene. The music idea was counter-productive. Her roommate's CD was of whales, so just when Sandy was drifting off to sleep, a whale wail would waken her. She quickly abandoned that as a sleep aid.

Another positive aspect of our follow-up session was that Sandy discussed Fear and Anxiety with her boyfriend. She felt very connected to him when he, too, cited the beach as his safe place. In essence, she had enlisted her boyfriend in her protest against Anxiety. Because she had reclaimed her sleep, equilibrium and calm, she and I agreed that there was not a need to meet again on this issue.

Several weeks later, she stopped by to thank me. It was just after Spring Break. She had spent the week with her grandparents (on the other coast from her home). She brought a basket of shells for me and said they were for me to give to other students who may feel as she had. I asked if it were okay to also share her story of shaking off Anxiety. She readily agreed.

Over the years, there have been quite a few students who feel the most secure and peaceful at the beach. When they identify the shore as their favorite place, I invite them to take a shell and I tell them Sandy's story of strength and generosity. Students seem to enjoy hearing of it. One of the most recent examples was this spring when I offered a shell to a student, Robin, from the Caribbean. She had grown up extremely poor and had survived severe physical abuse from her mother's boyfriend. The beach was where Robin would escape Helplessness. Her strong Christian faith was fortified at the beach, as she watched birds fly freely and felt the power of the sea. The offering of Sandy's shells and story recalled that story of her empowerment. It was crucial that I was able to hear Robin's narrative since I, an atheist, would never have assigned such a meaning.

DISCUSSION

Sandy's story serves as a lesson in just how important it is for the person and counselor to have common meaning. From hearing her presenting problem, one might have been tempted to assume that the invitation to Anxiety was the earthquake. With this imposed interpretation, some therapists may have proceeded with systematic desensitization or other such approaches to decouple Anxiety from Earthquakes. When Sandy had seen the intern, he, too, had assumed that this problem required attention to earthquakes. His unilateral, narrow definition of the problem, earthquake survival, had eroded his confidence. Since he had never dealt with this issue before, the earthquake had shaken him into Self-Doubt, too.

Fortunately, I have no expertise or experience with earthquakes, so I was comfortably in a position of what H. Anderson and H. Goolishian (1993) would describe as "not knowing." Since I was not saddled by the "expert" role, not knowing allowed me free rein to explore Sandy's meanings. That Sandy had experienced earthquakes with quite different reactions intrigued me. There were no other novel occurrences in her life at the time of or since this earthquake. What was causing her to edit her story at this point in her life? By revisiting the experience with her, we were able to define the source of Anxiety. The meaningful aspect of the day of the earthquake was that Sandy had to leave her (safe) house. Therefore, whether it were a fire, flood or earthquake, Sandy may have re-storied herself. In other words, the earthquake was the context, but not the content of Anxiety.

Since one of Sandy's foundations for feeling safe had been ruptured, it became important for her to site another "safe-house." The emotional ties to her mother's home had obscured her from seeing that she could and did internalize strength and support. By helping her to return to the beach, she was able to locate a buried story of equanimity in the presence of problems. I thought it imperative to join with Sandy in privileging her regained narrative of independence from Anxiety. Possibly there were other issues she could have explored with me. Perhaps other therapists would have suggested several more sessions. However, I thought it more important for her to determine her status than for me to second-guess her need. This is congruent with my desire to be collaborative and respectful. Sandy's sharing of her story and shells with others echoed the very traits she so admired in her mother: strength and generosity. Perhaps she would not have been able to claim these if she had not been encouraged to privilege her story over that of Anxiety's tale.

As noted in their Introduction, Epston and White (1992) see bearing witness and networking as important components of empowerment. By providing such an empowering narrative and token, Sandy has extended to others the ability to side-step problems. Sandy's and my collaboration started a network. Now I continue to serve as both witness and networker as I invite others on Sandy's behalf to also become both. Specifically, each time a shell is given, a unique story reveals itself, yet simultaneously shows its commonality with all the other narratives. What has been fascinating to me is how the same object, the shell, and the same place, the beach, can have such different meanings, and yet elicit the same effect. For Robin, the vision of birds and ocean brought into focus her spiritual story of being one of God's creatures. For Sandy, the tactile qualities of the beach helped her feel her strength and courage. Not only are their stories unique, the way in which they accessed their story is different. Robin had a visual memory and Sandy had a tactile one. And yet, their shared story line was one of reclaiming strength and safety.

What I like most about this case is how dynamic this single session continues to be. Rather than being a success story that started and ended with Sandy, she ensured that it only started with her. Sandy's narrative serves as a parable of how one can rewrite, edit or retrieve a preferred story of one's life. It also is illustrative of how important it is to join with someone in finding a common language to speak out against Problems.

QUESTIONS

1. *Please discuss the fact that this is a single session case with a follow up in a bit more detail. Why do you think it was workable in this single session format?*

I think it was due to the fact that Sandy's predominant narrative was that of a loved, loving and competent person. The earthquake shook the foundations of her safe house, which in turn, of her story.

Was this a conscious decision on your part?

Not until near the end of the session when I saw her remember her strength. However, as I was formulating a response to this question, I realized that many of the people I have seen, despite the number of sessions, often have a single session where their Problem gets encapsulated and lifted from their shoulders. Some therapists refer to this as the "aha! experience."

2. *A behavior therapist might call this a rapid desensitization, with the relaxation response quickly being substituted for anxiety. Can you discuss the differences that you see in your approach versus a behavioral one?*

The main distinction would have been for the therapist to identify the stimulus that needed to be desensitized, i.e., earthquake, rather than use Sandy's meaning (the house). A behavioral therapist would have thought that pairing relaxation with reintroduction to tremors would dislodge Anxiety's hold. My approach allowed Sandy to remember her ability to hold on to strength, not only at her mother's house, but also at the beach.

3. *What was your hypothesis as to why the client developed an anxiety response to earthquakes this time versus the other times that she was exposed?*

My understanding of Sandy's narrative was that, in fact, the quake was not the invitation to anxiety; the loss of the "safe-house" was. Therefore, it was important for me to encourage Sandy to recall other safety stories. Since it was clear to Sandy that quakes had not been the source of Anxiety in the past, she started to see herself as the problem.

Would this information make any difference in your treatment?

Yes, it is the difference that makes all the difference.

4. *You did not use the narrative technique of externalizing the problem in this case. Why not?*

Though it was not stated as blatantly as in this written piece, I thought of Anxiety as the problem, not Sandy.

5. *Was the length of the session longer because this was a single session therapy?*

It was about fifteen minutes longer.

6. *Would you typically use a longer than usual time frame for single session work?*

I do not set out to do single session therapy. It really depends on the person's identified need to continue or not. However, the first time I see someone, it often goes at least 60-70 minutes, depending on the issues raised and my schedule. I use the first session to get an "aerial" view of some of the stories of their life. Almost always there is a predominant disempowering story that obscures less privileged themes.

REFERENCES

Anderson, H., & Goolishian, H. (1993). The client is the expert: A Not-knowing approach to therapy. In S. McNamee & K. J. Gergen (Eds.), *Therapy as social construction* (pp. 25- 29). Newbury Park, CA: Sage.

Cade, B., & O'Hanlon, W.H. (1993). *A brief guide to brief therapy*. New York: W.W. Norton & Company.

Epston, D., White, M., & Murray, K. (1993). A proposal for re-authoring therapy; Rose's revisioning of her life and commentary. In S. McNamee, & K. J. Gergen (Eds.), *Therapy as social construction*. (pp. 96-115). Newbury Park, CA: Sage.

Epston, D., & Furman, B. (1994, June). *Conversations about conversations*. Presented at Therapeutic Conversations II, Reston,VA.

Friedman, S. (Ed.) (1993). *The new language of change: Constructive collaboration in psychotherapy*. New York: Guilford Press.

Furman, B., & Tapani, A. (1992). *Solution talk: Hosting therapeutic conversations*. New York: W.W. Norton & Company.

Lankton, S. (1993, November). *Building safety, belonging & other positive emotions through metaphor*. Presented at Advances in Treating Survivors of Sexual Abuse, Washington, D.C.

McNamee, S., & Gergen, K. J. (Eds.). (1993). *Therapy as social construction*. Newbury Park, CA: Sage.

O'Hanlon, W.H., & Weiner-Davis, M. (1989). *In search of solutions: A new direction in psychotherapy*. New York: W.W. Norton & Company.

Phillips, P. (1993, March). *Unpacking a brief case*. Presented at the annual meeting of Northeast Regional Counseling Center Directors, Hamilton, NY.

Phillips, P., & McGrath, R. (1994, October). *Tales from two universities: Narrative therapies*. Presented at the annual meeting of the Association of University & College Counseling Center Directors, Newport, RI.

White, M., & Epston, D. (1992). *Narrative means to therapeutic ends*. Australia: Dulwich Press.

Chapter 15:
The Runaway Client:
Working Through Interpersonal Anxiety

Michael G. S. Gottfried

SUMMARY. The case of a male graduate student struggling with excessive interpersonal anxiety and promiscuous sexual behavior is presented. The interpersonal issues were addressed within the therapeutic relationship drawing parallels to and from relationships outside of therapy. During the fifteen sessions of interpersonally focused therapy, the client made significant progress in his ability to form and maintain healthy relationships. *[Article copies available for a fee from The Haworth Document Delivery Service: 1-800-342-9678. E-mail address: <getinfo@ haworthpressinc.com> Website: <http://www.HaworthPress.com> © 2002 by The Haworth Press, Inc. All rights reserved.]*

KEYWORDS. Interpersonal anxiety, interpersonal therapy, family of origin, physical abuse

I am a newer PhD in counseling psychology, having finished my degree in 1999, a year after my internship. Most of my work has been in college counseling center settings. I also have extensive experience

Address correspondence to: Michael G. S. Gottfried, Student Counseling and Development Center, Valparaiso University, Valparaiso, IN 46383 (E-mail: mike.gottfried@valpo.edu).

[Haworth co-indexing entry note]: "Chapter 15: The Runaway Client: Working Through Interpersonal Anxiety." Gottfried, Michael G. S. Co-published simultaneously in *Journal of College Student Psychotherapy* (The Haworth Press, Inc.) Vol. 16, No. 3/4, 2002, pp. 239-254; and: *Case Book of Brief Psychotherapy with College Students* (ed: Stewart E. Cooper, James Archer, Jr., and Leighton C. Whitaker) The Haworth Press, Inc., 2002, pp. 239-254. Single or multiple copies of this article are available for a fee from The Haworth Document Delivery Service [1-800-342-9678, 9:00 a.m. - 5:00 p.m. (EST). E-mail address: getinfo@haworthpressinc.com].

with adolescents and families in inpatient, home-based and family therapy settings.

The foundation of my training was Rogerian. In working with adolescents, I soon saw shortcomings in a strictly client-centered approach. Additionally, I saw more and more systemic influences on my adolescent clients. I studied systems theories extensively during my masters program and was trained at an agency that was almost exclusively systems-oriented. Again, I found limitations in a single theoretical approach, especially when working with individuals. However, I still look for systemic influences with all my clients. In working with college students who have just left home, systemic influences are often very salient.

In developing my approach with individuals, initially I found myself using many cognitive-behavioral interventions and still do. However, I do not consider myself to be a cognitive-behavioral therapist because it isn't my primary frame of reference. I use cognitive-behavioral interventions as "micro" interventions when I see distortions, perceptions, or interpretations that contribute to the clients' central problems. On a "macro" level, I work interpersonally, looking for the aspects of the clients' interpersonal relationships, both in and out of the session, that keep them stuck. I see positive interpersonal relationships as the means by which most human problems are worked through. If clients had histories of satisfying and dependable intimate relationships, most wouldn't need to come to therapists; they would have discussed their problems and gotten the support and attention they needed to work through their troubling thoughts, behaviors, and emotions.

I conceptualize clients' interpersonal difficulties using John Bowlby's (1969, 1973) schema of attachment styles. Bowlby discusses people's internal working models of self and other, and hypothesizes that there are positive and negative versions of each. For example, someone who sees oneself as lovable and worthy of affection and sees others as generally responsive and dependable would have a secure style of attachment. Someone who has either a negative view of others or of oneself would have a variation of an insecure style of attachment. Attachment styles are thought to be formed at an early age with caregivers and persist into adulthood because of a self-confirming interpretation bias. Not only do people interpret events consistent with their schemas of self and other, but also they often help create a schema-affirming experience, an experience that proves their working models accurate. To access clients' attachment style, I generally look for their anxieties and hesitancies and explore these areas in more depth (Teyber, 2000). This helps us start a dialogue about their attachment style (without actually using the jargon) and helps flush out a pattern of relating or interpreting relationships that is central to their presenting problems.

Other significant influences on my approach to therapy come from feminist theory and existential philosophy. I keep attuned to the power balance in therapy and attempt to equalize it as much as possible, to collaborate instead of direct. I see clients having ultimate responsibility for authoring their lives. The universe is indifferent to them and the creation of their life is their responsibility.

DESCRIPTION OF CLIENT

Joe is a 26-year-old Caucasian gay male from the Midwest in the last year of a graduate program. He is of medium height, very thin, well groomed and was casually dressed. He is articulate and introspective, and shows no signs of thought disturbance. Joe was referred to therapy by several friends and finally decided to go, particularly since he was in training to be a therapist. He appeared mildly anxious, though I later learned his anxiety was great and was often masked well.

PRESENTING PROBLEM

Joe came to therapy for help with a problem that was becoming increasingly distressing for him. He would become intolerably anxious and then act out compulsively by meeting men for anonymous sex. He was becoming more upset with himself for doing so and concerned that it was not leading to the type of relationships he wanted and was leaving him feeling shameful and degraded.

While this was his most pressing issue, he initially presented with wanting to work through some residual feelings and thoughts about his family experiences growing up. While these issues were very distressing as well, they were not issues that he felt as responsible or shameful about, which is probably why he felt safer to bring them up initially.

SOCIAL/CULTURAL HISTORY/ENVIRONMENTAL CONTEXT

Joe was the second of two sons of an intact marriage. At the time of intake he reported no contact with any of his immediate family for at least 2 years. His father was alcoholic and physically abusive to Joe, his brother and mother. They lived outside of town with few neighbors around. Much of Joe's anxiety was a direct result of his upbringing. His father was wildly unpredictable and Joe lived in constant fear of his outbursts. Joe was unsure about how much his older brother was abused, but saw his brother as similar to their father in that he was belligerent and abusive (primarily verbally) to Joe. Joe described his mother as passive and nurturing when she could be. As an adult he realized how incapacitated she was by fear and abuse, leaving her mostly unable to be responsive to Joe's needs as a child. Joe stayed away from his family because he couldn't see any positive reasons to maintain contact. When he was in contact, they were generally withdrawn and sometimes asked to borrow money from him. He felt empowered by his ability to not have them in his life, though he occasionally experienced some guilt about this. Joe's brother was not functioning as well as Joe was, but since Joe felt both pushed away and leery of him, he kept his distance. He did maintain contact with one cousin with whom he was close, but was often frustrated because they are very different.

Joe was a first generation college graduate, and he financed and pursued college without familial support. He was particularly proud of this accomplishment. However, he occasionally felt much anxiety about whether he was competent enough for a masters-level education and resulting professional-level job.

Early on in high school, Joe realized he was gay. He has never talked to his family about his homosexuality though he thought they must suspect it, particularly his mother. When he realized he was gay and shared his realization with a friend's mother, she said that she had already known for several years. Apparently, it was clear to others before it was to him. He didn't see his sexual orientation as relevant to his anxiety or his issues with his family, though he wondered if his dad was particularly hard on him as a child because he suspected that Joe was gay. Joe talked about being very open and comfortable with his sexual orientation and even the often-negative response to it in our present society. At the point that he entered therapy, his being gay was a resolved issue for him.

Interpersonally, Joe struggled through some abusive relationships but was currently not in a dating relationship. He had identified the pattern of abuse stemming back to his father prior to coming to therapy.

ASSESSMENT/DIAGNOSIS/CONCEPTUALIZATION

Joe was dealing with the aftermath of a traumatic childhood and displayed symptoms consistent with posttraumatic stress disorder (PTSD). His symptoms included hyper-vigilance, exaggerated startle response, intrusive thoughts and anxieties, and avoidance of closeness in relationships.

His anxiety was manifested interpersonally, primarily in his approach-avoidant style in relationships. Joe would become so anxious that he was going to be rejected or attacked that he would withdraw from the relationship before either could happen. This was true for friendships, work and dating relationships, and the therapeutic relationship, as will be discussed below. Joe would get overwhelmed with anxiety, which he described as a near panic, and would then sometimes seek out an anonymous sexual encounter, which calmed him temporarily by distracting him from his anxiety. Because his anxiety felt overwhelming, Joe took great steps to avoid the feared situations and thus, never got the chance to see if his anxiety was warranted. He withdrew before he found out. This is not dissimilar to that of someone with a simple phobia who avoids a feared situation and never learns that the fear is unwarranted. Similar to treatment of phobias, treatment of interpersonal anxiety requires increased exposure to the feared situation.

In attachment terms, Joe has a preoccupied or resistant style of attachment, characterized by a negative view of self and positive view of others. It is typical for people with this pattern of attachment to crave close relationships yet be very anxious and unsure about them because of their poor self-image. This anxiety often propels people to sabotage or withdraw from relationships. For Joe, it meant that he feared rejection, abandonment or maltreatment from others and thus, would withdraw before finding out if his fears were accurate, or he would put himself in situations where maltreatment was likely. By doing the latter, his fear would be substantiated, proving to himself that he can predict others' reactions, thereby lessening anxiety temporarily.

COUNSELING GOALS

The primary goal with Joe was to process and lessen his anxiety regarding relationships and to explore connections to past abuse. To do this, I would have to establish a safe and secure relationship to keep Joe from withdrawing from therapy because of his anxiety. A strong therapeutic relationship would also help Joe change his attachment style to a more secure one. Bowlby (1988) writes that therapy is "a secure base" from which clients can try new behaviors and then return to a secure base, much like a child learning to swim returns to the side of the pool from time to time to feel the safety there before letting go again to try to swim. The development of a strong, positive relationship does two things: it gives someone like Joe a "secure base," and it allows him to have a corrective experience–one that challenges the accuracy of his current attachment style. If a therapist can be reliable, present and dependably a support of the client, then a client like Joe can start to wonder if at least some other people can be responsive to his or her needs. Thus, by forming a strong, positive relationship with the client and seeing them through their most troubling fears, clients can start to see relationships beyond therapy as dependable also. This was the ultimate goal with Joe. If he saw new possibilities for support and comfort in his current and future relationships, he would be much more equipped to handle the stresses he faced.

TREATMENT PLAN

Several content areas were part of the treatment plan for Joe: (a) explore and process feelings about physical abuse and family, (b) help him understand and prevent the anxiety that fuels promiscuous sexual behavior, and (c) help him set goals for future relationships, etc. The overarching method for achieving these and other goals was to help Joe manage his anxiety so that he could more naturally work through the areas that he avoided because of his anxiety. To do this, I had to become a holding place for his anxiety, to help guide him through it. I also needed to help him tolerate his anxiety long enough to see if it was warranted. As his tolerance for anxiety increased, it was expected that these other symptoms and avoidances would decrease.

COUNSELING PROCESS

During the time I saw Joe, several critical events and themes emerged that defined the therapeutic process. They are organized by theme or incidence with the time in therapy mentioned, though a few of these themes overlap temporally.

Joe was to be seen for 19 sessions over nine months, but four of those planned sessions were no-shows early on in therapy that he was "charged for" even though not seen. He was seen for two sessions before his first no-show. When he no-showed for the first time, I sensed that there was something happening between us that he was anxious about but wasn't sure what that was at that time. I didn't know if it was what we were talking about or if I was being tested in some way. I don't always call clients back who no-show early on in therapy. The Center was incredibly busy with a wait list and I sometimes think an early no-show is a sign of either a need that was met enough for the client's comfort or therapy is not a priority for that client right now. Usually, however, I sense that a no-show is a sign of something happening between us that is important and related to a client's issues, so I call, as I did with Joe.

Joe ended up coming back in for therapy for a session before the winter break. The no-show was because of another commitment, he told me. We had scheduled a time to meet in January. He no-showed again. I called him again and we met. He apologized profusely and said that he didn't know why he didn't show, he just didn't feel up to it. This pattern repeated twice more after other appointments were kept. Much later in therapy, I found out that my calling him each time was significant to him because it communicated that I still wanted to work with him even though he "messed up." That I could still feel positively toward him despite the no-shows helped him feel safer with me and less anxious about me rejecting him or getting angry with him.

Early on in therapy, Joe had an experience that triggered strong feelings. He was riding with his cousin and witnessed a dog being hit by another car. The driver paused, saw the whimpering dog, but then kept driving. Joe's cousin didn't stop either. Joe was furious with both the other driver and with his cousin and was very anxious about it, which he didn't understand. He could not let these feelings go. We explored them in his session the following day:

> Joe: I just don't get why I was so anxious. I'm still anxious about it!

> T: What does that feel like now?

> Joe: I feel this pit in my stomach, I half feel like I want to run out of here. I feel trapped. I'm trapped in my skin.

> T: When have you felt this feeling before?

> Joe: I don't know . . . .(long pause) . . . .When I was a kid I felt like this.

> T: Can you talk about it?

Joe: Yeah, I think so. I was about twelve I think. My dad was furious at my mother, I'm not sure why. It was just me and my parents, I don't know where my brother was at the time. I was up in my bedroom and my mom and dad were arguing in the kitchen. It was getting worse–I think he was hitting her–although I think I was mainly tuning it out at the time, because I remember not really being there but then hearing my mom yell my name and ask for help. I didn't know what to do so I tried to call 911. The only phone we had was in the kitchen so I had to go in there. My dad saw me trying to call and grabbed the phone from me and ripped it out of the wall. My mom was crying and there I was trying to help, but I didn't know what to do. I couldn't take on my father, he was huge compared to me . . . (pause) . . . I just remember feeling so helpless and guilty for not being able to do anything. And so anxious! God I was just so helpless! I couldn't do anything to help. (he appears close to tears, but stops himself)

(long pause)

T: How are you feeling right now?

Joe: Calmer. I mean what did I expect? I was twelve!

T: So you can forgive yourself somewhat?

Joe: Yeah, I think so. I think the thing with the dog just brought back that feeling. God what a horrible feeling.

The feelings he had watching the dog get hit and not being able to help were particularly intense because they were reflections of these earlier feelings that were previously not discussed or processed. Through this we learned that a lot of his anxiety comes from feeling helpless and then feeling guilty for it.

During the time that he was attending and then no-showing, he was set up with someone that he started dating. This was a significant thing for him because it brought up many of his issues. We explored many of these issues in therapy and helped him identify their origin or at least a pattern that was his own, as differentiated from the issues of the person he was dating. Joe felt incredible anxiety at times in that relationship. He felt like he had to initiate all the contact, that his date, Dave, showed only sporadic interest or initiative. Joe felt attraction to him but very limited connection. In discussing his anxiety, it seemed that what caused Joe the most anxiety was the indifference that he interpreted coming from Dave. He didn't know if Dave was going to approach intimacy or withdraw. This was a bit of a revelation to Joe. He related some of the anxiety to early family experiences of not knowing what mood his father was going to be in. The anxiety and uncertainty finally became too much for Joe, and he ended the brief relationship. The pattern of his withdrawal from relationships due to anxiety was becoming clearer. We talked about this pattern and explored how it played out across situations.

Around the time of that session, he had a relapse, and engaged in an anonymous sexual encounter. Both Joe and I were able to get clearer about how much anxiety played a part in this behavior. He was very anxious about the loss of his relationship, the upcoming job search, and his approaching graduation. He realized how much the anonymous encounter was fueled by anxiety and, through this realization, he became more focused on dealing with the anxiety to prevent doing such again.

About halfway through individual therapy with me, Joe started participating in a support group for gay men. He exhibited a pattern of attendance to group that was similar to his individual therapy attendance. In talking about the similarities and differences between his behavior in group therapy and individual therapy, he realized that he tests people by "failing" them first. He tested me by "failing" me as a client. That is what made my calling him back so important to him. He "failed" me but I was still okay with him.

> Joe: I don't know, I just can't get myself to go sometimes. I really wonder if they like me. They seem to already be comfortable with each other.

> T: So you feel out of place there.

> Joe: Yeah, I feel very out of place, though there really isn't any reason for it. I mean they're nice to me and everything. I just can't go there sometimes.

> T: What makes it unbearable?

> Joe: I don't know. I should be able to go, I feel kind of stupid for it but I just can't go sometimes.

T: This same thing happened with us when you first started here. There were several times that you felt you just couldn't come here but now you're coming regularly. Do you think there is a pattern here?

Joe: Well, I always do that. I have a real hard time starting something.

T: What do you think that's about? Let's look at our example. What happened here that made it okay to come more regularly?

Joe: Well, it helped a lot that you called when I missed an appointment.

T: How did that help?

Joe: Well, I guess it showed me that it was important to you. I also felt that after screwing up so many times that if you were still wanting to meet with me that I guess I could be okay with you.

T: In a way you were testing me to see if you could trust me?

Joe: Yeah, I guess so.

T: Do you think that you're doing that here, with the group?

Joe: (pause) Yeah I think that might be a big part of it. I mean I really want to be part of the group, I just don't think I'm up to dealing with it sometimes. I'm too anxious.

T: And testing to see if people are still okay with you after you pull back helps you feel less anxious?

Joe: Definitely.

In talking further, we realized that he does this in a variety of settings. His anxiety not only led to withdrawal, but his withdrawal was a test to see if his anxiety was realistic (based on how others respond to his withdrawal). After talking with the group facilitator, he returned to therapy, with one more no-show, and was able to work past his anxieties and feel accepted by the group. This testing behavior was a significant concern for him in starting a new job.

Joe landed a job as a therapist at a residential center. After about a month, he began to pull back, call in sick, and once didn't even call in. While at work he thought he was doing a horrible job and was very anxious that he would be fired, despite the positive feedback that he was getting. He became aware of how he was starting to create what he feared and he attempted to change his behavior. His employer even allowed him to take some time off because his anxiety was too high to work. We discussed how his difficulties at work related to the pattern of testing and withdrawing that we had previously identified:

T: So how might this situation be similar to what happened here in therapy, or with the group?

Joe: I guess I could be testing them. I just feel so anxious.

T: You're expecting them to figure out that you're a fraud and fire you.

Joe: (laughs) Yeah I guess I am. It doesn't make much sense though. I mean everyone has been real nice to me there. They seem to value my input. They've been telling me that I'm doing good so far.

T: So, do you think there are other ways to see if you need to be anxious there besides withdrawing and tempting them to fire you?

Joe: I don't know. I've done this a lot. I'd like to do it different. I just get so anxious I can't be there.

T: But when you do make it there, it goes okay?

Joe: Yeah, it generally goes pretty well.

T: Wouldn't it be powerful to do it different this time, so you could see if you really needed to put yourself through this anxiety or not?

With his employer's patience and his new ability to refrain from withdrawing completely, he was able to return to work and eventually feel like he was doing an adequate job.

The attention to his primary pattern of failing others to see if they were safe helped Joe see how much he does this testing and helped him weigh the costs of doing so. His not withdrawing completely, as he had often done, provided a healing experience for him; he realized that if he hangs in there, his anxiety is usually shown to be unfounded. What facilitated this change was our identifying the many times and places in which he anxiously acted out by withdrawing and how that invariably kept him from achieving what he wanted to accomplish. Through the several experiences that "passed" his tests (individual therapy, group therapy, and his job site), he was able eventually to see that maybe his "tests" kept him from having other positive experiences as well.

OUTCOME/TERMINATION OF COUNSELING

Joe was much less anxious by the end of therapy. He hadn't had compulsive sex in several months, and he was not withdrawing from the supportive relationships he had around him. He had started to be more direct, honest, and use his assertiveness skills in his relationships, partly because he was less anxious about losing them. I knew that Joe would be graduating and no longer eligible for services so I began early to prepare for termination. Given his interpersonal anxieties and tendency to withdraw prematurely, I wanted to make sure that he had an opportunity to end our relationship formally and differently by talking well in advance about his feelings and thoughts about it ending. Ironically, he got called into an emergency meeting and had to miss our last session, which couldn't be rescheduled, but he did call and process termination over the phone. He said that he was upset about missing it since he was trying to do things differently (i.e., not withdraw).

DISCUSSION

Working through Joe's childhood abuse and interpersonal anxiety in a short-term model was difficult. To do so, I focused on the current manifestations of that abuse, going back to memories of the original experience when it seemed important to do so, when his current problems related back. By working through the current manifestations, the internal representations changed. For Joe, feeling more and more like he could trust others to not reject him and learning that his anxiety is tolerable helped lessen his anxiety enough to work through other residuals of the abuse.

Therapy also helped him to shift his attachment style slightly. Bowlby (1988) believed that effective therapy moves people from insecure styles of attachment to more secure styles. This was evident with Joe. By the end of individual and group therapy, he was starting to see more safety and reliability in others and more worth in himself. He still had internal work to do, but the groundwork had been laid. He could build on his success.

Erik Erikson (1968) theorized that the developmental task of young adulthood is to work out the conflict of intimacy versus isolation. Joe's presenting problems reflected this conflict: his compulsive sexual behavior and his anxiety in relationships became more and more troubling to him as his desires for a satisfying relationship became greater. It became more necessary for him to deal with this anxiety if he was going to be able to develop healthy relationships.

Attention to the process was crucial for Joe. We got as much or more information from examining how we talked as from discussing what we talked about. This also made therapy more powerful by focusing on what was currently happening within the session instead of outside events exclusively. An interpersonal approach emphasizing interpersonal issues allows many changes to be attempted in session, while giving clients a place to process these changes immediately. Attention to themes of interpersonal behavior across situations helped Joe realize that it was probably his distortion and not a reflection of what was actually going on in the situation. Additionally, it helped tally the consequences of this pattern of behavior, which in turn, made Joe more and more uncomfortable with it and more ready to change.

What helped Joe the most was his courage as he worked hard to tolerate high levels of anxiety with little support outside of therapy, and no support or contact from family. Given his situation and background, I was often struck by how intensely he had to work and I felt inspired by his effort.

QUESTIONS

1. *Did you consider referring Joe for an evaluation and possible use of anti-anxiety medication? Why or why not?*

Early on in therapy, Joe and I talked about anti-anxiety medication as an adjunct to therapy. He was opposed to medication at that time and was even more opposed later when he started seeing progress without it.

I generally discuss medication with clients with more than mild anxious or depressive symptoms. My general rule of thumb in recommending medication is assessment of current functioning in and out of therapy. If clients are able to function fairly well, then I do not generally recommend medication until other therapeutic interventions are attempted. If clients are unable to function adequately in their work, school, and relationships or are impaired in their ability to benefit from therapy, then I recommend combining medication with therapy.

2. *Your calling Joe when he missed some early appointments seemed to make a difference in establishing a trusting relationship with you. Would you typically do this with clients? Do you have specific criteria as to when you would call a client who no-shows?*

More often than not, I call clients who no-show for two reasons. First, as in the situation with Joe, I often think that there is a clinical reason for a no-show, that it is an expression of what is happening, or not happening, between the client and me. Sometimes not showing is an interpersonal test, as it was with Joe: 'Is my therapist going to become angry with me?' 'Is the relationship important enough to my therapist to pursue it when I pull back?' Sometimes no-shows are an expression of anxiety, as they often occur after a particularly intense session. Additionally, a no-show is sometimes an indirect expression of anger or disappointment with counseling or with me, and attending to that in the next session can be very fruitful.

The second reason I call clients after they do not show is to communicate how important I regard our appointment time. In doing so, I gently encourage them to be direct with me about their reason for not showing. Even if clients do not want to continue therapy, my calling communicates that the commitment of making the appointment was important to me, I am concerned about them, and I am curious about their absence. However, I am careful to communicate concern instead of shaming clients for missing their appointments.

Often, clients no-show when they are feeling a little better, much like many patients who don't return to their physicians once their symptoms subside. Generally, I do not call clients if I decide that my calling would impede clients from working on taking more responsibility for their lives. I also choose not to call if the client came in with just a situational problem that resolved itself within a week or two. In such cases, our meeting has been more akin to a brief consultation than therapy.

3. *You mentioned that you often use cognitive behavioral techniques, yet there is not mention of any relaxation methods or stress inoculation procedures in this case. Did you use any of these techniques? Why or why not?*

Since Joe was in training to be a therapist, he had some familiarity with relaxation and stress management skills. While we did discuss these skills, particularly early on in therapy, they were not a major focus of our work. My references to using these skills in anxious situations periodically throughout therapy, and practicing them when not particularly anxious, were not very helpful. Addressing the cognitive and interpersonal aspects of his anxiety proved to be more successful. His anxiety was so great that he could not utilize relaxation skills very well when anxious until he had achieved better control of his negative interpretations and irrational fears.

I tend to use relaxation skills with all clients who present with stress or anxious symptoms, but they prove to be more helpful for some clients than others. For Joe, he could only use them after he worked on the thoughts and interpretations that contributed to his anxiety. He would then use them with no intervention from me necessary.

4. *You were able to make progress in changing Joe's attachment style in a short time, even though that is considered by some to be a rather difficult process. Can you discuss your views on how it happened so quickly?*

Although I was able to make some progress in changing Joe's attachment style, his attachment style was only starting to change during therapy; he had not yet developed a consistently secure attachment style. Nevertheless, progress was made more quickly than with many other clients. I think what helped accelerate this process was the fact that he was challenged as to the adequacy of his attachment style by many different situations and relationships simultaneously. Much of my work with him was persistently showing how the various situations we discussed were all related to his general approach to interpreting and interacting in relationships. Over time, and with the group therapists working on similar themes, Joe was able to start to challenge his fundamental views of himself and others. With most clients, it takes longer for experiences that disconfirm views of self to accumulate and for the client to understand and incorporate them.

A second factor was timing. Joe was ready to make changes in his life. He was looking forward to working as a professional therapist as he was nearing graduation, and he felt compelled to function better in general and in work situations. Also, he came to therapy already starting to realize his role in his problems. Increasingly, he was noticing that he was experiencing relationships similarly across situations and over time, suggesting to him that something about him was at least, in part, responsible for his problems.

5. *Joe claimed that he was very comfortable with his sexual orientation, yet he was involved in compulsive sexual behavior. This is often a sign of poor adjustment to sexual orientation, but you interpreted it as related primarily to his need for anxiety release. Can you discuss this a bit more?*

I agree that compulsive sexual behavior is often a sign of poor adjustment to sexual orientation, and I explored this early on with Joe. I think that often, compulsive sexual behavior is acting out impulses more intensely because they are, at other times, suppressed by internalized or experienced homophobia. A pendulum swings one way (suppression) and it very often has to swing as strongly the other way (compulsively acting out). I have worked with other gay men for whom this was an issue. As I've helped them deal with their internalized homophobia by examining it in a safe and valuing relationship, the compulsive behavior has subsided and they have become more comfortable with their sexual orientation.

But this explanation for Joe's compulsive behavior didn't seem to apply when we explored it. Joe was aware of the homophobia in our culture, but didn't experience much of it internally. For Joe, the sexual intimacy was not what was the most anxiety-producing; it was emotional intimacy. Given his abusive history with his father and brother and previous abusive intimate relationships, emotional intimacy with men was particularly anxiety-producing.

REFERENCES

Bowlby, J. (1969). *Attachment and loss: Vol. 1: Attachment.* New York: Basic Books.

Bowlby, J. (1973). *Attachment and loss: Vol. 2: Separation: Anxiety and anger.* New York: Basic Books.

Bowlby, J. (1988). *A secure base: Clinical applications of attachment theory.* London: Routledge.

Erikson, E. H. (1968). *Identity: Youth and crisis.* New York: Norton.

Teyber, E. (2000). *Interpersonal process in psychotherapy.* (4th ed.). Pacific Grove, CA: Brooks/Cole.

Chapter 16:
Harm Reduction:
From Substance Abuse to Healthy Choices

David A. Diana

SUMMARY. Working with clients with both substance abuse and other Axis I mental health concerns is becoming more and more common on a college campus as well as in the general population. By utilizing both brief therapy techniques and a harm reduction approach, the therapist engages the client where the client is ready to begin in an attempt to motivate the client toward healthier choices. This case study examines the inter-relationship among alcohol abuse, attention-deficit disorder, anxiety, and depression. *[Article copies available for a fee from The Haworth Document Delivery Service: 1-800-342-9678. E-mail address: <getinfo@ haworthpressinc.com> Website: <http://www.HaworthPress.com> © 2002 by The Haworth Press, Inc. All rights reserved.]*

KEYWORDS. Alcohol abuse, brief therapy, co-existing disorders, harm reduction, motivational interviewing, substance abuse

Over the past 13 years, I have worked in a variety of mental health and substance abuse outpatient programs as well as at colleges and uni-

Address correspondence to: David A. Diana, Director of Alcohol and Other Drug Programs, Smith Hall, First Floor, Hobart and William Smith Colleges, Geneva, NY 14456 (E-mail: Diana@hws.edu).

[Haworth co-indexing entry note]: "Chapter 16: Harm Reduction: From Substance Abuse to Healthy Choices." Diana, David A. Co-published simultaneously in *Journal of College Student Psychotherapy* (The Haworth Press, Inc.) Vol. 16, No. 3/4, 2002, pp. 255-268; and: *Case Book of Brief Psychotherapy with College Students* (ed: Stewart E. Cooper, James Archer, Jr., and Leighton C. Whitaker) The Haworth Press, Inc., 2002, pp. 255-268. Single or multiple copies of this article are available for a fee from The Haworth Document Delivery Service [1-800-342-9678, 9:00 a.m. - 5:00 p.m. (EST). E-mail address: getinfo@haworthpressinc.com].

versities. While pursuing my graduate degree in clinical psychology, I worked with many clients with a variety of mental health issues who also experienced difficulties with mood altering substances. During my second-year long practicum, I received training that combined both mental health issues and substance abuse work in a comprehensive multi-disciplinary approach. I carried this philosophy with me, and was able to incorporate the principles in my position as director of counseling services at a small liberal arts college in the Midwest, and later as program coordinator for an outpatient chemical dependency program in a rural county in upstate New York.

Currently, I am in my second year as the Director of Alcohol and Other Drug Programs, and I work with a variety of clients who present with both substance abuse and other Axis I mental health concerns. By combining brief therapy, motivational interviewing, and a harm reduction approach to engaging clients, I am partnering with the client in an attempt to assess the degree of change the client is willing to explore. Most clients in treatment on a college campus engage in six or fewer sessions, which makes this approach appealing for clients unsure of whether they want to abstain totally from substances. The goal is to engage students in an attempt to explore their choices and reduce the risks associated with heavy drinking or other substance use.

The vast majority of college students do not abuse alcohol (Perkins & Berkowitz, 1986; Perkins, Meilman, Leichliter, Cashin, & Presely, 1999) or will outgrow heavy drinking and alcohol-related problems without ever seeking assistance from a therapist (Marlatt et al., 1998; Jessor, Donovan, & Costa, 1991; Zucker & Fitzgerald, 1991). My experience over the past decade in working with a college student population is that most college students do not meet the DSM-IV criteria for substance dependence, though some meet the criteria for substance abuse. Therefore, if the diagnosis is alcohol abuse, and the student does not want to abstain from alcohol, the next best approach is to inoculate students against harm by giving them the necessary tools to keep them safe (Marlatt et al., 1998).

The art of psychotherapy, often referred to as treatment in the alcohol and other drug (AOD) field, depends a great deal on how the therapist can mobilize clients' resources to help themselves. The ultimate brief therapy is single session therapy (SST). One premise in SST is the notion that the therapist's assessment and treatment plan must "mobilize and intensify" clients' "positive expectation toward recovery and change" (Talmon, 1990). When working with a client who has co-existing substance abuse and mental health issues, utilizing both brief therapy techniques and a harm reduction approach can do just that. If we therapists think that students who have been using substances for whatever reason are going to abstain because we say so or our agency says the person must do so, we are kidding ourselves. Perhaps a more effective approach when dealing with substance-abusing clients or students is to work with them where they are. By combining brief therapy, motivational interviewing, and a harm reduction approach to treatment, we have a better chance of reducing alcohol and other drug related problems in college students as well as in the general population.

DESCRIPTION OF CLIENT

Rob was a 21-year-old Caucasian male junior majoring in business, and of medium height and weight. He was casually dressed and well groomed for the initial interview. His presenting concern focused on his difficulty concentrating in class and staying on task when studying.

PRESENTING PROBLEM

Rob presented to our office after being suspended for a semester due to an alcohol-related incident. He was on academic probation and the Dean suggested that he seek assistance to explore what led to his suspension. He was diagnosed with Attention Deficit Disorder (ADD) when he was 18 and his physician prescribed Ritalin. While the Ritalin helped his concentration in class, he still had difficulty focusing on his work when studying at home. His chief complaint was not getting his class work done while he constantly thinks about what the future holds for him. His persistent worry about the future and his lack of motivation to go to class created additional concern for Rob, to the point where he questioned whether college is where he should be.

Rob appeared to be very open and honest during the interview. His motivation for treatment at this time seemed to be at the encouragement of the Dean, but he did say he wanted to know if he had a problem with alcohol and whether his ADD could be treated differently since he felt the current medication regime was not working well. During this session, he was very anxious and moved restlessly in his chair. He was forthcoming with information but tended to avoid direct eye contact. His mood was within the normal range but his affect was relatively flat. Rob described how, at times, he would have certain thoughts about failing and not succeeding in college. These thoughts were recurrent and persistent. He tried to think about other things but could only suppress these worries for a short period of time. Thoughts of failure usually occurred when he was trying to focus on his academic work or when he was lying in bed trying to fall asleep for the night.

PSYCHOSOCIAL HISTORY

Rob is the younger of two sons. His parents have been married for more than 20 years but his father had two daughters from a previous marriage, making them Rob's half-sisters. He describes his family as "well to do," living a pleasant lifestyle in New England. He describes his parent's relationship as very "loving and nurturing," and said both his parents were very supportive of him. He described his mother as a "stay at home mom" who raised him while his dad worked and took care of the family finances. Throughout his childhood, his father was constantly on the go due to business. Consequently, Rob always felt closer to his mother and it was not until he entered college that he and his father started connecting around how Rob was doing in his classes and what Rob was going to do after college.

Rob also described his relationship with his only brother, a 22-year-old college graduate, as "very close." They talked regularly by phone and got together on breaks either at the family's main residence or their second home in the South. Rob saw his two older half-sisters occasionally, usually during the holidays and sometimes in the summer as well.

Rob attended boarding school in New England where he participated in soccer and was an average student, often struggling to pass his coursework. He was very popular in school, had a variety of friends, and always seemed to have a steady girlfriend. But his relationships were strained constantly by conflict over whether he would spend time with her or with his male friends; a theme carried over to his college girlfriend of almost three years. On one occasion, when he wanted to spend time with his male friends, they had a heated argument and she slapped him. Rob did not respond in a physically violent way but was verbally abusive. He took responsibility for his own verbal violence, but downplayed her physical violence.

Rob experimented with a variety of mood-altering substances while in boarding school; it was routine for him and his friends to drink alcohol and smoke marijuana every weekend. He had not smoked marijuana since his first year of college, but continued to drink alcohol regularly at least two or three times a week, consuming at least six and sometimes as many as 10 or 12 drinks in a single sitting. Consequently, he experienced nausea, vomiting, and headaches due to his drinking, and he occasionally missed classes due to drinking the night before. He has also slept away his Saturday and sometimes Sunday due to drinking on a Friday night. Rob was a member of a fraternity and was currently living in the fraternity house on campus at the time of therapy.

ASSESSMENT AND DIAGNOSIS

Rob presented with a variety of DSM-IV symptoms including anxiety, depression, alcohol abuse, and attention-deficit/hyperactivity. Since many mental health issues like anxiety and depression can be masked by alcohol, I felt it was important to see if Rob was willing to work toward reducing his current amount of alcohol. We could then get a baseline for his behavior and see if the alcohol might be contributing to his symptoms and if there was an underlying bio-chemical concern where medication might be necessary.

I used a motivation approach (Miller & Rollnick, 1991) to assess what goals Rob would like to emphasize to help build our relationship and to empower him to guide his therapy.

COUNSELING GOALS

Because substance abuse and mental health difficulties are so often linked, it is important to include substance abuse screening as part of every mental health assessment no matter what the client's presenting concern (Washton, 1993), especially because of the high incidence of substance use disorders among young adults. Thus, every college counseling center therapist, counselor, or psychologist should consider incorporating an accurate substance use screening into their assessment process.

My primary goal with Rob was to help him address his alcohol abuse and to encourage him to establish and maintain a balanced lifestyle. By teaching him how to anticipate, identify, and manage high-risk drinking situations, he would have a variety of behavioral tools to use whenever necessary. By reducing Rob's alcohol consumption and motivating him toward a balanced lifestyle, we could then start to address his anxiety and depressive symptoms. Although this conceptualization utilizes motivational interviewing within a cognitive-behavioral framework, we cannot negate the possibility that medication might be an additional therapy to consider in conjunction with this approach.

TREATMENT PLAN AND COUNSELING PROCESS

I feel it is crucial to set the tone of the treatment process during the initial assessment by being non-judgmental and expressing empathy. By working with the client and rolling with the resistance, I can engage clients to look at what brought them into my office, and assess their motivation to change.

Miller and Rollnick (1991) utilized Prochaska and DiClemente's (1986) stages-of-change model in the context of their motivational interview approach, in order to understand the ambivalent client and bolster interest and desire to change behavior. This approach provides a comprehensive assessment with respectful and objective feedback. By utilizing the motivational approach in the screening process I am emphasizing the client's responsibility for change (i.e., "If you wish, I will help you learn how to help yourself."). A variety of choices and a range of options are provided to enhance the commitment to making therapy work. Additionally, I express empathy versus attacking the resistance, and I reinforce optimism and hope by using "can do" messages, as illustrated by the following interaction:

T: What brings you here today?

Rob: I was suspended from school because of an incident and the Dean recommended that I talk to someone about this.

T: I'm curious, were alcohol or other drugs involved in this situation?

Rob: Yes, I did drink that night, but it was not a lot.

T: What would be a lot for you? Ten to 12 drinks in one sitting?

Rob: No, not that many, usually I have six to seven beers.

T: Would it be fair to say that you had at least six to seven the night of the incident?

Rob: At least.

T: I'm wondering if you are concerned about your alcohol use?

Rob: I think that night I drank too much, but I don't think that I have a problem with alcohol.

T: It sounds like that you had at least seven drinks or more the night of the incident. Is this accurate?

Rob: Yes.

T: So, I am wondering if you are willing to take a look at the amount of alcohol you consume and perhaps instead of six to seven drinks, set a limit of three to four drinks?

Rob: I'd like to try this.

The integration of motivational interviewing and cognitive-behavioral skills training is the key component of Brief Alcohol Screening and Intervention for College Students (BASICS, Diemeff, Baer, Kivlahan, & Marlatt, 1999). BASICS provides the client with information and skills that facilitate moderate drinking within the context of motivating the client to achieve and maintain a balanced lifestyle.

During the second and third sessions, accurate information about alcohol is provided, primarily to debunk the myth that "more is better." Here students are encouraged to examine their beliefs regarding alcohol and what they hope to get out of drinking. The biphasic response to alcohol can be explained in simple terms: most people feel an initial high as they have one to two drinks; as they continue to drink, they feel tired and lose that "buzzed" feeling. Thus, the stimulating effects of alcohol are diminished and continued drinking only leads to depressive symptoms, which can include passing out or becoming unconscious. In contrast, one can minimize the depressive effects by curtailing drinking alcohol so that one's blood alcohol content (BAC) does not go beyond .06%. As illustrated by the following:

Rob: I like to drink in social situations, it helps me to relax.

T: This makes sense. Most people feel a "buzz" after one to two drinks. What happens though, once the buzz wears off, is that one feels tired. One might continue drinking to try to get the buzz back but, in reality, the more you drink and exceed the .06 BAC, the more likely you are to feel depressed. It is referred to as the "point of diminishing returns."

By focusing on Rob's view of alcohol while providing an atmosphere that supports self-efficacy and, at the same time, provides accurate information about alcohol, Rob was willing to reduce his consumption to one to two drinks once a week by our fifth session. This reduction provided the opportunity to further explore his thought processes. Rob continued to struggle with worrisome thoughts about the future that seemed to distract him when he sat down to do his coursework. Here the solution focused on exercise, guided imagery, and utilizing positive self-talk to cope with his anticipatory anxiety about the future.

Rob discussed how he enjoyed riding his bike, but hadn't done so in months. I encouraged him to ride at least two times a week, and he ended up establishing a three times a week schedule. Every Monday, Wednesday, and Friday morning he would ride for 30 minutes before his first class. As a positive consequence, he noticed a considerable difference in his energy level, and this helped him feel good. I observed that he smiled more in our sessions and appeared more relaxed.

Over the course of sessions 7 and 8, we discussed a variety of stress management techniques that Rob could incorporate into his weekly routine. He described how he enjoyed going to the family house in Florida since he could walk along the beach, which provided the type of atmosphere that helped him feel the most relaxed. Rob was able to get to Florida during the October and March breaks and this helped, but when he could not go there physically, I suggested he go there in his mind. The following transpired during our session:

> T: You mentioned that you feel most relaxed when you are in Florida at your parents' second home.
>
> Rob: Yes, it is so relaxing, I am able to swim in the ocean, take long walks and watch the sunset.
>
> T: I would like to try a relaxation technique with you; it is called guided imagery. Would you be willing to try this with me?
>
> Rob: Yes.

T: Okay. Close your eyes and start your breathing like we have practiced before: deep breath, in your nose and out your mouth.

Rob: (He continues to breathe with his eyes closed)

T: Picture yourself on the beach (Pause).

You notice everything around you (Pause).

You feel very relaxed (Long pause).

Continue to breathe in and out in and out (Pause).

It feels good to be here, you feel safe and secure (Pause).

You can feel the sand between your toes (Pause).

As you walk along the beach you can hear the seagulls (Pause).

You can hear the waves crashing on the beach (Pause).

You continue to walk along the beach; this time you can feel the cool ocean water on your feet as the wave breaks upon the shore. (Long pause).

The warm sun feels wonderful on your face (Pause).

Rob continued to either abstain or consume only one to two drinks once a week. He reported that he felt much better on Saturdays and was motivated to get work done before socializing. Rob's exercise and relaxation routine provided him additional tools to cope with the college's demanding academic program. In our final four sessions, we focused largely on exploring his thought processes. Rob continued to have days when thoughts about the future would overwhelm him and he would not get his coursework completed in time for class. Though he was passing all of his courses, he contemplated whether college was right for him, thinking in direct conflict with his belief that he needed to achieve his degree in order to have professional and financial success.

We then started to counter Rob's cognitive distortions with positive self-talk techniques in order to reframe his thinking of himself and the world around him. He began to recognize that his definition of success centered around his father's expectations of him. He struggled between his deep respect for his father and his own ideas about what it means to be successful. Rob shared his father's thinking that he would like to work in the business field, but he was not sure whether he wanted to travel as frequently as his father or be away from his future family. This opened the door for exploration concerning the influence of his father's experience as well as his own interests in Rob's goals. In our next session we discussed what he uncovered:

T: Last week we talked about your expectations of success and how they are similar and different from your parents. What did you journal about this?

Rob: I was intrigued by the fact that I constantly want to be like my Dad, but then again I don't.

T: What do you mean?

Rob: I respect my Dad for all he has done for our family. He is a very hard worker and we have many wonderful things because of his hard work, but I do not want to sacrifice not being around for my wife or children.

T: It seems that hard work is something that your family values; at the same time you struggle with what it means to be available as a husband and father.

Rob: Exactly!

T: I wonder if both are possible?

Rob: (Becoming tearful) This is something that I am not accustomed to. I think I "think too much" about things and it gets me into trouble.

T: It is okay to cry if you want to. It sounds like you can be hard on yourself?

Rob: I guess I can be like Dad in some ways, have a good job, and the financial means to support my family, but I can also be there for my family, if I choose to.

TERMINATION PROCESS

During the initial assessment, we had talked about the timeframe of our weekly sessions lasting approximately 45-50 minutes in length and continuing for approximately 12-15 weeks, which coincided with the semester calendar and made for an easy transition as we approached the semester break. Rob's high-risk drinking diminished over the course of his therapy, and his overall physical health improved once he established a moderate form of exercise on a regular basis. His academic work remained about average, and he continued to receive assistance through the Academic Achievement Center. His anxiety about the future did not occur as frequently, according to his self-reports. His journals also indicated that at times his anxiety still interfered with completing his homework. This contributed to his self-doubt regarding his ability to succeed in college.

I suggested early in the therapeutic relationship that Rob have a neuropsychiatric evaluation. At the time, Rob preferred to do this in his hometown, and it took longer to arrange than if he had opted to see someone locally. He was aware that medication might be helpful and was planning on seeing the psychiatrist during the break.

I informed Rob that he could continue meeting with me when he returned in the Spring semester if he felt it would be helpful. We discussed some signs and symptoms that might signal that he should return for more counseling. I complimented him on his commitment to meeting weekly and on his openness to explore a variety of personal issues that can provoke unsettling or unpleasant feelings.

DISCUSSION

The link between substance abuse and mental health concerns is vital for every therapist, clinician, counselor or psychologist to understand. Co-existing disorders among the general population range from 50-80% among clients seeking treatment; therefore, every college counseling center professional should be conducting a substance abuse screening in conjunction with a mental status exam. When working with college students with no preexisting psychiatric history, substance abuse often produces behavioral symptoms that mimic almost any type of psychiatric disorder. For example, in Rob's case, his alcohol abuse, which is a central nervous system (CNS) depressant, can produce symptoms of depression and anxiety. If students' substance abuse is not properly identified, he or she is likely to be treated only for mental health concerns, which then allows their alcohol or other drug abuse to escalate.

Many college students, like the general population, have a difficult time giving up their patterns of use and abuse. It does not make sense to expect clients to immediately abstain from the substances that have helped them cope or have given them some type of relief. Rather, it is more feasible to view progress as a multi-dimensional process fostering gradual reduction of substances, within the framework of motivating the client to change based on where the client is in the stage of change process. This approach is client-centered and does not view the client's behavior as being "in denial," but rather more successfully works with resistance in an attempt to move the client toward a healthier and balanced lifestyle.

Rob's desire for autonomy coupled with his opposition to authority is typical of most young adults during this developmental phase. His identity formation was complicated by his ambivalent relationship with his father, and his self-worth seemed defined by obtaining his degree with the goal to be financially "well-off." By incorporating brief therapy within a harm reduction and motivational approach to viewing the concerns he presented, I helped Rob recognize his resources and strengths and develop solutions to his difficulties. By empowering him to think about his choices and rolling with his resistance, I partnered with him in an attempt to engage him to reduce his abuse of alcohol as well as explore ways to cope with his anxiety. Due to the limitations of the brief therapy model, we did not take the time to explore in depth Rob's family dynamics and his relationship with his significant other.

QUESTIONS

1. *The client seemed rather compliant in the first session considering it was a forced referral. How do you handle cases where the client is less inclined to be cooperative?*

No matter what the situation that brings someone into therapy, the key is meeting the client where they are at the time of the initial session. By doing this, I begin the process of establishing the relationship and building rapport. For example, I might ask the client, "What do you hope to gain from our meeting?," or "What would you like to gain with the time that we have together?" Therefore, I move in the direction the client views as important, not what I might interpret as the problem.

2. *You chose to focus on the drinking problem first, yet one could argue that the client's attention deficit disorder is at the root of his problems with worry about the future and self-medication. Can you discuss this a bit more? Were you able to follow up to see if he received treatment for the attention deficit problem?*

The client did receive a full neurological assessment to determine what role the attention deficit disorder might be contributing to his difficulties. Based on the neurologist's report, it was determined that the client's symptoms were not indicative of attention deficit and he referred the client to a neuropsychiatrist for possible SSRI medication.

3. *The client had some major issues with his father. Was transference an issue in counseling? Can you comment on the relationship between you and the client?*

Certainly in any therapeutic relationship the issue of transference might surface. A theme that did surface related to availability of others, in particular his father. One week, I had to cancel due to an emergency. The next session, the client seemed upset and we processed how he was disappointed that we did not meet the previous week. We explored the connection between how this situation related to how he was feeling about his father in general. Because the client had been working with me for some time, this helped the client explore his feelings about his relationship with his father.

4. *What strategies did you use to get the client to practice regular relaxation and to exercise?*

Part of the strategy in working with clients who might be abusing substances is to focus on wellness. The client became interested in the notion of his wellness lifestyle. I gave him a handout depicting a wellness wheel and we started to talk about the various components that comprise one's wellness. As we processed, the client started to recognize that some areas of his wellness lifestyle were in check, while other areas he needed to improve on. Based on this, the client decided he wanted to exercise more and find ways to improve his concentration. It was then suggested that regular moderate exercise and relaxation techniques might be a way for him to achieve his goal. By practicing and following-up with the client in our sessions, this helped to keep the momentum going.

5. *Was there any discussion or therapeutic work regarding the cli-
    ent's friends and peer pressure to drink? If this did exist, how did
    he learn to overcome it?*

During the initial session and throughout the therapy this issue was
presented to the client. The client stated that he did not drink because his
friends pressured him. He stated that his friends understood if he continued to have behavioral problems he might be asked to leave the college
permanently. The client did not feel that peer pressure was something
that contributed to his use of alcohol.

REFERENCES

Berkowitz, A. D., & Perkins, H. W. (1986). Problem drinking among college students:
    A review of recent research. *Journal of American College Health*, 35, 21-28.
Dimeff, L. A., Baer, J. S., Kivlahan, D. R., & Marlatt, G. A. (1999). *Brief alcohol
    screening and intervention for college students: A harm reduction approach.* New
    York: Guilford Press.
Flegenheimer, W. V. (Ed.). (1982). *Techniques of brief psychotherapy.* New York: Ja-
    son Aronson, Inc.
Jessor, R., Donovan, J. E., & Costa, F. M. (1991). *Beyond adolescence: Problem be-
    havior and young adult development.* New York: Cambridge University Press.
Marlatt, G. A. (Ed.). (1998). *Harm reduction: Pragmatic strategies for managing
    high-risk behaviors.* New York: Guilford Press.
Miller, W. R., & Rollick, S. (1991). Motivational interviewing preparing people for
    change. New York: Guilford Press.
Perkins, H. W., Meilman, P. W., Leichliter, J. C., & Presley, C. A. (1999). Misperceptions
    of the norms for the frequency of alcohol and other drug use on college campuses.
    Journal of American College Health, 47, 253-258.
Prochaska, J. O., & DiClemente, C. C. (1986). Toward a comprehensive model of
    change. In W.R. Miller and N. Heather (Eds.), *Treating addictive behaviors: Pro-
    cess of change* (pp. 3-27). New York: Plenum Press.
Talmon, M. (1990). *Single-session therapy: Maximizing the effect of the first (and of-
    ten only) therapeutic encounter.* San Francisco: Jossey-Bass Publishers.
Walter, J. L., & Peller, J. E. (1992). *Becoming solution-focused in brief therapy.* New
    York: Brunner/Mazel Publishers.
Washton, A. M. (Ed.). (1993). *Psychotherapy and substance abuse: A practitioner's
    handbook.* New York: Guilford Publication.
Zucker, R. A., & Fitzgerald, H. E. (1991). Early developmental factors and risk for al-
    cohol problems. *Alcohol Health and Research World*, 15(1), 18-24.

Chapter 17:
Finding the Silver Lining:
Counseling a Couple in Conflict

Paul L. Toth
Brady R. Harnishfeger
Andrew Shea

SUMMARY. The authors introduce the reader to a college couple with whom the therapist used a short-term counseling model. Specific principles of short-term couples therapy are identified and discussed in the context of how these principles were applied to the clinical work with them. John Gottman's (1999, 2000) concept of the "dream within the conflict" is reviewed, followed by a transcript of a counseling session demonstrating how it was used therapeutically within a short-term couple therapy model. *[Article copies available for a fee from The Haworth Document Delivery Service: 1-800-342-9678. E-mail address: <getinfo@haworthpressinc.com> Website: <http://www.HaworthPress.com> © 2002 by The Haworth Press, Inc. All rights reserved.]*

KEYWORDS. Couples, counseling, conflict, college, early-adult

---

Address correspondence to: Paul L. Toth, Counseling and Psychological Services, Indiana University Health Center, 600 North Jordan Avenue, Bloomington, IN 47405 (E-mail: ptoth@ Indiana.edu).

[Haworth co-indexing entry note]: "Chapter 17: Finding the Silver Lining: Counseling a Couple in Conflict." Toth, Paul L., Brady R. Harnishfeger, and Andrew Shea. Co-published simultaneously in *Journal of College Student Psychotherapy* (The Haworth Press, Inc.) Vol. 16, No. 3/4, 2002, pp. 269-285; and: *Case Book of Brief Psychotherapy with College Students* (ed: Stewart E. Cooper, James Archer, Jr., and Leighton C. Whitaker) The Haworth Press, Inc., 2002, pp. 269-285. Single or multiple copies of this article are available for a fee from The Haworth Document Delivery Service [1-800-342-9678, 9:00 a.m. - 5:00 p.m. (EST). E-mail address: getinfo@haworthpressinc.com].

This chapter outlines the application of a short-term therapy approach to couples counseling in a university counseling center within a university health care center. Counselors there are encouraged to work within a short-term or solution-focused framework. Couples counseling in this setting is less common than individual or group counseling. The therapist who worked with this couple employs cognitive/behavioral techniques and is guided by social learning theory. Solution-focused, interpersonal communication and Gottman's approaches are utilized within this general framework.

The authors first introduce a college couple with whom the therapist used a short-term counseling model. Next, specific principles of short-term couple's therapy are identified and discussed in the context of how these principles were applied to the clinical work. Then, John Gottman's (1999, 2000) concept of the "dream within the conflict" is reviewed. Finally, we present a transcript of a counseling session, demonstrating how it was used therapeutically within a short-term couple therapy model. As only one of the three authors actually conducted the therapy, the term "I" will be used to indicate the therapist.

To keep the case more manageable, we focus on only one issue and formulate so as to suit it for use with a variety of couples. The Gottman material seemed a natural choice. This means, however, that some of the information is not historically accurate. For example, our conclusion is, in part, hypothetical. The session numbers are not accurate but the description of the effect counseling had in this couple's life is.

Moreover, we each work differently with couples. The section of the chapter covering the Meanings Interview was written by author Shea as he had the most experience using this intervention.

THE COUPLE

"Ellen" and "Greg" met in college and had been living together for two years. Both were of European descent and were in their early to mid-twenties. Greg was an undergraduate at the university, who for six years had been compiling credits toward a bachelor's degree in accounting while working part-time at a local bookstore. Ellen was employed as a professional in the community. They had no children.

Both Greg's father and mother died in very recent years. Greg and Ellen had ended their relationship before Greg's parents died but Ellen reconnected with him after their deaths to offer comfort, and they soon moved into an apartment.

Greg came to the counseling center seeking help for depression. He had been experiencing depressive episodes when he was eighteen years old prior to the illnesses and deaths of his parents and had been helped by counseling and medication, but his symptoms had reoccurred about four months prior to his first individual counseling session. After two more months, Greg reported that Ellen's distress about his depression was causing tension in their relationship, and asked her to attend a session with him.

APPLYING THE PRINCIPLES OF SHORT-TERM COUPLES COUNSELING

The counseling of Ellen and Greg illustrates many of the principles of short-term couple therapy outlined by Donovan (1999), including: (1) finding the focus of treatment, (2) managing affective intensity, (3) encouraging the alliance, and (4) arranging an emotionally affirming experience.

"Finding the focus of treatment," determining what the therapeutic focus of treatment will emphasize, may occur rapidly if a couple comes to counseling already agreeing upon the "presenting problem." Or, the process may take more time as the clinician assesses, suggests and/or negotiates the focus of treatment. For Greg and Ellen, the treatment focused on reducing tension in the relationship caused by the stress of Greg's depression. This focus required that they listen to each other's needs and hopes, whereas Greg had tended to attempt to "fix" Ellen's distress instead of listen to her. This vignette is from the first therapy session:

Ellen: I just can't go on like this.

Greg: Like what?

Ellen: You always pulling away from me. Yesterday I needed to talk to you about my job. You don't even understand how much I hate it.

Greg: (long pause) Maybe if you just looked at the job as a part-time thing. Or, if you talked to Marcel about how bored you are he'd give you something different to do.

T: You know Greg, I think that you're very important to Ellen and she wants to talk with you about some of her distress. It seems that she needs you to listen right now and you want to solve her problem.

"Managing affective intensity" means seeing how affect can be addressed therapeutically, assuming that effective therapeutic change can best occur when emotional intensity is present between couples. Thus, this principle reflects how the clinician encourages, redirects, moderates, validates, or rewards affective expression in therapy. As with nearly all couples who seek counseling, Ellen and Greg were experiencing emotional distress. The therapist worked with them by encouraging them to speak about concerns from their own viewpoints ("I" messages) to reduce blame and criticism, reduce emotional flooding by taking breaks from one another when emotional intensity becomes overwhelming, and listening to the other's distress instead of trying to solve problems. The vignette continues.

T: So, I want you try something a little different this time. Greg, I want you to hold off making any suggestions to Ellen. Try to just listen, and then tell her what you've heard her say. Okay? Go ahead Ellen.

Ellen: (looking at Greg) My job sucks! I'm not challenged at all. I run out of work to do. Marcel treats me like a 13-year-old. What am I doing working there? It really brings me down.

T: Without trying to fix the problem, Greg, can you tell Ellen what you heard?

Greg: (to Ellen and the therapist) Yeah, her job sucks! I knew that.

Ellen: (to Greg) But how am I to know you understand what I've said unless you let me know?

Greg: Well, you put up with a lot so that I can go to school. I hate to see you going through this.

Ellen: (tearing) Thanks.

"Encouraging the alliance" reflects the importance of creating a positive therapeutic connection between the couple and therapist. Effective short-term couple counseling fosters and encourages the therapist/couple alliance through the therapist communicating to the couple an understanding and validation of the values, beliefs, and emotions that relate to the couple's struggles with the presenting problem. The vignette continues.

T: (to Ellen) How does it feel to have Greg tell you this?

Ellen: It helps to know that he notices what I do.

T: Sure it does. (to Greg) Even though it may have seemed like Ellen should have known that you understand her, do you see how making it plain to her can help?

Greg: Yeah, yeah I do. But it's hard to do when I know how frustrated she can get, and angry too. I get a bit scared and want to run away.

T: What happens when you run away?

Greg: It just gets worse. I feel paralyzed and Ellen gets pissed off.

T: You did a great job of expressing yourself to Ellen when you told her "I hate to see you go through this." How did saying that feel?

Greg: It was scary, but not too bad. I'm glad I said it.

Ellen: I really liked hearing you say it.

"Arranging an emotionally affirming experience" means setting the stage in therapy for couples to experience "a new ending to an old beginning." The therapist may offer clients a new perspective from which to view the presenting problem or may help them develop new skills they can utilize when the problem or conflict arises, a principle particularly relevant to the therapeutic intervention in the counseling session examined later in this chapter. Utilizing Gottman's (1999) concept of "the dream within the conflict," the therapist was able to offer Ellen and Greg an opportunity to discover new ways to view old conflicts. Through this exploration, they were able to deepen their intimacy and discover new ways to discuss old problems. The following section explores the concept of the "dream within the conflict."

FINDING THE "DREAM WITHIN THE CONFLICT"

Creating shared meaning is one of the foundations in Gottman's concept of a healthy relationship (Gottman, 1999; 2000). Each person brings to the relationship his or her own "life-dream" comprising his or her hopes and expectations for what life should be like. Of the many discrete components in each person's life-dream, the most important components include one's definitions of trust, security, individual freedom, interdependence, and familial duties. Others are the roles of religion and spirituality, fun, family rituals, expressions of emotion, expressions of opinions, and attitudes toward money, sex, rules, and being a member of a family.

To create shared meaning the therapist helps each partner bring his or her life-dream into the other partner's awareness. Because there are many obvious and subtle ways the components of one's life-dream can cause conflict with a partner's life-dream, the therapist helps make each partner's dream known to the other and then aids the couple to mesh their dreams together to form a common understanding.

If, as often happens, people are unaware of the components of their life-dreams, they are probably unaware of their partners', and therefore unaware of how these two dreams are competing for fruition. Gottman (2000) uses a *Meanings Interview* to make each partner's individual dream accessible breaking dream components into four areas: goals, symbols, roles, and rituals. Some examples of questions in each area are:

> *Goals:* What are your life goals (professionally, personally, as a couple)? Why do you have these goals?

> *Symbols:* What does "being a couple," "love," "fun" mean to you? How did you come to these definitions?

> *Roles:* What does being a "girl or boy friend," "student," "son, daughter, brother, sister," or "friend" mean to you? How do you balance these roles? What experiences led you to believe in these role definitions?

> *Rituals:* How do you spend weekends, evenings, anniversaries, birthdays, holidays? Where do these rituals come from? (Gottman, 2000).

The "Meanings Interview" can help a couple understand that they can create a new culture with their partner based on an understanding of their own individual and family culture. In each of the four areas, the origins of each component, and the discrepancies and commonalties between partners' components, should be discussed. Since perfect overlap in these areas is highly unrealistic, partners must find a way to be respectful of their own and their partner's dreams, hence creating their own culture—a shared dream, a shared meaning.

The Meanings Interview was done with Greg and Ellen within the first few sessions; due to the nature of their responses it would be difficult to capture the entire interview here. For the most part, their discussion around the meanings they ascribe to Roles and Rituals seemed to be without issue; their struggles seemed more associated with the meanings they ascribed to certain Symbols and Goals. Generally, they were both rather clear about their professional goals and why each had come to those goals. Discussing their goals as a couple became more complicated. Each wanted to get married and to marry each other, but the circumstances that were needed for them to be comfortable moving into marriage were quite different. A most telling portion of the interview occurred when they discussed what "trust" meant.

> T: (to both) Okay, so what about trust, what does trust mean? How do you know that you trust each other? And how do you know the other trusts you?

> Ellen: (uneasy laughter) I don't think he (then turning to Greg) you trust me at all.

> Greg: (smiles) Have you given me reason to trust you?

This portion of the session is clearly bringing them to a long simmering issue. Apparently, sometimes Ellen had been less than completely forthright in describing past interactions with an ex-boyfriend.

> T: (to both) Okay, before this becomes a discussion of specific experiences between you two, let's stay with each of you describing difficulties you have had with trust in your families of origin.

> T: (to Greg because it seems he has a more difficult time trusting than does Ellen) Why don't you start, what can you recall about whom you could or couldn't trust in your family of origin?

Greg: (defensively) Well, it's not my father, I mean I knew that he cared about us, and about me.

T: (moving toward Greg) Okay, I know that you loved him a great deal, but was there stuff he did that made you wonder if you could trust him at times, or around certain circumstances?

Greg: (less defensive) Well, it wasn't him so much as it was his job. He had to move around so much. I never knew how long I would be able to stay in one place, or how long I would be able to have my friends.

T: (to Greg) Okay, so what do you wish he could have done differently?

Greg: I know he loved his work, so I don't think I would have minded moving if I just knew more about when and why we were moving.

T: (to both) Okay, so based on that portion of your life experience, trust is very connected to you being informed. (to Ellen) Can you see why it is so important to Greg that you share *all* the facts?

Ellen: Yes.

So, through this discussion about the meaning of the term "trust," Ellen is better able to share information with Greg without experiencing him as being intrusive or manipulative. In addition, as Greg becomes more aware of what trust means to him and why, he can learn to distinguish Ellen from his family of origin, and perhaps be less demanding of information from her.

Gottman notes that, couples sometimes engage in seemingly unwinable, intractable fights that are symptomatic of one or both partners reactions to having their personal dreams being ignored by the other. Therefore, the key to decreasing damage and increasing understanding is to recognize each other's dream within the conflict. Gottman's (1999) intervention comprises five steps:

1. each partner becomes aware of her or his own dreams within a given conflict, via the emotional and cognitive reaction one has when one's own personal life-dream is not fulfilled.

2. each partner shares his or her own dream as well as listening to the other's dream. Gottman suggests that each partner write down his or her unfulfilled dream including the history of that dream, and the emotional reaction she or he is having to it. Then, each partner takes some time (15-20 minutes) to share the information while the other listens empathetically. Listening means suspending judgement and thus helping the partner explore their dream and its relationship to the conflict.
3. each partner then acknowledges the stress of this intervention, especially the risks of sharing one's dream, and tolerating of the other's dream. The couple should take time to help each other feel safe and secure.
4. each partner and the couple makes peace with the conflict, knowing these conflicts are *never solved*. Gottman instructs partners to define aspects of the conflict they cannot give up and those about which they can be flexible. The therapist strives to help the couple make the former category as small as possible, while the latter as large as possible, so as to promote a temporary compromise. Both partners should accept the compromise and revisit it in 2-3 months, repeating the earlier intervention.
5. each partner, with the goal of recreating a spirit of thanksgiving, expresses gratitude for the relationship and for each other.

The following section describes a session demonstrating how the therapist employed Gottman's "dream within the conflict" intervention to help deepen Greg and Ellen's empathy for the other, helping them experience emotional resolution and support in the midst of their conflict.

Ellen and Greg were locked in a disagreement over finances. Ellen wanted them to consider marriage. Although Greg was comfortable with the idea of being married to her, he thought that they had been too financially irresponsible to take on this commitment. They had experienced a hurtful argument the previous weekend with each critical of the other. Unable to resolve the conflict, they wanted to discuss their argument in the counseling session. I reminded them of communication techniques that could be helpful: speaking non-judgmentally from one's own experience; listening without criticizing; respecting the other's position; and, lowering defensiveness by accepting a small portion of their partner's point of view, as examples.

They were instructed to speak to each other for 10-15 minutes about the conflict without the therapist interrupting. I would help them process the interaction afterward (Gottman, 1999).

Greg: (beginning softly) Why don't you begin? You didn't get the chance to finish what you wanted to say last Sunday.

Ellen: That's right. Thank you (with a bit of an emotional edge).

Greg: Go ahead.

Ellen: (tearing, her speech slowing down and becoming softer) I'm just so frustrated (crying heavily now). Getting married is something I want and you'll have no part of it.

Greg: Well, that's not exactly true. I want to be married some day too. It's not that I don't have that hope. I'm just not ready. We're just not ready yet.

Ellen: Why not? I'm afraid you won't think we're ever going to be ready.

Greg: (expressing some anger) We're not ready! Don't you agree?

Ellen: (to the therapist) We haven't managed our money well. Our credit cards are way out of hand.

Greg: (to Ellen) We're just not grown up enough yet. We have to prove to ourselves that we can take care of our finances before we take a step as important as getting married. We have to be our own parents and keep an eye on our spending. We can't keep spending more than we earn and expect to set up a life together, have children and buy a house.

Ellen: (frustrated and somewhat angry) But we have the money. We may not have been as financially responsible as, looking back, we would have liked to have been, we might not have been as frugal as we would hope to be in the future, but we have the money to pay off our debts.

The couple informed me in the first session that though they were experiencing deficit spending, Greg had received a substantial trust fund from his parents' estate and they were in sound financial shape. However, he did not want to withdraw money from the trust fund to pay off past debts.

Greg: (defensive and somewhat angry) I don't see how we can take on such a commitment if we haven't been responsible in our financial matters.

Ellen: (crying) We don't have to punish ourselves. And I think that's what you want to do, punish us. It sure feels that way to me. I just don't think that we need to punish ourselves.

This conversation continued for a few more minutes. Then I broke in.

T: Well, you've been talking for about ten minutes or so, let's take a look at what's been going on. (pause) Though financial responsibility is important to you and getting married is a big decision, you've been talking about more than getting finances arranged so that you can get married.

Both Ellen and Greg sighed, smiled (through some tears) and acknowledged my statement with something like "No kidding."

T: What do think has been going on?

Ellen: Getting married and really starting a new kind of life together with Greg is so important to me. We're the only one of our friends who isn't married or making plans for marriage, having children and owning a home. I've given up a lot–I've put my life on hold for Greg to finish school here–and I'd like to be settled. If I can't have the career I dreamed of, I should be able move on with my life in other areas.

T: You feel like you've given up a lot to be here with Greg.

Ellen: Yes I have. I'm stuck in this job that doesn't challenge me. And I live in a dinky apartment. I wonder sometimes how committed you really are, Greg. I'm not moving on with the plans for my career and I'm not settled either.

T: It sounds like some hopes and dreams that have been frustrated. You know, when anyone's dreams are frustrated, other parts of their relationships are sure to be affected. Ellen, I want you to talk with Greg about the dream that you're afraid isn't going to work out.

Ellen then talked in detail about how much she cared for Greg and her knowing that he cared for her as well, but felt that their relationship was incomplete. Moreover, she felt "stuck in this crappy little town" without being a part of it. She talked about how her dream as a loving partner and mother and a successful, self-confident career woman had diminished. She expressed to Greg that she had two important dreams in her life: (1) having a satisfying and happy marriage and family life; and (2) having a successful and challenging career. She now felt as if she would achieve neither.

I asked Greg to tell Ellen what he had heard her say and Greg was able to do so with sensitivity and empathy. I then invited Greg to explore his dreams with Ellen.

> T: You know Greg, you were able to be quite helpful to Ellen just now by listening to her and showing that you care about her dreams. Maybe you could talk with her about some of your hopes around this same issue.
>
> Greg: Well, I'm still concerned about the way we spend our money. (pause)
>
> T: Hmm . . . My hunch is that this has something to do with your Mom and Dad.
>
> Greg: Yea, that's true. Hmm . . . I think it does.
>
> T: Could you talk with Ellen about this?
>
> Greg: (to Ellen) I guess it has to do with my parents, especially my Dad and the money he left me. (pause) I feel like I owe him.
>
> T: Can you tell Ellen what you think you owe him?
>
> Greg: He left me this inheritance. It's like as long as I have it, they're around in some way.

Greg then talked about how he wanted to pass this legacy on to his own children in order to honor his parents. He was afraid that using the money to pay off their credit card debt would dishonor his parents' memory since the credit card purchases were for "unessential items."

This session ended with both Ellen and Greg feeling relieved and satisfied that they had been heard.

The next two sessions were spent, in part, exploring these dreams. Greg was able to redefine ways to honor his father and mother, and Ellen decided to put one dream temporarily on hold (the challenging career) while exploring further the possibility of being married. More importantly, both were introduced to the idea of listening to and reflecting on their own and their partner's dreams, which helped each of them gain a new understanding of the other, and in turn, reducing Greg's depression and raising his satisfaction with the relationship.

By the sixth session, Ellen and Greg expressed satisfaction with their progress and agreed their relationship had significantly improved. Although they still argued on occasion, their conflicts lacked the emotional "sting" of previous arguments. Both were more willing to "agree to disagree." They agreed with me that this improvement in their functioning "was only the beginning" and that they would need to work to maintain their gains. At the same time, I assured them that, when future conflicts arose, their new skills could be brought back into play to keep the conflicts manageable.

As the sixth session drew to a close, I initiated the topic of when to reschedule, suggesting they consider returning for a "check-up" session in about three weeks. They agreed and, after the seventh session, they decided to return for a "booster session" in about six weeks. As of this writing, Ellen and Greg continue to come to counseling on occasions needed to clarify issues regarding Greg's depression.

DISCUSSION

This couples' experience is congruent with outcome research indicating that marriage counseling can not only increase marital satisfaction, but has potential for treating depression effectively and even preventing depressive symptoms (Beach, Fincham, & Katz, 1998; Beach, Smith, & Fincham, 1994; Waring, 1994). This counseling began as treatment for Greg's depressive symptoms. Couples counseling was indicated as Greg's reactions exacerbated his tendency to avoid Ellen, which then heightened tension and distress within the relationship. Using Gottman's techniques for finding the couple's dream within their conflict, the couple was able to experience conflict in a new way. Ellen and Greg learned that they could not only survive conflict in their relationship, but grew closer by exploring it in a more intimate way. Facing, rather than avoiding distress in his relationship, Greg's sense of optimism and internal positive attributions grew. This served to improve the quality of his relationship with Ellen and reduced his depressive symptoms. What had begun in Greg as a negative pattern of self-doubt, feelings of failure, and avoidance, had become a positive pattern of facing conflict, growth in self-confidence and deepening intimacy.

The above analysis assumes a model where symptoms, per se, have causative roles in the depression. It may also be that deficits in the relationship between Greg and Ellen's were a causal factor or that the symptoms were more reflections of the depression rather than causes of it.

QUESTIONS

1. *Greg's depressive symptoms appeared not to play a role in the couple's counseling, yet you mentioned that these symptoms were causing stress in the relationship. Can you comment on this and in particular how individual symptoms and pathology fit with Gottman's theory?*

Greg's most pronounced depressive symptoms included less confidence and more negative talk about himself. He experienced a vigorous internal negative critic that handicapped his efforts to help himself. He isolated himself socially, became increasingly irritated with Ellen and pulled away from her, sexual and emotional intimacy were compromised and they felt isolated from one another, which, in turn, exacerbated Greg's depressive symptoms, especially his negative self-talk. I surmise Gottman would look upon depression as he would any other problem or challenge for the couple. Most importantly, the couple would need to keep talking about the problem in a non-judgmental, empathic way using "I statements," avoiding criticism, validating emotions, being understood and expressing affection (Gottman, 1999). It can be quite difficult for a depressed person to engage in this type of interchange, but it can help the person feel more optimistic about himself and the relationship and help ease some of the negativity that accompanies depression. By investigating the dream within the conflict, Greg and Ellen engaged in positive communication patterns; they felt a deeper understanding by and for the other. A sense of connectedness and empowerment was developed which helped Greg look at himself as a proactive participant in the relationship instead of a burden to his partner (or her as a burden to him), resulting in an increase in optimism and positive self-regard.

2. *Can you discuss in a bit more detail how developmental issues were involved in the case? For example, was Ellen at a different developmental stage because of her readiness for marriage?*

Ellen and Greg's struggles can be framed in part in terms of developmental issues, or perhaps developmental incompatibility. Chickering's (e.g., Chickering and Reisser, 1993) theory of student development, and especially the task of "developing purpose" (aspiring toward meaningful vocational goals and developing a commitment to lifelong partnership), seems particularly relevant to understanding some of the struggles between Ellen and Greg. Some of Ellen's anger and frustration with Greg stemmed from her feeling blocked or unsupported in her desire to achieve her vocational goal of a "challenging" career, and personal goals, such as marriage, owning a home, and having a family. Greg seemed not to share these goals or, at least did not feel particularly strong about pursuing them at this stage in his life. Yet, once Ellen and Greg were able to explicitly identify their own "dreams behind the conflict" and able to understand and validate each other's dreams as important to that individual (whether or not they were shared), the capacity for accommodating these developmental differences through compromise and negotiation became available.

3. *Gottman's idea of exploring a "shared dream" seems to apply well to this young couple. What happens if the couple runs into major conflicts with regard to the shared dream? What is the therapist's role in discussing a possible incompatibility of dreams and goals?*

If a couple's goals appear incompatible, the therapist would try for a temporary compromise that should be revisited in about six months time. During that six month period, one would expect that the couple could grow closer and thereby reduce some of the major conflict, but the couple might continue to struggle fruitlessly, and couples would grow more distant from each other. Gottman suggests that not all couples are bound to succeed. Although Gottman does not directly say it, one may surmise that if two people are having such difficulty reaching any compromise on an issue, such difficulties may portend relationship failure.

4. *Sexual issues are not discussed in this presentation of the case. Were those issues discussed in the case? How do they fit with Gottman's model?*

Greg and Ellen's sexual difficulties were discussed early in the treatment. At that time I (Paul Toth) had not been introduced to Gottman's research but had taken couples through the sensate focus protocol (with some supervision through the Kinsey Institute at Indiana University). This treatment helps couples explore love making (rather than only intercourse) through attention to their own and their partner's sensual needs and pleasures; and it involves learning to communicate one's own needs and listening to the other's. This helped the couple work through their sexual troubles and to begin to learn to communicate more positively. It also helped set the stage for them to further their understanding of their partner through working to the dream behind their conflict. Their sexual problems were symptoms of the deeper conflict, fear of sharing deeper intimate goals regarding marriage and career.

Gottman discusses sexual issues as a form of communication difficulty: "No other area of a couple's life offers more potential or embarrassment, hurt, and rejection than sex. No wonder couples find it such a challenge to communicate about the topic clearly" (Gottman, 1999, p. 200). He encourages couples to learn to talk to each other about sex in ways that helps each person feel safe. The senate focus intervention that I introduced to the couple helped to improve their ability to identify and clearly state their needs. The process is similar to the *shared meaning* exercise: Until each partner is clear about his or her own position (i.e., sexual needs or goals, roles, symbols, rituals), the couple will struggle as unspoken expectations and hopes clash.

5. *Please comment on how the therapist can develop an alliance with the couple versus becoming aligned more with one partner than with the other.*

The therapist's development and maintenance of a therapeutic alliance with the couple is critical for maximizing positive outcomes; it is important that the therapist not align more with one partner than with the other. Several strategies can help couples therapists maintain this delicate therapeutic balance.

One is to frame couples therapy at the outset, with the therapist emphasizing to the couple the difference between individual and couples therapy. The therapist indicates that couples therapy focuses on the couple and on the couple's relationship with each other; the relationship itself is the "client" and the therapist's role is fostering collaboration between the partners. Thus, the therapist explains he or she is interested in helping their relationship, not just one individual in the relationship.

A second strategy for developing a therapeutic alliance with the couple is goal setting and developing a treatment plan. The therapist should facilitate development of mutually agreed upon goals. Mutually exclusive goals make collaboration difficult and set the stage for the therapist to be perceived as siding in support of one goal over another and hence one partner over the other. Similarly, the therapist should foster the development of a treatment plan agreeable to both parties. By adopting the goals and treatment strategies the couple has developed, the therapist becomes an ally of the couple and their relationship.

A third strategy relates to listening non-judgmentally to client's stories. The therapist should validate each person's views without showing preference by emphasizing the subjective quality of experiences (no one's perception is "right" or "wrong"), and the importance of partners learning to understand and respect differences in each other's views rather than agree on whose is "right." Finally, the therapist can further develop a neutral position by offering each partner opportunity to respond to the comments made by his or her partner, so that it becomes clear that the therapist is aware of and respects both viewpoints. The therapist may then offer a perspective to better accommodate the views of both parties and facilitate more collaboration.

REFERENCES

Beach, S. R., Fincham, F. D., & Katz, J. (1998). Marital therapy in the treatment of depression: Toward a third generation of therapy and research. *Clinical Psychology Review, 18*, 635-661.

Beach, S. R., Smith, D. A., & Fincham, F. D. (1994). Marital interventions for depression: Empirical foundation and future prospects. *Applied and Preventive Psychology, 3*, 223-250.

Chickering, A.W., & Reisser, L. (1993). *Education and Identity* (2nd ed.). San Francisco, CA: Jossey-Bass.

Donavan, J. A. (1999). *Short-term couple therapy*. New York: Guilford Press.

Gottman, J. M. (2000). *Clinical manual for marital therapy: A research-based approach*. Seattle, Washington: The Gottman Institute, Inc.: Seattle, WA.

Gottman, J. M. (1999). *The seven principles for making marriage work*. New York: Crown.

Waring, E. M. (1994). The role of marital therapy in the treatment of depressed married women. *Canadian Journal of Psychiatry, 39*, 568-571.

Chapter 18:
Synthesis and Summary

James Archer, Jr.
Stewart E. Cooper
Leighton C. Whitaker

The sixteen cases just presented offer a fascinating view of the kind of brief therapy work that is being done with young adults. We were gratified to find therapists who could present such an exciting and interesting variety of case situations. We see in these cases theoretical orientations ranging from time-limited psychoanalytic therapy to a one session (narrative) approach. Additionally, the four hallmark characteristics of brief therapy seem to be present in all of the cases. These include: a rapid and effective therapeutic alliance; a specific focus typically with a structured approach by the therapist; an assumption that the clients are resilient and can move rapidly; and encouragement to have the client do considerable work outside of the counseling office. Further, in examining the cases it seems clear that developmental issues were important, often at the heart of the therapy. Many of these cases also highlight the importance of cultural issues and reflect an understanding by the therapist of how cultural dynamics affected the interaction and the case conceptualization.

Our purpose in this chapter is to summarize how and why each case worked in a brief therapy context as well as how developmental and cultural issues played out in the therapy. The cases all had some of these elements in common, yet each also reflected the uniqueness of the client and the therapist.

[Haworth co-indexing entry note]: "Chapter 18: Synthesis and Summary." Archer, James, Jr., Stewart E. Cooper, and Leighton C. Whitaker. Co-published simultaneously in *Journal of College Student Psychotherapy* (The Haworth Press, Inc.) Vol. 16, No. 3/4, 2002, pp. 287-295; and: *Case Book of Brief Psychotherapy with College Students* (ed: Stewart E. Cooper, James Archer, Jr., and Leighton C. Whitaker) The Haworth Press, Inc., 2002, pp. 287-295. Single or multiple copies of this article are available for a fee from The Haworth Document Delivery Service [1-800-342-9678, 9:00 a.m. - 5:00 p.m. (EST). E-mail address: getinfo@haworthpressinc.com].

287

In the therapy with a young man who had a bee phobia presented by Dr. Chris Gunn, several factors contributed to a successful conclusion. Dr. Gunn's sensitivity to the cultural norms in which the client was immersed allowed for a rapid and effective alliance. For example, Dr. Gunn respected the young man's need for control and distance and did not push discussion of "deeper" issues, such as sexual orientation. Dr. Gunn was also able to use language and metaphors that resonated with the client. The therapy seemed to help the client come to accept an identity (as the sensitive one in the family) with which he had previously been uncomfortable. In the long run, this may have been an even more important outcome than the obvious progress regarding the phobic fear of bees. It allowed the young man to continue to develop an acceptable sense of identity and to accept his strengths and reinterpret what he had seen as weaknesses.

Two of our authors present relatively brief treatments of posttraumatic stress as a result of sexual assault. These cases have often been thought to require longer-term therapy, so the approaches taken by these therapists and the client and process variables are quite interesting to examine. In the case presented by Dr. Vivian Barnette, the client was a young African American woman who was raped by several men. She displayed many typical PSTD symptoms and felt considerable guilt about the rapes. At first she seemed embarrassed to discuss her case with Dr. Barnette, who is also African American, perhaps partly because the client had a White boyfriend, but in the end this cultural similarity seemed to aid the development of trust. The client had been raised in a religious family where premarital sex was not considered appropriate, and her relationships with her father and her current fiancé were complicated by feelings related to the rape. The therapist, by forming a rather quick and effective therapeutic alliance, was able to gain her trust and use brief psychodynamic therapy to help her better understand how her role with her father and the family was affecting her feelings toward herself and others. Cognitive therapy was also employed to help her cope with specific symptoms and to work toward more positive beliefs about herself and her role in the rapes. Dr. Boyd did more than assist the client in overcoming posttraumatic stress related to the rapes. By helping her better understand the "little girl" relationship she had with her father, Dr. Boyd was able to help her continue her development toward adulthood and avoid a potentially lasting developmental block because of the sexual assault.

The PSTD case presented by Dr. Jaquie Resnick involved a young woman who had been date raped three months prior to counseling. The client had a history of being stalked and came from a dysfunctional family background and thus had poor boundaries and low self-esteem played out in a history of exploitive relationships with men. According to Dr. Resnick, her development, already complicated by this history, was further interrupted by the rape trauma. At the beginning of therapy, the client appeared to be very angry at her mother and men in general. Dr. Resnick developed a structured treatment plan incorporating elements of cognitive, feminist, humanistic, and psychodynamic therapy. The plan included: normalizing the client's feelings in the context of rape trauma syndrome, establishing trust and safety and empowering the client in the relationship, reframing self talk, supporting coping strategies and supporting and identifying the client's resilience, identifying destructive behaviors and providing alternative options, and exploring ways in which her family of origin issues complicated dealing with the assault. Dr. Resnick used a structured approach incorporating many of the well-established principles of rape trauma treatment to make excellent progress with a client who had to deal with rape trauma within the context of difficult family issues.

Dr. Jeffrey Pollard intervened with a young man who was a mandatory referral from the college judicial system for violating an order not to pursue an ex-girlfriend by being in the area where she lived. Dr. Pollard assessed the problem as an obsession with the ex-girlfriend. The client had had previous counseling for substance abuse. Dr. Pollard's primary approach was to move the client through Prochaska's stages of readiness (contemplation and preparation) into an action stage where he was able to change the obsessive thinking and behavior that were causing him problems. Dr. Pollard indicated how he typically expresses empathy and understanding about the client's feelings, about being coerced into counseling, at the beginning of therapy. In this case, he initially focused on discussing the situation resulting in the referral and the client's feeling about having no choice or control. Dr. Pollard moved the client into contemplation and commitment to change by encouraging self-evaluation and an understanding that he could be free to choose his behavior. The client also began to gain insight into his obsession and his interaction style and how developing skills to deal with his compulsive behavior might be in his own best interests. Eventually, the therapy moved into the action stage where Dr. Pollard was able to use several breathing and behavioral strategies to help the client gain control of his impulses. One of the major curative factors in this case seems to be the therapist's ability to let the client gain some control over the interaction, while at the same time encouraging movement toward insight and change. In terms of developmental issues, this case provides a good example of how helping a young person confront a challenge related to problems that are pre-pathological (not yet reaching diagnostic levels) can work toward preventing the further evolution of the problem thinking and behavior.

Dr. Harry Piersma presented a very interesting case of a young woman who had avoided difficult and unresolved issues related to her past by being very active in athletics and other programs where she could avoid developing intimate relationships. After an extensive initial assessment, which Dr. Piersma feels is necessary for successful brief therapy, it was determined that the focus of therapy would be on how the client's relationship with her mother could be used to help her understand her presenting problem of conflict with her supervisor. A goal of examining how she could achieve more intimate and satisfying relationships with both males and females was also established. Much of the content of therapy was focused on the "schema" of unrelenting perfectionism that the client had developed due to fear of criticism by her parents. Understanding of this schema allowed her to challenge her fear and move on developmentally by forming close relationships and learning to handle criticism.

Dr. Phil Meilman provided an excellent example of how intermittent therapy can work over the course of a student's college career. Most of the five segments of counseling focused on the client's relationships with women and his self-concept. The client used counseling as a kind of crisis management, coming in whenever he needed help with a pressing concern. Dr. Meilman used a direct problem-solving approach and at the same time helped the client gain insight into the dynamics of his self-doubt. Further, Dr. Meilman used colorful and direct metaphors. In response to the case study, the client mentioned that one of the metaphors Dr. Meilman used, "waiting for rigor mortis to set in," had a very powerful impact on his thinking. The brief evaluative reaction by the client to his counseling together with the case study enriches this case study.

In the case presented by Dr. Jeff Brooks-Harris, a young man explores his grief over a best friend's suicide ten years earlier. According to Dr. Brooks-Harris, this grief had interfered with the client's development and made it difficult for him to form close relationships. One of the most critical incidents in the therapy was use of an empty chair technique enabling the client to say goodbye to his friend and to resolve to move on with his life. This second phase of counseling Dr. Brooks-Harris labeled experiential. In the first, cognitive, phase, the client gave up his belief that the only way he could work through his grief was to process feelings and reactions with his friend's parents who refused an overture to do so. In the third and last phase of the therapy, a narrative approach was used to help the client tell his story in a different way and develop a new understanding and meaning to this traumatic event in his life. The therapist in this case used several active and structured approaches in the seven sessions that allowed this to occur. Also, the client's previous relationship with Dr. Brooks-Harris in a men's group provided a quick and effective alliance.

Dr. Lynda Field's case of a Haitian-American student with separation/individuation issues illustrates the importance of multicultural counseling theory and technique. Dr. Field's knowledge of specifics about her client as a female from the Haitian culture and her in-depth application of multicultural counseling theory enhanced the therapeutic alliance and treatment success. Her assessment of the acculturation level of the young woman was central. This case also serves as an excellent illustration of the principles and practices of brief therapy in a college context. Dr. Field described key prognostic precursors, such as motivation, that were brought into the therapy by the young woman as well as the active stance and use of between-session homework that she employed as a therapist.

Dr. Steve Dubrow-Eichel's case of working with a young male member of a "High Demand Group" (HDG, sometimes referred to as a cult) presents a very interesting special issue. Some students on every campus join in such organizations. This case conveys the client's engagement in therapy and the subsequent unfolding of his potential and autonomy. Dr. Dubrow-Eichel described how he achieves these results by combining developmentally based psychotherapy with time limited intermittent sessions and motivational interviewing, avoiding replicating the control battle between the young man and his parents, instead joining with him in a way that made change possible. Additionally, his working with the parents early in the process was very helpful in reducing some of their reactivity and anxiety, which had contributed to the very behaviors that were of concern to them. Dr. Dubrow-Eichel makes an excellent case for the benefits of brief intermittent therapeutic contact when spread out over several years, especially in HDG situations.

The case of a grieving graduate student of Cambodian descent presented by Drs. Knott and Ngo represents another extensive use of multicultural counseling theory and techniques. Their having "insider" information concerning the clients' Cambodian cultural background was crucial. Their brief presentation of a model for recovery from major loss illustrated how the young woman needed assistance in moving through the intermediate stage (adaptation) to the ultimate stage (accommodation) of loss in coming to terms with the death of her brother, her role in providing support to him and, through this process, her dealing with her mother, and getting on with her own life. She needed to experience grief and express bereavement over both the death and her own victimization experiences, including the cultural sanctions against her informing her mother and looking for support from her. The case also provided a particular template for conducting brief therapy as Dr. Knott helped the young woman through exposition, diagnosis, contracting, implementation, evaluation, and termination.

Dr. Dennis Heitzmann discussed counseling a female athlete with an eating disorder, an increased form of psychopathology on campuses noted by directors of college counseling centers across the nation. The young woman in his case needed to take time off campus to assist her process of individuation. Such a step is not atypical for recovery from eating disorders among college students, particularly those with severe disorders. Dr. Heitzmann and his client happened to share a strong interest in running and physical fitness. Given her misuse of exercise as a coping mechanism for emotional and self-esteem issues, this commonality was very helpful in her recovery. Dr. Heitzmann also demonstrated the use of empirically supported treatment methods for eating disorders. He used several cognitive and behavioral techniques to help her talk about her concerns and issues and to make adaptive changes in her perspectives, attitudes, behavior, and life choices.

The case of treating a Caucasian female who raised as a minority in a foreign country, presented by Dr. Edward Delgado-Romero, is very informative in its coverage of acculturation issues. Moreover, the case involved a unique combination of her being a "global nomad" (in this case an American raised in a culture foreign to the parents who were living and rearing their children overseas) in therapy with a first generation Columbian-American therapist. Dr. Delgado-Romero made the helpful nature of shared acculturation experiences clear. In particular, their commonality of living outside of their native cultures fostered accurate empathy and a stronger working alliance. He described the healing when his client discussed painful issues with him without replicating negative relational experiences she had undergone with her own parents. His description of his awareness and resolution of his countertransference issues toward the ex-boyfriend demonstrated the importance of understanding and using the dynamics in the counseling relationship. This case showed how the client's vague, diffuse issues were resolved when clarity of details and expression of emotion were encouraged. At the beginning of this case, her presenting issue was vague depression and low energy. By the end of counseling, she had done a good deal of working through unresolved concerns and achieving separation and autonomy.

Dr. Paula Phillips described an effective single session treatment for a female with earthquake induced posttraumatic stress disorder (PTSD). Many students who go to college mental health services do so for only one or two sessions; for the right person with the right issue, effective changes can result. This case is interesting in its emphasis on forming a very rapid collaboration with the client and on explicating the problem and forming a team against it. The client indicated Insomnia, Mood, and Stress as areas for improvement. The counseling center's use of a one-word A-Z diagnostic descriptor term is intriguing. Dr. Phillips describes how she used narrative therapy to get the young woman to become aware of the meaning of events, places, and relationships at a deep level and how she then used imagery based techniques to decrease anxiety and enhance coping mechanisms. Her use of seashells, symbolizing calmness, relaxation, and control, was creative and innovative. The seashells take on further meaning when Dr. Phillips explains that they have been used successfully with other clients and were in fact donated by a client.

Dr. Michael Gottfried's treatment of interpersonal anxiety for a young gay male conveyed the importance of the interpersonal approach to counseling. His work emphasized Bowlby's attachment theory and its implications of using therapy as a "secure base." For example, the way that his client's attachment meta-position played out in interpersonal situations as an often repeated acted out ritual became a focus of therapy. The client acted out sexually when his anxiety got too high or left relationships rather than risk abandonment. Of equal or perhaps greater importance was how the client's interpersonal pattern manifested in the counseling process itself. Dr. Gottfried's calling his client after missed sessions, and not reacting with anger, was helpful and allowed for successful processing and insight in subsequent sessions. Counseling also covered the working through of early childhood abuse experiences and how they impacted his client's current anxieties, hyper-vigilance, and acting out behaviors.

Dr. David Diana presented the counseling case of a young male adult with substance abuse problems and "attention deficit disorder." This case is important in its focus on substance abuse, a very difficult issue on all college campuses. Dr. Diana's emphasis on using a combination of the harm reduction model along with "motivational interviewing" represents application of some of the most current models of substance abuse counseling. In this case, his use of these approaches enabled him to successfully join with his client rather than engender resistance by a "just say no" tactic. Additionally, he highlighted the high level of co-mobidity of substance abuse and mental health issues, and the con- comitant importance of doing chemical abuse/dependency screening at intake. Many therapists working in college mental health fail to assess and check for substance abuse problems, yet such difficulties can un- derlie other symptomatology. The young man's academic probation and several other life concerns were a direct result of his drinking be- haviors. The importance of Dr. Diana's keeping current with the treat- ment of substance abusers was apparent in this case. He used detailed knowledge of successful drinking practices to help his client buy into counseling. His presentation also illustrates the primacy of resolving substance abuse issues first in a chemical dependency model of recov- ery. Specifically, the substance abuse behavior was reduced, the identi- fication and working through of underlying issues could begin.

The case by Drs. Toth, Harnishfeger, and Shea is our only example of brief couple's counseling. Conjoint therapy is the treatment of choice in certain circumstances and is conducted in most college counseling cen- ters. These therapists highlighted concepts and techniques from John Gottman, one of the key figures in the field of marital therapy, in their treatment of this young man and woman facing relational difficulties. Their case also incorporated the conjoint therapy theories of Donovan, both in concept and illustration. They demonstrated how their counsel- ing helped the couple define the focus of treatment, manage their high levels of affect, come together as a team to discuss their problems, and have an emotionally affirming experience. It is with the latter agenda that these authors used Gottman's "dream interview" technique. Their use of this intervention may be especially informative to those who have not been exposed to this method. The underlying focus, helping the couple identify congruencies and discrepancies in goals, symbols, roles, and rituals, was helpful. The exchange rather than the resolution of their dreams was the most salient factor. It is important to note that al- though this was a couple's counseling case much of the work, particu- larly the sharing of dreams, provided a mechanism for personal reflection and development for each member of the dyad.

We conclude this book by offering two final perspectives. First, while some clients will always need extended and/or extensive therapy, we believe that the majority of university students can make significant positive use of brief therapy, both short term and intermittent, to overcome major developmental blocks and to facilitate critical personal growth. The willingness of clients, represented by these cases, to struggle through pain and risks is impressive and inspiring. Second, working with the authors, our fellow professionals and therapists in a variety of counseling settings with college students, has been very satisfying and a unique learning experience for us. We feel privileged that these therapists have given us an inside view of their work and of the very creative and successful ways they have managed to provide help to their clients in relatively brief time periods. We are also fascinated by the way that these counseling cases seem to open developmental growth for the clients involved, and how counseling helps to prevent the possibility of much more severe pathology emerging in the future. Working with these cases and these therapists has renewed our energy and optimism about counseling and therapy and has strengthened our commitment to strive toward making counseling available and accessible to young people.

Index

Abuse (physical), interpersonally based therapy and, 239-254
ADD (Attention Deficit Disorder), 257-258
Adler, A., 226
Alcohol abuse, 255-268. *See also* Substance abuse
American Psychological Association. *See* APA (American Psychological Association)
Anderson, H., 234,237
Anti-Social Personality Disorder *vs.* impulse-control disorders, 68. *See also* Impulse-control disorders (following and low-level stalking behavior)
Anton, W.D., 140,150
Anxiety attacks
  DSM IV diagnosis for, 16
  interpersonally focused therapy and, 239-254. *See also* Inter-personally focused therapy
  introduction to, 1-10,13-14,287-295
  motivational interviewing as treatment for, 255-268
  REBT (Rational Emotive Behavior Therapy) as treatment for, 13-25. *See also* REBT (Rational Emotive Behavior Therapy)
  reference and research literature about, 24-25
  supervisory conflict and, 85-100. *See also* Supervisory conflict

APA (American Psychological Association), 136,150,192
Archer, J., 1-12,287-295
Arnett, J.J., 2,10
Arredondo, P., 136,151
Association of Death Education and Counseling, 172
Athletes, brief psychotherapy and. *See* Sports psychology, brief psychotherapy and
Attention Deficit Disorder. *See* ADD (Attention Deficit Disorder)
Attig, T., 180-181,189

Baer, J.S., 261,268
Bandura, A., 7,10
Barnette, V., 27-41,288
Baron, A., 5,10-11
BASIC ID (Behavior, Affect, Sensation, Imagery, Cognition, Interpersonal, Drugs/biology) system, 8
Baumeister, R.F., 195,207
Beach, S.R., 281,285
Beck, A.T., 6-7,10,14,86
Beck, J.S., 124,134
Behavior, Affect, Sensation, Imagery, Cognition, Interpersonal, Drugs/biology system. *See* BASIC ID (Behavior, Affect, Sensation, Imagery, Cognition, Interpersonal, Drugs/biology) system
Benjamin, L.S. *See* Smith Benjamin, L.
Benjamin-Dartigue, D., 139, 151
Bereavement

Super, D.E., 2,12
Supervisory conflict
  case study of
    client background, 87-91
    counseling process, 87-91
    discussion about, 96-98
    DSM-IV diagnosis, 87-91
    introduction to, 85-87
    questions about, 98-99
    treatment, 92-96
  introduction to, 1-10,85-87,
    287-295
  reference and research literature
    about, 99-100
  schema-focused therapy as treat-
    ment for, 87-93

Talmon, M., 8,12,256,268
Teyber, E., 210,215,224,240-241,254
Time limited dynamic
      psychotherapy. *See* TLDP
      (time limited dynamic
      psychotherapy)
TLDP (time limited dynamic
      psychotherapy)
  vs. BID (brief intermittent devel-
      opmental) therapy,
      154-155. *See also* BID
      (brief intermittent develop-
      mental) therapy
  case study using
    case conceptualization, 31
    client biographical sketch,
      28-29
    client family/personal history,
      29-31
    DSM IV diagnosis, 29
    introduction to, 27-28

multicultural considerations,
    31-33
presenting problem, 29
questions about, 38-40
treatments and interventions,
    33-38
introduction to, 1-10,27-28, 287-295
PTSD (posttraumatic stress syn-
    drome-delayed onset), treat-
    ment for, 27-41
reference and research literature
    about, 41
Toth, P.L., 269-285,294
Transtheoretical Analysis, 65-84

Walker, A., 192
Waring, E.M., 281,285
Washton, A.M., 259,268
Weiner-Davis, M., 8,12,227,237
Wheelis, A., 203,207
Whitaker, L.C., 1-12,287-295
White, M., 129,134,226-227,234,237
Whitman, W., 193
Wilson, R.R., 14,24-25
Winsdale, J., 8,12
Wolpe, J., 7,12

Yalom, I., 18
Young, J.E., 86-88,99-100

Zeig, J.K., 14,25
Zucker, R.A., 256,268